The Rise
of Settler Power
in Southern Rhodesia (Zimbabwe),
1898–1923

The Rise
of Settler Power
in Southern Rhodesia
(Zimbabwe),
1898-1923

James A. Chamunorwa Mutambirwa

Rutherford • Madison • Teaneck
Fairleigh Dickinson University Press
London and Toronto: Associated University Presses

© 1980 by Associated University Presses, Inc.

Associated University Presses, Inc.
Cranbury, New Jersey 08512

Associated University Presses
Magdalen House
136-148 Tooley Street
London SE1 2TT, England

Associated University Presses
Toronto M5E 1A7, Canada

DT
962.75
M87
1980

Library of Congress Cataloging in Publication Data

Mutambirwa, James A. Chamunorwa, 1938–
    The rise of settler power in Southern Rhodesia
(Zimbabwe), 1898–1923.

    Bibliography: p.
    Includes index.
    1. Rhodesia, Southern—Politics and government—
1890–1965. I. Title.

DT962.75.M87   1980   968.9'102   78-75181
ISBN 0-8386-2267-4

Printed in the United States of America

For my parents, brothers, and sisters

Contents

Preface

On November 11, 1965, Ian Smith, prime minister of Southern Rhodesia, unilaterally declared Rhodesia independent (U.D.I.) of Great Britain. Prior to this illegal act the Rhodesian government had spent many months negotiating for a settlement with the British government. The main points of disagreement concerned those provisions in the proposed constitution that stated that there must be after the granting of legal independence unimpeded progress toward majority (African) rule. There are 7 million Africans and about two hundred and fifty thousand Europeans in Rhodesia. The Rhodesian government maintained that to accept this would endanger all the principles of Western Christian civilization. In seizing independence the Rhodesian government claimed that it sought to preserve government in "civilized and responsible hands" for the foreseeable future.

After more than eighty years of constant contact with the Africans of Southern Rhodesia, the Europeans still considered the Africans uncivilized and irresponsible. Why was this so? The Europeans had always argued that they came to Rhodesia to spread civilization.

U.D.I. was not only a challenge to the Africans of Rhodesia it was also a challenge to the British government, which as the colonial power had the constitutional responsibility to grant legal independence. And it is not surprising that the racist Ian Smith's illegal government has survived all these years primarily because of South African support.

In 1966 the Rhodesian African nationalists started a guerilla war in response to the challenge of U.D.I. that was intended to deny the African majority political power for all time. With the collapse of the Portuguese colonial empire in 1974 and the independence of Mozambique in 1975 (Mozambique has an eight hundred-mile long border with Rhodesia), the guerilla war against the Rhodesian white settlers has been intensified. And the war of liberation will continue to escalate until the Africans achieve majority rule.

U.D.I. provoked the question: How did such a state of affairs come about? And why did the British government not send troops to put an end to Smith's rebellion? It is the purpose of this book to answer these questions by looking at the period from 1898 to 1923. The conflict evident since 1965 and that has now broken out into a full-fledged guerilla war has its roots in these years. How did the European settlers' small voice of 1898 rise to a crescendo, drowning all opposition, in 1923? What was British policy toward the Africans in the years before Rhodesia attained self-government?

Both the British South Africa Company and the British government had hoped that they could use the settlers as pawns in their own plans; the Company to develop the country and make money, the British government to use the British Rhodesian vote against the Boers in South Africa. The settlers were the connecting link with the other elements of the British population in South Africa and were, therefore, aware of the animosity between the British and the Boers and of the need to keep the British stronger. From the beginning the British government and Rhodes considered Rhodesia's occupation as a possible solution to the South African problem.

Southern Rhodesia from the very beginning presented the British Colonial Office with the problem of determining what kind of relationship should exist between the blacks and the whites. Rhodesia could neither be another Australia nor New Zealand where the white population outnumbered the indigenous people. The problem in Rhodesia, as in South Africa, was complicated by the presence of a very small European population that was vastly outnumbered by the Africans. And further European immigration was discouraged by the gloomy economic prospects of the country. The question then was which interests, African or European, should be paramount. The nature of Rhodesia's colonization ensured the paramountcy of European interests. The colonization cost the British government nothing. The expenses for the occupation and conquest were paid for by the British South Africa Company, while "the Rhodesian settlers paid in blood . . ."[1]

Archibald Colquhoun, the first administrator in Mashonaland, in 1906 wrote a book, *The Africander Land*.[2] He devoted the first 127 pages to a discussion of what he called the real South African problem—the black cloud. He began the first chapter by asking: "is South Africa a white man's country?"[3] By a white man's country Colquhoun meant "a country where the white man can efficiently and economically fill every grade, unskilled as well as skilled, in the hierarchy of the community, where he is at liberty to carve out a fortune, where his fate is in his own hands, and where he can build up a political and social system on his own model."[4] But how was this to be done?

In America the European settlers did not try to assimilate the Indians into their social system. They essentially exterminated the Indians. Nor did the New Zealanders and Australians try to assimilate the Maoris and Aborigines. In the three areas the indigenous people were not useful as laborers. Thus the economic development of the United States, Australia, and New Zealand was undertaken without the participation of the indigenous people. In Southern Rhodesia and South Africa things were different. First it was impossible to exterminate the Africans. They could and indeed did resist and even, as in Rhodesia in 1896–97, threatened European supremacy. Secondly, the Europeans needed the Africans as cheap laborers.

Rhodesia was a white man's country whose future lay in a federated South Africa. This was a determining factor in British policies toward the Africans in Rhodesia. White supremacy was to be achieved and maintained by concentrating all political, economic, educational and military power in the hands of the Europeans. Legislation was manipulated to exclude Africans from acquiring political power. To the British Colonial Office at the turn of the century a policy of White supremacy in Rhodesia was essential to achieve overall British policies in South Africa.

In 1923 the settlers emerged victorious over both the Company and the British government when they refused to enter into the Union. It is ironic that the Rhodesian settlers refused to join the Union in 1922 for the same reason Rhodes had wanted Rhodesia brought into the Union—fear of Boer dominance.

Ideally, research on this topic should have been carried out in Rhodesia. As an officer of the Zimbabwe African National Union (ZANU) from 1965 to 1968, a return to Salisbury was then impossible for me.[5] However, I believe that the materials consulted in London—at the Public Record Office, the Royal Commonwealth Society Library, the Institute of Commonwealth Studies at London University, and the British Museum—and also at Rhodes House at Oxford are sufficient. Because the British South Africa Company was required to submit its minutes and records to the colonial office, I was able to see most of the Company's metropolitan documents that were not destroyed during the war. I was also able to read the dispatches of the resident commissioners in Salisbury as well as the high commissioners with headquarters in South Africa. Looking at these previously used materials from my perspective as an African I was able to see them in a fresh light.

This book, then, is primarily concerned with the rise of settler power in Rhodesia and with the evolution of British African policy in Southern Rhodesia between 1898 and 1923. It is an attempt to present to the reader the history of the political, social, and economic relations between the whites and the blacks in Rhodesia.

This is not the first time that someone has written on the period. A few Europeans, both liberal and conservative, have written on these formative years of Rhodesian history.[6] Stanlake Samkange, a Rhodesian African historian, has written on the period prior to 1898 and does not, therefore, address himself to the problems of settler power and pressure.[7]

This book grew out of the material presented as a Ph.D. dissertation at Columbia University. I am grateful for the help that my sponsors Professors Graham Irwin and Marcia Wright gave me. Dr. Jackson Chirenje and Dr. Charles Utete kindly made criticisms and suggestions that enable me to see the black-white problem in Rhodesia from a wider perspective. But I, alone, am responsible for the interpretations and for whatever mistakes remain.

Rutgers University   J.A.M.
Newark, New Jersey

NOTES

1. Ethel Tawse Jollie, *The Real Rhodesia* (London: Hutchinson and Co., Paternoster Row, 1924), p. 21.

2. Archibald R. Colquhoun, *The Africander Land* (New York: E.P. Dutton and Company, 1906).

3. Ibid., p. 1. Rhodesia at this time was considered a part of South Africa.

4. Ibid., p. 2.

5. I was the ZANU representative in North America during this time.

6. The liberal point of view is best portrayed by Terence Ranger in his book, *The African Voice in Southern Rhodesia: 1898–1930* (London: Wm. Heinemann, Ltd., 1970). He also briefly describes the period after 1898 in chapters 9 and 10 in his book: *Revolt in Southern Rhodesia 1896–7* (London: Wm. Heinemann, Ltd., 1967). Also representing the liberal point of view is John H. Harris' book, *The Chartered Millions: Rhodesia and the Challenge to the British Commonwealth* (London: Williams and Norgate, Ltd., 1926). For the conservative view, see L. H. Gann, *A History of Southern Rhodesia: Early Days to 1934* (London: Chatto and Windus, 1965) and H. M. Hole's two books: *The Making of Rhodesia* (London: Macmillan and Co., Ltd., 1926) and *Old Rhodesian Days* (London: Macmillan and Co., Ltd., 1928).

7. Stanlake Samkange, *Origins of Rhodesia* (London: Wm. Heinemann, Ltd., 1968). British and Rhodesian official documents as well as many works on Rhodesia refer to the "Matabele" and "Matabeleland." These spellings are incorrect. I have used the correct form employed by African writers like Samkange and Nathan Shamuyarira, i.e., "Matebele" and "Matebeleland." "Ndebele" and "Matebele" can be used interchangeably.

The Rise
of Settler Power
in Southern Rhodesia (Zimbabwe),
1898-1923

1
The Reasons for British Occupation

The British conquest of Rhodesia was a partial fulfillment of Cecil Rhodes' dream of bringing the African continent under the British flag. He, Alfred Milner, and Joseph Chamberlain were the foremost spokesmen of the idea that empire and expansion were the most profitable duties of Englishmen. Rhodes insisted that British expansion would be a blessing not only to England but also to mankind. "Having read the histories of other countries," Rhodes once said, "I saw that expansion was everything, and that the world's surface being limited, the great object of present humanity should be to take as much of the world as it possibly could."[1]

The ambitions of Rhodes, Milner, and Chamberlain were, of course, not unique. British colonization of Rhodesia in 1890 formed a part of the general expansion of European power in Africa during the last quarter of the nineteenth century. British imperialistic expansion in North and South Africa was partly impelled by the British possession of and desire to safeguard India. In 1885, Milner said:

It would be simply disastrous if we turned our whole attention to the Suez route to the neglect of the Cape route, a route commanded by no other Power, dependent upon no delicate piece of engineering, but open sea all the way, a broad and safe high road for the greatest of maritime nations. It is not to Egypt, but to the Cape Colony, not to Gibraltar and Malta and Suez, but to St. Helena and Simon's Bay and Mauritius that we should turn our attention, in view of the defence of our Indian and Australasian possessions.[2]

17

To secure her hold upon India, England found it necessary to control and safeguard waterways to the subcontinent, the Suez Canal and the Red Sea, as well as both Egypt and South Africa. England had first occupied the Cape in 1795, when she was at war with France, but she gave it up in 1802. When war between France and Britain broke out again, the English reoccupied the Cape in 1806, this time for good. The prime objective of England on both occasions was to prevent the French from controlling the sea route to India.

A factor of great importance in the revival of British imperialism was the activity of other European powers. The nineteenth century witnessed a tremendous growth of nationalism in Europe. By 1870, Italy and Germany had emerged as unified nations, and the aggressive national spirit evolved in those nations during their struggles for unification, became, in each case, an impulse to imperial expansion. Expansion became identified with glory. Treitschke, the German nationalist historian, wrote: "Every virile nation has established colonial power."[3]

Otto von Bismarck, the German chancellor, did not embark on expansion immediately after the unification of Germany in 1870, although the Colonial party wanted him to do so. But in 1884, Bismarck, finally won over to the Colonial League's expansion policy, declared protectorates over Togoland, next to the Gold Coast (now Ghana); the Cameroons, where British trade had hitherto predominated; South West Africa; and East Africa. Germany showed signs of stretching east from South West Africa and joining hands with the expansive Boers of Transvaal. Bismarck's activities alarmed Britain and caused her to increase the area under her control in Africa. Sir Harry Johnson wrote: "It was the German intervention which stirred up British enterprise in Africa."[4] Consequently, at Rhodes's insistence, the British government forestalled the Germans by declaring a protectorate over Bechuanaland (now Botswana) in 1885, thus preventing the Boers from blocking the route from the Cape Colony to Central Africa.

As a result of Germany's moves in Africa, Britain needed South Africa to prevent any threat to India. But a factor of great importance, if one is to understand not only the history of Southern Rhodesia but also of British policies there, is the fact that in order to ensure the security of the sea route to India round the Cape, the British had to be the preponderant power in South Africa. In other words, the Boer ambitions of expansion had to be checked, particularly since the Boers were flirting with the Germans. Furthermore British control of South Africa was necessary to protect British mining interests in the Boer-dominated Transvaal.

The story of the colonization of Rhodesia has been adequately told by Stanlake Samkange in *Origins of Rhodesia*.[5] Here it is only necessary to note that, beginning in the 1880s, the Boers of the Transvaal showed interest in what later became Southern Rhodesia. Paul Kruger, president of the Transvaal Republic, sent messengers to Lobengula, king of the Matebele, and even concluded a treaty of friendship with the Matebele monarch. These Boer overtures caused Rhodes, who questioned the validity of Kruger's treaty, to initiate his own contacts with Lobengula. The upshot of all this was that in 1889 Rhodes persuaded the British government to grant him and his British South Africa Company a charter to occupy Lobengula's territory.

One of Rhodes's fondest dreams was to color the map of Africa red. Since Boer occupation of Rhodesia could have closed the route to Central Africa, the occupation of Rhodesia was a partial fulfillment of Rhodes's dream. His dream, moreover, coincided with the British policy of surrounding the Boers, a policy that Rhodes also advocated. Kruger had dreams of establishing a federated South Africa under Boer dominion and free from British influence; Rhodes also sought a united South Africa, but as a member of the British Empire.

The animosity between the Boers and the British dates back to the time when the English occupied the Cape. At that time the population of the Cape was quite diverse, consisting of the Boers, descendants of the Dutch; the San; the Khoi-Khoi; and the Bantu. The Boers looked upon all nonwhites as inherently inferior people who could never aspire to being more than hewers of wood and drawers of water. "There were frontiersmen [Boers]," wrote Walker, "who said openly that African natives were children of Ham and might therefore be treated if necessary as men hated of God. Even those who did not go so far took it for granted that they themselves were in all things privileged as against brown men and black."[6] On the other hand, the British felt that the nonwhites were still barbarians, but with time, hundreds of years maybe, could be raised from their "abyss of barbarism." The two white races had different attitudes towards the nonwhites and therein lay some of the causes of animosity between Boer and Briton. In the 1820s, the British tried to Anglicize the Cape by making English the official language and by replacing Roman Dutch law with the English judicial system. The Dutch system of local government was also abolished. Commenting on the coming of the British, Hofmeyr wrote: "So there came into juxtaposition two powerful self-conscious nations . . . the possessors of distinctive traditions which neither would readily see destroyed. There arose differences of outlook, divergences of opinion, conflicts of sentiments. Thus were born controversy and strife. . . ."[7]

The period beginning in 1820 saw the arrival of more English at the Cape. In 1819, the British government voted to pay fifty thousand pounds for the passage of five thousand emigrants. In Britain, this period also witnessed the climax of evangelicalism, a religious movement that exercised much influence, not only in London but also in Cape Town, and whose effects on the history of the empire were to be enormous. The evangelicals, who held that the Europeans at the Cape were generally oppressing the nonwhite people, founded and maintained great missionary societies. One of these, the London Missionary Society, led by Dr. John Philip, was very active at the Cape. In 1828, Dr. Philip published a book, *Researches in Africa,* in which he exposed the ill treatment of the nonwhite people at the Cape. As could be expected, this book was received with indignation at the Cape. The book exasperated the colonists, for in the same year the Cape Assembly passed the Fiftieth Ordinance which made the Khoi-Khoi equal to the Europeans before the law. Under the ordinance, the Boers could no longer compel the Khoi-Khoi to work for them. The very idea that the Khoi-Khoi, or nonwhites in general, could be treated as equals before law courts was blasphemy to the Boers, since it cut deeply into their philosophy of racial superiority. In a letter published in the *Cape Monthly Magazine* of September 1876, explaining the reasons for the Great Trek, Elizabeth Steen Kamp, the sister of Piet Retief-leader of the Great Trek, wrote complaining of:

the shameful and unjust proceedings with reference to the freedom of our slaves; and yet it is not so much their freedom that drove us to such lengths, as their being placed on an equal footing with Christians, contrary to the laws of God and the natural distinction of race and religion, so that it was intolerable for any decent Christian to bow down beneath such a yoke; wherefore we rather withdrew in order thus to preserve our doctrines in purity.[8]

Of this period Hofmeyr commented that the Boers denied the missionary view that all men were equal before God: the missionaries "emphasized ideas of social and political equality which could not be acceptable to those who had, as a result of their practical experience, convinced themselves of the black man's inferiority."[9]

In 1833, the British abolished slavery not only at the Cape but throughout the Empire, except India. The Boer farmers were irked by the abolition not only because they were opposed to it but also because they felt that the compensation paid them for their slaves was inadequate. The British government was prepared to pay only 1.25 million pounds for thirty-nine thousand slaves valued by the slave owners at between 2 and 3 million pounds. Furthermore, the claims of the Boer farmers had to be approved in London where payment was to be made.[10]

Thus, the causes of Boer discontent were manifold and led to hatred of the British and their system of government. The frustrated Boers decided to leave the Cape and to escape British authority. The spirit of the Boers is best portrayed in the famous Piet Retief Manifesto, clause nine of which reads: "We quit this colony under the full assurance that the English Government has nothing more to require of us, and will allow us to govern ourselves without its interference in the future."[11] Away from British control the Boers could treat the nonwhites as they pleased without fear of British interference. They would, as they stated, establish the proper relations between master and servant.

The Great Trek, as this movement was called, started in 1836, and by 1846 ten thousand people had left the Cape. As the trekkers moved away from the Cape, they ran into the Bantu with whom they were to fight several wars.[12] The trekkers were seen by the British as potential enemies who, if their power were allowed to extend unchecked into the interior, might one day endanger the vital trade route to India. Two British historians, Robinson and Gallagher, have observed that from the beginning of the Great Trek:

> The imperial strategic interest became entangled with the wanderings of the trekkers and their colonization of the interior. Their independence and animosity, the Colonial Office feared, might one day endanger the control of the coastline. In pursuit of order and security, the empire gradually extended paramountcy in one form or other over the entire region occupied by the trekkers.[13]

The British, however, maintained that they still had authority over the Boers in South Africa no matter where the Boers went. One result of this policy was the Transvaal War of 1880–81, which ended in the defeat of the British. Before the battle of Majuba Hill the British had tried other means to retain their preponderant position in South Africa. In 1874, Lord Carnarvon, the colonial secretary, had advocated a Confederation of the four South African provinces. This scheme for confederation failed because the Boers realized that the British were not genuinely seeking to establish an independent state but rather their own political supremacy. The Boers also feared that under a confederation their institutions and language would be replaced by English as had happened at the Cape in the 1820s. Furthermore, the approach to African affairs by the two races was different. For example, in the Cape, coloreds and Africans could vote, whereas in the Transvaal they could not.[14]

Despite the British defeat at Majuba the British government did not give up the idea of retaining supremacy in South Africa. After 1881 a reappraisal of methods was necessary. From then on British policies in South Africa were to be achieved not by the direct involvement of London but by the activities of local British politicians in South Africa.[15] "The surest way of preserving the Empire intact was through the efficacy of local freedom, to be guided by local opinion, and to allow the colonies to develop according to their own inclinations and interests."[16] Rhodes took over the aggressive or expansive role that the British government had hitherto played. Rhodes entered the Cape Parliament in 1881, the year in which Britain was humiliated at Majuba. Commenting on Rhodes's timely entry into South African politics, De Thierry wrote:

The political conditions of South Africa during the past twenty years called for such a man as Cecil Rhodes, and for no other. So low had the fortunes of Britain fallen in this part of the world, that an eclipse was imminent; to avert which nothing would have been successful but statesmanship, original, audacious, independent and with a perfect command of means.[17]

Amery wrote that Rhodes believed "in imperial expansion through colonial expansion. His ideal was the creation of a united Realm of South Africa. . . ."[18] Rhodes attributed the failure of Lord Carnarvon to achieve confederation to the fact that the colonial secretary had tried to impose it from above. When Rhodes entered the Cape Parliament he tried to conciliate the Boers with the hope that he could gain their support for a federation, and thus achieve South African unification from below.

When Rhodes obtained a charter for the British South Africa Company he intended not only to bring new territory under the British Empire but also to contain Boer expansion once and for all. The occupation of Rhodesia in 1890, as far as Rhodes was concerned, was intended to achieve this latter aim. But Rhodes also had in mind that Rhodesia would be a base from which further expansion northwards could be undertaken. Moreover, the men who occupied Rhodesia expected to find deposits of gold richer than those of the Witwatersrand in Transvaal. Rhodes believed that an El Dorado in Mashonaland would be followed by an influx of British immigrants into the country. "If the New Rand were found," wrote Walker, "the rush of Europeans thither would make Charterland and not the Transvaal the coming economic centre of South Africa capable of dictating, in conjunction with the Cape, the terms of the economic federation and possibly of the political federation which was to follow."[19] From the very beginning of the British occupation of Southern Rhodesia, Rhodes saw Rhodesia as a key factor in the future of South African politics.

NOTES

1. A. Vindex, ed., *Speeches of Cecil Rhodes* (London: Chapman and Hall Limited, 1900), p. 7.

2. Quoted in W. B. Luke, *Lord Milner* (London: S. W. Patridge & Co. 1901), pp. 91–92.

3. Quoted in Mary Evelyn Townsend, *European Colonial Expansion Since 1871* (New York: J. B. Lippincott Company, 1941), p. 34.

4. Quoted in Charlotte Maurice Touzalin, "The Rise of the Empire Builders (1870-1899)," (Master's Essay, Columbia University, 1921), p. 18.

5. Also see, Ronald Robinson and John Gallagher, *Africa and the Victorians* (New York: St. Martin's Press, 1961).

6. Eric Anderson Walker, *The Great Trek* (London: Adam and Charles Black Ltd., 1934), p. 64.

7. Jan H. Hofmeyr, *South Africa* (London: Ernest Benn Ltd., 1931), p. 65.

8. Quoted in John Bird, *The Annals of Natal 1495 to 1845*, vol. 1 South Africa (Pietermaritzburg,: P. Davis & Sons, 1888), p. 459.

9. Hofmeyr, *South Africa*, p. 60. Also see Walker, *The Great Trek*, p. 77.

10. Ibid., pp. 90–91.

11. *Grahamston Journal*, February 2, 1837. Quoted in G. W. Eybers, *Select Constitutional Documents Illustrating South African History 1795-1910* (London: George Routledge & Sons Ltd., 1918), pp. 144–45. The Boers also left the Cape because the British government despised them. See James Anthony Froude, *Two Lectures on South Africa* (London: Longmans, Green and Co., Ltd., 1880), p. 13.

12. Monica Wilson and Leonard Thompson, eds., *The Oxford History of South Africa*, vol. 1. *South Africa to 1870* (New York: Oxford University Press, 1969), p. 409. See pp. 410-21 for the series of wars fought between the Boers and the Africans.

13. Robinson and Gallagher, *Africa and the Victorians*, p. 54.

14. See Eric A. Walker, *A History of Southern Africa*, 3rd ed. (London: Longmans, Green and Co., Ltd., 1964), pp. 356–86.

15. In 1853 the Cape Province received representative government, but the governor held all power. From 1872, when the Cape was granted responsible government, the governor's powers were reduced to those of a constitutional head who acted on the advice of the Cape government.

16. G. B. Pyrah, *Imperial Policy and South Africa 1902-10* (Oxford: The Clarendon Press, 1955), p. 3.

17. C. De Thierry, "Rhodes," *The Empire Review* 3 (1902): 384.

18. L. S. Amery, *The Times History of The War in South Africa 1899-1900*, vol. 1 (London: Sampson Low, Marston & Company Ltd., 1900), p. 103. Also see Chapter 5 "Eliminating the Imperial Factor" in Felix Gross, *Rhodes of Africa* (New York: Frederick A. Praeger, 1957).

19. Walker, *A History of Southern Africa*, p. 430.

2
The Settlers

The word *settlers* is used to describe the Europeans who came to live in Southern Rhodesia *after* 1890. Even the Europeans referred to themselves as settlers. Not much is known about the backgrounds and lives of the first settlers or pioneers, as they called themselves, who numbered 196: They wrote very little about their experiences. "That so few personal reminiscences have been bequeathed to us by the pioneers and early settlers,"[1] wrote Jones, "is hardly a matter of surprise. They were modest and unassuming people who would naturally have been averse to placing on paper any anecdotes which might be interpreted as an effort on their part to blow their own trumpets. Their numbers included no great diarists to jot down the daily happenings. None of them were literary men. . . ."[2]

Almost all the settlers came from South Africa in search of gold. They arrived in Salisbury on September 12, 1890, and two weeks later the settlers who had marched in a column disbanded and scattered throughout Mashonaland prospecting for gold. The early settlers lived very simple lives. They lived in grass huts, ate African food, and drank African beer. Ethel Tawse Jollie, wife of the first administrator in Mashonaland, tells us that "the first six months found even the Company's police almost without boots. . . ."[3] Most of the early settlers had very little money and almost no personal belongings. Carruthers, a miner reminiscing about his early days, told the author Neville Jones that "it was my habit to strip when at work, to save washing and often walked without trousers on long tramps."[4]

News of the successful arrival of these first settlers in Salisbury brought other settlers from South Africa. They came during the rainy season and many of them experienced great difficulties.

Very often they had to wait several days or even weeks until flooded rivers subsided, and many of them died of malaria and hunger.[5] In 1893, the European population in southern Rhodesia had increased to 1,122[6] and to 4,863[7] by 1895. During the 1896–97 Chimurenga (War of Liberation) in which about three hundred whites were killed, many Europeans returned to South Africa. By the end of 1896 the white population had dropped to 2,737.[8] After 1897 the European population steadily increased, and by 1901 it was up to 11,032 and to 15,000 by 1903.[9] The African population for 1902 was estimated at 514,813.[10]

As the white population increased and as the dream to find gold disappeared, the economic pursuits of the European settlers began to diversify. Some became storekeepers and hotelkeepers, others took to farming, and still others became laborers of the British South Africa Company mining interests and its subsidiaries. Some farmers grew maize (corn), wheat, barley, oats, tobacco, potatoes, and citrus fruits. Other farmers raised cattle, sheep, goats, chickens, and pigs.[11] Percy Hone, the historian, tells us that some Europeans worked as teachers, doctors, lawyers, artisans, builders, blacksmiths, plumbers, and engineers.[12] In 1909, Hone made a comparison of European occupations for the years 1904 and 1907. Although he did not specify how many miners or clerks or teachers there were, his study is, nevertheless, interesting because it sheds light on the division of labor in the European community.

Hone divided European occupations in both the rural and urban areas into five categories:

Year	Occupation	Males	Females	Total [a]
	Professional	1,387	187	1,574
	Domestic	217	1,603	1,820
1904	Commercial	1,884	55	1,939
	Agricultural	879	150	1,029
	Industrial	3,103	82	3,185
	Professional	1,147	261	1,408
	Domestic	196	2,326	2,522
1907	Commercial	1,749	55	1,804
	Agricultural	1,095	79	1,174
	Industrial	3,482	96	3,578

a. In 1904 the European population had declined to 12,596. Decline was due to the depression that followed the Boer War. By 1907 the population had increased to 14,000 but still below the 1903 level of 15,000.

In 1907, there were 1,400 white miners and by 1909 the number had increased to 1,700.[13] From Company documents one can estimate the average monthly salaries for most European employees in Southern Rhodesia for 1912. Only a few occupations and salaries of the Europeans are listed here to save space. The average monthly salary for an artisan was about £24; a baker £20; a blacksmith £30; a bricklayer £30; a clerk £25; a miner £30; a male domestic servant £8; a female domestic servant £4; a laborer £26; and a mine manager £70.[14]

These figures suggest that the majority of the settlers were wage earners and not men and women of great means. Their dreams of an El Dorado evaporated in a few years and life turned out to be difficult for the settlers.[15] The first fifteen years of white settlement were gloomy and insecure. In 1893 the Matebele War broke out; in the 1896–97 Chimurenga over one tenth of the European population was killed; and from 1899 to 1902 the Boer War made the economic and political outlook of Rhodesia even more uncertain.

Yet eventually, the Europeans succeeded. Perhaps the reason for their success lies in the fact that ever conscious of their very small number they were united and their attitudes and behavior toward the Africans were the same[16] The sense of insecurity—the fear of being swamped by the Africans—led the Europeans to develop and maintain policies that were intended to keep the Africans at a distance educationally, socially, economically, and politically. The settlers practiced politics of exclusion. To give up or share privileges with the Africans was thought to be detrimental to the interests of the white race. Small and struggling as the European population was, to have allowed the Africans to compete for jobs with Europeans would have reduced wages and would have lowered the Europeans' standard of living. Thus the high level of European living depended on preventing black-white competition.

As has been stated, the settlers came to Rhodesia not for humanitarian but for economic reasons. In that fact lies the cause of the black-white problem in Rhodesia. To succeed in the gold mining venture, even if gold had been found in abundance, because of their lack of capital, the settlers required cheap African labor. And because cheap African labor was necessary, the settlers intended consciously or unconsciously from the very beginning of their activities in Rhodesia and even before they left South Africa, to interfere with the African way of life. In the early years the settlers used outright force to secure labor and later they introduced taxes as "legal" means to force Africans to seek work to secure the necessary money to pay these taxes. Chapter 6 provides a full discussion of the labor shortage, but it should be emphasized here that when the Africans were forced, whether by brute force or legal means, to work for the Europeans they lost their freedom—the freedom to live as they had done before the coming of the Europeans. And the loss of freedom (which is the essense of settlerism) was more important than any small and side benefits that may have accrued to the African during his period of employment. Moreover, despite the many claims that have been made of the benefits of the money economy and European colonialism in general to the Africans,[17] it was the paramount interests of the settlers that were served when Africans worked for the Europeans. Any gains by the Africans were only incidental and were, in fact, minimal.

The promise of three thousand acres of land to each settler even before setting foot in Rhodesia threatened African land, the mainstay of the Africans' economic activity. Indeed a few years after occupation of Rhodesia by the settlers, reserves were established to "accommodate" the Africans. The African methods of agriculture at the time have been described by some as wasteful. The Africans practiced shifting cultivation—working a piece of land for three or four years at a time and then moving on to another piece of land or another place altogether. Forcing Africans to abandon shifting agriculture was seen as a great advance. Montague Yudelman, who has studied land tenure among the Africans of Rhodesia, tells us that by practicing shifting cultivation, the abandoned land "was left to revert to bush until fertility was restored."[18] According to Yudelman, this method of agriculture, given the abundance of land and the lack of capital, was sound.

Individual acquisition of the land by the settlers was contrary to African customary laws of land tenure. Under African customary law the land belonged to the entire tribe and even the chief could not give it away. There was no individual private ownership of land. But, according to Yudelman, the settlers "as inhabitants

. . . (did) not regard all the land as an African heritage but rather as an important element in a sociopolitical framework designed to protect European levels of living."[19] The sequestration of African land is important not only because it undermined and limited African economic activity but also because it served the economic and labor interests of the Europeans.

The setting up of reserves reduced African land and in effect meant reduction of the productive capability of the Africans simply because they had less land to support themselves. When Africans started to avail themselves of the opportunities that the market presented to their products, they affected European interests. Their products competed with those of the Europeans. Even as late as 1910, when European agriculture was reasonably well established, the director of (European) agriculture wrote: "The difficulty of the farmers is not in the production . . . but in the assurance of a market at reasonable prices, the demand by mines and prospectors for . . . food, meat, potatoes, pumpkins, being of an erratic and unreliable character."[20] The Company, to prevent competition between the settlers and the Africans, did very little to develop the agricultural and pastoral capabilities of the Africans.[21] "Land policy" wrote Yudelman, "was an important element in this general philosophy of noncompeting groups and in maintaining European standards."[22] It is interesting to note that in Kenya after the introduction of white settlers as farmers at the beginning of the twentieth century not only were African reserves set up but the European farmers, eager for cheap labor, argued that the reserves were too big. And the cultivation of cash crops like coffee and cotton by Africans, hitherto encouraged by the British government, was now discouraged, and the Africans of Kenya produced less in 1920 than they had produced in 1913.[23]

The introduction of the reserves was also intended to provide settlers with labor. Reserves were scattered all over the country surrounding European farms so that the European farms were surrounded by sources of labor. After the reserves had been delineated in both Kenya and Rhodesia the settlers clamored for their reduction. The more land the Africans had, the more the Africans produced and therefore the more they could sell. This would increase competition for markets between the Europeans and the Africans, and if the Africans had more to sell, they would then have enough money to pay taxes and there would not be sufficient motivation for them to work for the Europeans. Professor Gann writes:

> The employers' position worsened when some African villagers started to sell part of their crops. The growth of new townships and compounds had the unintended effect of creating a small market for African produce; mine-owners, prospectors and even white farmers all bought native grain and meat, thereby helping to spoil their own local labour supplies. . . . Acreage under cultivation increased. . . . Employers soon took note: Southern Rhodesia natives . . . did not make good workmen, for the high price of grain was spoiling the labour market. . . .[24]
>
> [We find similar policies pursued in Kenya.] Labor supply has had its effect on theories of taxation and land ownership. The settlers have advocated high taxes to force natives to work for wages to pay them. Taxes are collected at the proper time to encourage native labor for settlers during harvest. . . . Settlers have wanted to limit the native holdings of land to force them out to work. . . . They have preferred to force natives to live in small groups in alienated areas to provide a permanent labor supply.[25]

Conflict over land and labor were proof of the incompatibility of settler and African interests. These two major issues dominated the black-white relationship in Rhodesia even after 1923. The company had the power to establish reserves, and even after their establishment, the company could move Africans to a new reserve if minerals were discovered on the old reserve. The company imposed taxes on the Africans and determined how much was to be spent on African education or reserve development. The company and the settlers used their political power to ensure their predominant social and economic position.

The significance of the land and labor policies of the Europeans in Southern Rhodesia, the setting up of reserves and the introduction of taxes, lies in Africans' loss of the freedom to determine their lives. These land and labor policies were the mechanisms used to reduce the area of freedom of the Africans.

After African military power had been broken, company settler disputes dominated Rhodesian politics. The settlers organized themselves into political groups to apply pressure on the company and sometimes they sent petitions to the British government to secure redress of their grievances. None of the political associations formed proved to be long lasting. In most cases the associations were formed to meet the needs of the moment and were then disbanded. The associations would hold rallies and the pressing issues of the day would receive wide discussion in the press.[26]

In 1897 the Europeans in Matebeleland formed a debating society that demanded settler representation in the Legislative Council. In 1904 the company claimed ownership of all the unalienated land in Rhodesia; in response the settlers, to dispute the claim, held a conference attended by delegates from the major towns of Rhodesia in June 1904. In July of the same year a delegation was sent to England to meet with the board of directors to discuss the land claims of the company. Nothing definite came out of the London meeting with the board of directors. But the dispute had charged the political atmosphere in Rhodesia and, as a consequence, in Matebeleland on July 20, 1904, the Matebeleland Political Association was formed "for the purpose of promoting and advancing, politically and financially the best interests of this country. . . ."[27] About this time a similar organization, the Mashonaland Political Association, was formed in Mashonaland to serve the same purpose. Before the visit of the board of directors in 1907 two political associations, the Mashonaland Progressive Association and the Rhodesian Constitutional League, were formed to present settler grievances before the directors. After meeting with the directors the league was dissolved because it had achieved its purpose. "Today" wrote the leaders of the league, "the situation is totally changed. . . . The Directors have visited us, have in the main admitted the justness of our complaints, and further have already taken practical steps towards many much desired reforms. . . . We are practical men . . . and are ready to meet them (the Directors) in (a) . . . spirit of conciliation. As proof of our seriousness we hereby declare that the Constitutional League no longer has any reason for existence and is hereby dissolved."[28] However, in 1912 the league was resuscitated when the political future of the country became an issue because the charter was to expire in 1914. The most important settler political association, the Responsible Government Association, which demanded self-government for Rhodesia, was formed in 1917. The farmers had their own pressure group as well. In 1902 they formed the Rhodesian Agricultural Union, which was affiliated to the South African Agricultural Union. By 1910 the Rhodesian Agricultural Union had at least twenty-five local branches.[29] These settler organizations or pressure groups directly influenced the members of the Legislative Council, many of whom belonged to one of these organizations. From 1909 onward the political future of the country was determined not by the company nor by the British government but by the settlers. And in the struggle between the settlers and the company the Africans, politically, came out a very poor third.

NOTES

1. Neville Jones, *Rhodesian Genesis: The Story of the Early Days of Southern Rhodesia compiled from the Reminiscences of the Pioneers* (Glasgow: The University Press, 1953), p. 30.

2. Ibid., p. xii.

3. Ethel Tawse Jollie, *The Real Rhodesia* (London: Hutchinson and Co. Paterhoster Row, 1924), p. 17.

4. Jones, *Rhodesian Genesis*, p. 48.

5. W. D. Gale, *Heritage of Rhodes* (London: Oxford University Press, 1950), p. 28. Also see E. F. Knight, *South Africa After the War: A Narrative of Recent Travel* (London: Longmans Green, and Co., Ltd., 1903), pp. 306–9.

6. *The Guide to South Africa for the Use of Tourists, Sportsman, Invalids and Settlers, 1903–1904*, p. 292.

7. Ibid., p. 105.

8. Ibid.

9. Ibid.

10. Ibid.

11. Percy Hone, *Southern Rhodesia* (London: George Bell and Son, 1909), pp. 200–212.

12. Ibid., p. 20.

13. *The Guide to South and East Africa for the Use of Tourists Sportsman. Invalids and Settlers*, 1913, p. 235.

14. Ibid., pp. 156–58.

15. During the first few years of settlement Rhodes spent between £40,000 and £50,000 from his own pocket helping destitute settlers. Jollie, *The Real Rhodesia* p. 27. The Company also helped. Knight, *South Africa*, p. 309.

16. This does not mean that Europeans had no differences among themselves. They had. For instance up to 1908 (European) farmers objected to prospectors (white) taking horned cattle over their land in case they were diseased; farmers also objected to uncontrolled right of prospectors' cattle to graze on their farmlands; farmers resented the indiscriminate cutting down of trees on their lands. But these conflicts were resolved by negotiations or by arbitration by the Company. Hone, *Southern Rhodesia*, pp. 293–94.

17. L. H. Gann and P. Duignan, *Burden of Empire: Appraisal of Western Colonialism in Africa South of the Sahara* (New York: Frederick A. Praeger, 1967).

18. Montague Yudelman, *Africans on the Land: Economic problems of Agricultural Development in Southern, Central, and East Africa with Special Reference to Southern Rhodesia*, (London: Oxford University Press, 1964), p. 11.

19. *Ibid.*, p. 19.

There is controversy on the use of the word *tribe*. Early usage by Europeans had pejorative connotations. Hence some young African historians prefer the use of *nation* rather than tribe. Although many of the characteristics of nation (and nationalism) and tribe (and tribalism in a sociological sense) are similar, usage of the word *nation* in this context might be confusing and misleading. Therefore throughout the book the unsatisfactory word *tribe* is used but not in a pejorative sense.

20. Report of the Director of Agriculture for the Year Ended 31st December 1910, p. 1. African agriculture was handled by the Native Department.

21. Rodney has observed that: "Failure to improve agricultural tools and methods on behalf of African peasants was not a matter of a bad decision by colonial policy makers. It was an inescapable feature of colonialism as a whole. . . ." Walter Rodney, *How Europe Underdeveloped Africa* (Dar-es-Salaam, Tanzania: Tanzania Publishing House, 1972), p. 240.

22. Yudelman, *Africans on the Land*, p. 20.

23. M. R. Dilley, *British Policy in Kenya Colony*, 2nd ed. (London: Frank Cass & Co., Ltd., 1966), p. 181.

24. L. H. Gann, *A History of Southern Rhodesia: Early Days to 1934* (London: Chatto & Windus, 1965), pp. 174-75. Also see Rodney, *How Europe Underdeveloped Africa*, p. 255.

25. Dilley, *British Policy*, p. 214.

26. Very little information is available about the leadership and membership of the associations or organizations mentioned later. It is, however, a safe assumption that organizations work for the benefit of their membership, and that these organizations were pressure groups that put pressure on the company and the British government to secure advantages for the whites in Rhodesia. In the existence of these organizations lay the power of the settlers.

27. *The Bulawayo Chronicle*, July 23, 1904, p. 1.

28. Quoted in M. E. Lee, "The Abrogation of the Charter Movement in S. Rhodesia 1898-1907," Henderson Seminar no. 16, (November 6, 1971), p. 18.

29. Report of the Director of Agriculture for the Year Ended 31st December, 1910, p. 8.

3

The Triumph of the Company, 1890–1897

The economic and political relations that were to obtain between the Africans and the settlers after the British occupation of Rhodesia had been accomplished were clearly defined in the 1889 Royal Charter. Under the charter the British South African Company's economic activities were to be restricted to mining. Lobengula had signed the Rudd Concession in order to rid himself of the many Europeans who pestered him for permission to exploit minerals in his kingdom. Throughout his negotiations with Rhodes's agents and in his correspondence with Queen Victoria, Lobengula strove to keep the "intending new settlers" under control.

While negotiating for mineral concessions in Rhodesia, Rhodes purposely did not include land as one of his demands. He knew that Lobengula would not grant land concessions. Gibbs's analysis was correct when he wrote:

> Rhodes and the Company knew well enough that the Rudd Concession gave them no power in the land other than to enter it and dig for gold. Even Lobengula was unlikely to be so foolish [as] to give more. Nor had Rhodes been so foolish as to ask for it. Getting what Lobengula was prepared to give, he could take the rest without asking.[1]

Rhodes clearly had no intention of respecting the limitations imposed on him and on the company by the Rudd Concession and by the 1889 Royal Charter. Even before the pioneer column had been assembled in 1890 Rhodes promised to the adventurers who composed it free land grants of over three thousand acres per man. "The fact that Lobengula had granted no land rights, no powers to

34

make laws, nor authority to settle disputes," wrote Hugh Marshall Hole, an official of the company at the time of occupation, "was tacitly disregarded. Preparations were made for allotting farms to those Pioneers who would undertake to occupy them. . . ."[2] It is highly probable that the British high commissioner at Cape Town knew of Rhodes's promises of land grants to the members of the pioneer column. However, the high commissioner did not oppose Rhodes because he was as eager as was Rhodes to see Rhodesia under the British, and not the Boer, flag.

As Lobengula became aware of Rhodes's real intentions, he appealed directly to the British government for help and called upon it for an assurance that Rhodes and the company would respect his authority. Lobengula even sent three envoys with a letter to Queen Victoria to express his deep concern, but the British government completely ignored his plea.[3] The Matebele king then tried to beat Rhodes at his own game. Lobengula was convinced that as long as Rhodes had no title to the land, he (Lobengula) would have the upper hand. In 1891, Lobengula therefore granted a hundred-year land concession to a German financier, E. A. Lippert, who was a rival of Rhodes's. As Hole puts it, "the chief [agreed] all the more readily as he thought by this means [he would] avenge himself on Rhodes's Company for gaining a stronger position than he had expected."[4] Another authority explains Lobengula's reasoning:

> Lobengula . . . knowing that Rhodes's people and Lippert's people were enemies—enemies like the Matabele and Zulus who would fight each other to death rather than dwell in the same land—without a qualm—signed another concession giving Lippert what he asked. For if Rhodes had the right to dig for gold, and Lippert the right to own the land, they would fight and destroy each other and the land would remain for the Matabele people.[5]

The reaction of Rhodes and the company to the news of the Lippert Concession was predictably hostile. Initially Rhodes wanted to challenge the concession's legality. Such an action, however, would have played into the hands of the company's opponents who would then have been able to question the legality of Rhodes's mineral rights. Obviously, the land grants Rhodes had promised to the pioneers who entered Mashonaland in 1890 embarrassed the company since the company had no right to grant any land. The Colonial Office was aware of this.

> I am to observe that Lord Salisbury is doubtless aware that the British South African Company has found itself hitherto somewhat embarrassed by the fact, on which those opposed to it were not disinclined to dwell, that the "Rudd Concession" obtained from Lobengula in 1888 did not in terms purport to grant more than mining rights in his territories, and that therefore it had but an imperfect right if any at all, to grant such titles to immovable property as were necessary for the development of a civilized community and operations south of the Zambezi.[6]

To avoid adverse criticisms the company decided to buy the land concession from Lippert. The company paid Lippert £30,000 and gave him some shares of its stock.

Lobengula's attempts to divide and rule were frustrated by Rhodes who was prepared to pay any price to get what he wanted. When told that Lippert had sold his concession to the company, Lobengula, who had treated the Europeans well, felt only disgust and contempt for the white men whom he rightly felt could not be trusted to respect any agreement. It fell on John Moffat, who had known Lobengula as a young man but was now assistant British commissioner in Bechuanaland, to convey the sad news to Lobengula. "The Chief was a good while before he took in the idea, as his impression was that there was a radical antagonism between the two parties, and he is not very cheerful about it."[7]

With the acquisition of the Lippert Concession, the company thought that it could legally make land grants and went ahead to do so. Later the Lippert Concession was to be declared invalid by the British Privy Council.[8] But the British government of the day gave its emphatic support to the acquisition of the Lippert Concession by the company. Lord Knutsford, secretary of state for the Colonies, signified this official approval when he wrote, through his secretary, to the company:

> I am to state, for the information of the British South Africa Company, that Lord Knutsford approves the concession in

question and transfer to the Company, subject to the terms of the Company's Charter, and on the express condition and reservation that the Company do not assign the Concession or transfer any share in the profits arising out of it, either to any person or body politic or corporate, without knowledge and sanction of the Secretary of State.[9]

Under the terms of the Royal Charter, the company could acquire a concession with the approval of the secretary of state.[10]

Lobengula, in granting the Lippert Concession, had obviously sought to strengthen his position rather than to weaken it. From his point of view the transfer did not alter his political position vis-a-vis the company since the concession was a hundred-year lease in which Lippert's powers had been so defined and stipulated as not to usurp Lobengula's authority. It is unthinkable that a man of Lobengula's awareness should have deliberately surrendered his authority. The company, in buying the concession, had sought, first, to eliminate a potentially dangerous rival, and, second, to deny to Lobengula a legal base from which to challenge its power. The company, to further its commercial aims, claimed powers that Lobengula had never given to Lippert. "Wide, however, as were the powers granted by Lobengula," wrote Williams, a sympathetic biographer of Rhodes, "they were nothing to the fantastic superstructure of rights subsequently built upon this document by the Company."[11]

The pioneers who entered Mashonaland in 1890 came primarily to seek their fortunes in gold. Many were not interested in owning land; in fact, some of the pioneers disposed of their land grants on their way to Mashonaland. Because the early settlers were preoccupied with the search for gold, because Mashonaland was sparsely populated, and finally because the farms pegged out were in most cases not occupied or settled, land alienation in Mashonaland did not cause much initial hardship for the Mashona. In fact, in this early period of European occupation, the Mashona thought that the Europeans were nothing more than hunters or gold seekers who would leave the country before long.[12]

In Matebeleland the situation was quite different. The pioneer column had deliberately sidestepped Matebeleland because of Lobengula's hostility. Theoretically, Lobengula, according to the terms of the company's charter, had political authority in both Mashonaland and Matebeleland. Rhodes and his advisors were also aware of the real threat to the company posed by the military organization of the Matebele. Rhodes and the company were convinced that their economic activities could not produce satisfactory results unless Matebele power was broken up. "To some of Rhodes' advisors," wrote Williams, "the danger of a conflict with the Matabeles was no objection: the Matabeles, they argued, would have to be suppressed sooner or later, and the sooner the better."[13]

Failure to find the expected rich gold deposits in Mashonaland led to the speculation that the El Dorado was in Matebeleland. But Lobengula stood in the way. In London, meanwhile, the price of the stock of the chartered company had begun to fall. It was thought that once Lobengula was removed, gold mines could be exploited in Matebeleland and the company's financial prospects would become brighter. The opportunity to destroy Lobengula's military power came in July, 1893, when the company alleged that some Africans in the Fort Victoria area had stolen its telegraph wire. To punish the offenders, the company impounded the Africans' cattle which, however, belonged to Lobengula. When Lobengula realized that some of his cattle had disappeared, he sent an *impi* to punish the Mashonas whom he mistakenly thought had stolen the cattle.[14] From this seemingly trivial incident broke out the 1893 Matebele war in which Lobengula was defeated.

The cattle incident gave Dr. Leander Starr Jameson, a friend of Rhodes's who later became premier of the Cape Colony, the opportunity he had long sought not only to destroy Matebele power but also to exploit the resources of Matebeleland for the benefit of the company. In mid-August 1893, Jameson made known the infamous Victoria Agreement that offered huge bonuses to those willing to undertake an expedition against Lobengula. The terms offered are important as they clearly indicate the utter disregard of the Company for the interests of the Africans. These terms also show the ruthless acquisitiveness of the "prospective settlers" and point to the danger the Africans faced if and when in the future these men should be given a say in the government of the territory. The following were the conditions of service.

1. That each member shall have protection on all claims in Mashonaland until six months after the date of cessation of hostilities.

2. That each member will be entitled to mark out a farm of 3,000 (three thousand) morgen in any part of Matabeleland. No occupation is required, but a quit-rent will be charged on each farm of ten shillings per annum.

3. That no marking out of farms and claims will be allowed, or held valid, until such time as the Administrator and the Commanders of the different columns consider the country sufficiently peaceful, and a week's clear notification will be given to that effect.

4. That members be allowed four (4) clear months wherein to mark out and register their farms, and that no such marking out or registration will be valid after that time, with the exception of the rights belonging to members of the force filled, invalided, or dying on service.

5. The Government retain the right at anytime to purchase farms from members at the rate of £3 (three pounds) sterling per morgen, and compensation for all improvements. This does not include the purchase of claims already pegged out on farms.

6. That any member of the Victoria Force is entitled to 15 (fifteen) claims on reef and 5 (five) alluvial claims. . . .

7. The "Loot" shall be divided: one-half the B.S.A. Company, and the remainder to officers and men in equal shares.[15]

It is interesting to note that the first five clauses of the Victoria Agreement are concerned with land and that none of the eleven clauses mention the Matebele. In the aftermath of the war their land was open to the invaders without any consideration for the welfare of the Matebele. The "loot", i.e., all the cattle of the Matebele, was, in fact, confiscated by the victorious company. After the Matebele War of 1893, the Matebele had their lands confiscated. They remained, or returned to the lands on which they had lived before the war, not as owners of the land but, according to the conquerors, as squatters on European property.

During the Matebele War, Sir Henry Loch, the British high commissioner for South Africa, expressed the desire that the British government take over the peace negotiations at the end of the hostilities. Loch, it appears, was of the opinion that only a peace settlement between the British government and Lobengula would produce stability in the whole of South Africa. Before the war ended, the Colonial Office informed the company that

> the settlement will necessarily involve considerations far wider than any affecting the interests of the Company and its rights under the Charter, and bearing directly upon the peace and security of South and Central Africa generally, and it is there-fore needless to point out that Her Majesty's Government are bound to keep the supreme control of that settlement in their hands. It appears . . . fairer to the Company that Sir Henry Loch, as representing Her Majesty's Government, should con-trol negotiations from the outset than that the Secretary of State should find himself obliged, at a later stage, to reject any arrangement, or material part of an arrangement, already provisionally made by the Company, a result which would greatly weaken the influence of the Company among the natives".[16]

Rhodes, however, did not want the British government to be involved in any peace settlement. In a cable to the board of directors, Rhodes urged the directors to insist on the exclusion of the British government. He argued: "British South Africa Com-pany have asked British Government nothing, and surely they have right, in terms of Charter, if victorious, to settle the question with Lobengula, subject only to approval of Marquess of Ripon [the Colonial Secretary]."[17] Both the board of directors and the colonial secretary agreed to this plan. But as we have seen, the Victoria Agreement clearly indicated that Jameson and Rhodes did not wish for any peaceful settlement. They sought instead to expropriate Lobengula's "land" and cattle through outright mili-tary victory. Any peace settlement would have meant first that Lobengula's power, though reduced, would have remained, posing a possible threat in the future, and second, that "if the High Commissioner took over the negotiations for peace with Lob-engula then the promise of land, cattle and gold Jameson had undertaken to pay the invaders from Matebeleland spoils would not be honoured and the Company would be in trouble with its mercenaries."[18] The outbreak of the 1896–97 Chimurenga sug-gests that the British government's fear that a settlement in which it did not play an active role would not produce lasting peace was justified.

The results of the 1893 War were tragic for the Matebele, as has been noted. The men who took part in the expedition against the Matebele had over 6 million acres from which to peg out farms, and by August, 1894, some 5.4 million acres had been alienated.[19] The war made the Matebele technically landless. It was in the power of the British government to repudiate the cattle stealing and land sequestration that took place. However, it was difficult for the authorities in London to know exactly what had happened because they had no representative in Southern Africa except for the British high commissioner in Cape Town, more than a thousand miles away from Rhodesia.

In July, 1894, the British government recognized the defeat of Lobengula and by an Order in Council brought Matebeleland under the administration of the British South Africa Company. The Order in Council also sought to protect the interests of the Matebele. Aware of what had happened to the land of the Matebele, the British government demanded that a land commission be set up to

> deal with all questions relating to the settlement of natives in Matabeleland. It shall without delay assign to the natives inhabiting Matabeleland land sufficient for their occupation, whether as tribes or portions of tribes, and suitable for their agricultural and pastoral requirements, including in all cases a fair and equitable proportion of springs or permanent water, it shall also direct the Administrator to deliver to them cattle sufficient for their needs; and the Administrator shall give effect to such direction.[20]

The Matabeleland Order in Council of 1894 thus recognized, and indeed, set a tacit seal of approval on the company's violation of Matebele economic and political rights. The British simply failed to exercise the powers they possessed, as explicitly laid down in the 1889 Charter, to control and regulate the activities of the company. Alienation of African land, because land was the source of all African economic activity, has been the root cause of the economic, political, and social problems that have plagued Rhodesia ever since the days of the early settlers.[21] Under African customary law the chief held all the land in trust for the whole tribe. In West Africa, British land policy stipulated that neither concession nor conquest could destroy African customary land law and that even when paramountcy changed, as, for example, from an African chief to a white power or the company, the new rulers merely became the new trustees of the national interest. Writing about Rhodesia, John Harris, secretary of the Aborigines Protection Society, reminded the British government of its legal and moral responsibility to the Africans of Rhodesia:

> Why is Rhodesia Britain's "acid test" in Colonial policy? The answer is as simple as it is definite and challenging. British Colonial policy is at the parting of the ways in Rhodesia, because the question raised is whether a wrong having been clearly proved Great Britain should now deliberately choose to persist in that wrong and uphold all its consequences, or conversely, whether, that wrong having now been demonstrated, the British people should choose to do the Right.[22]

It seems obvious that British land policy in Rhodesia followed a pattern different from its policy in West Africa because of settler pressure. The conquest of Matebeleland had been undertaken by settlers who had been lured there by the company. Even Rhodes was aware of the significance of settler involvement: he told the conquerors of Lobengula that by their military conquest they had become owners of the land.[23]

In 1888, as in 1889 and 1890, Rhodes and the British government argued that Lobengula "owned" Mashonaland and Matebeleland and that his authority in the area was paramount and should be respected. But after Lobengula's defeat, Sir Henry Loch, the British high commissioner, took a different position. This was undoubtedly the result of the influence exerted on him by Rhodes, who was the prime minister of the Cape Province at this time. Before the end of the hostilities Loch had called for British control of the settlement, but after the war he supported Rhodes's arguments with regard to the size of Matebele lands. In 1894, Loch, to prove that the Matebele had not suffered any serious loss in land, argued, in a dispatch to the secretary of state:

> From the information collected by me before the war, I am of opinion that a circle drawn at 60 miles radius from Buluwayo would have embraced the whole of the land in actual beneficial

occupation by the Matabele nation and their slaves. . . . If, then, we take the area inhabited by the Matabele nation, as thus defined, we find that they were in beneficial occupation of a country of between 10,000 and 11,000 square miles.

It may be assumed since the war the slaves have deserted their former masters and, under these circumstances, I think it probable that the total area of the two native reserves, estimated at about 6,500 square miles, will be sufficient if the land be suitable and the Land Commission, who have acquired local knowledge, appear to be satisfied with this.[24]

From 1894, British land policy in Matebeleland (as well as political policy) was directed mainly at securing land that was sufficient and adequate enough for the agricultural and pastoral purposes of the Matebele. It was for this purpose that a Land Commission was set up in 1894. The commission was composed of three people: Judge Vincent of the Matebeleland High Court, a member selected by the secretary of state, and another selected by the company but appointed by the high commissioner.[25] The two other members selected for the commission were Captain Lindsell and Captain Heyman, both of whom had taken part in the war against Lobengula. It is difficult to see how commissioners who had staked their lives on conquering the Matebele could be expected, so soon after the campaign, to be impartial and fair to the Matebele. Nevertheless, the commission was theoretically appointed by the British government to inquire as fully, as competently, and as fairly as possible into the land requirements of the Matebele. The commission did not even bother to travel throughout the greater part of the land they assigned to the Matebele and, therefore, did not know whether the land was suitable for agriculture or had sufficient water. The commission relied heavily on second-hand evidence and did not even know the size of the African population of Matebeleland. No land surveys were available to the commission, nor did it bother to make any.[26] Yet before the end of 1894 the commission had recommended, with the approval of the administrator and the British high commissioner, the establishment of the Gwaai and Shangani reserves.

In January, 1895, the British government approved the report of the Land Commission. The report was bitterly attacked by Henry Labouchere, editor of *Truth*, and by the Aborigines Protection Society. They complained that the rights of the Matebele had been totally ignored and also charged that the land was completely unsuitable for agriculture and was without sufficient water for the needs of those who would live on it. This criticism prompted Sir Richard Martin, the deputy British commissioner in Rhodesia, to conduct his own inquiry. Martin discovered that the Gwaai and Shangani reserves were totally inadequate; they fell far short of the requirements of the Matebeleland Order in Council of 1894.[27] The Colonial Office described the entire Land Commission report of 1894 as a farce.[28] In any case, very few Africans, if any at all, went to live in the newly created reserves.

A full discussion of the policy of reserves is undertaken later,[29] but it is appropriate here to note the effect of European land alienation on the Africans of Rhodesia in the period 1890 to 1896. Africans, particularly in Mashonaland, did not immediately feel the impact of European land alienation. Most of the settlers had an interest in gold, not land; therefore, they merely pegged out the land, left the Africans living on it as they had before, and went in search of gold. By October, 1892, although approximately three million acres of the land had been alienated, less than a third of this was occupied.[30] Two major grievances [that were the main causes of Chimurenga] were the attempt by the settlers to force Africans to work on their farms and the attempt by the company to impose a tax on them. However, even after the Europeans had come, the Africans experienced little change, because they continued to live on the land that they had occupied before the settlers had arrived. In 1914 the Southern Rhodesia Native Reserves Commission reported:

The members of the original pioneer force, some 200 in number received the right of selecting farms of 1,500 morgen in Mashonaland. . . . Rights to mark out farms were also granted to members of the police force taking part in the occupation within a specified period, and a number of rights lapsed owing to non-fulfillment of this condition. On the whole the number of farms occupied in Mashonaland during the first three or four years after the arrival of the pioneers' expedition was small in proportion to the vast area opened up, and the indigenous native tribes scattered through the country were not exposed to any pressure or inconvenience from the presence of the European settlers.[31]

In Matebeleland after the 1893 War, the Matebele returned to their "homes" where they had lived prior to the fighting.

> Partly owing to their natural aversion for abandoning districts which they had occupied for several generations, and partly because of the distance of the reserves from their existing kraals, the Matebele did not at once, nor indeed for many years, avail themselves of the Gwaai and Shangani Reserves, and no efforts were made by the Government to induce them to settle on the ground provided for them. They remained scattered about the country in the districts where they had resided before the occupation.[32]

This situation, at the time, benefited both the company and the settlers, who were primarily preoccupied with the search for minerals. Despite the wholesale land alienation that followed the 1893 War, only nine hundred acres were actually under cultivation by the Europeans in Matebeleland in 1895.[33] Therefore, even in Matebeleland, the effects of the ruthless land alienation did not immediately produce profound difficulties for the Matebele. Most of the settlers preferred to be absentee landlords so that they could both prospect for gold and collect rents from the Africans living on "their" land. In 1914 the Southern Rhodesia Native Reserves Commission observed:

> The first tendency of the settler was to encourage the Matebele to remain on the farms for the sake of their labour. The natives were regarded as tenants, and in many cases they were glad to enter into arrangements whereby in consideration of a small annual rental or of an undertaking to furnish labour for their landlords at stated seasons, they should enjoy undisturbed possession of their old village site and lands.[34]

The effects of land alienation were eventually to be felt by the Africans, for the accommodation by European landlords of African "squatters" on their land was only temporary. As the African population and the number of their cattle increased, their demand for land for agricultural and pastoral purposes began to press on the European landholdings. The European settlers, the company, and the British government sought ways to provide land for the future needs of the ever-increasing African population. The problem was compounded by the fact that beginning in 1907, when the company had finally realized that Rhodesia was not an El Dorado, the company sought to recoup profits from its investments by selling more land. However, there was still another obstacle to be overcome by the company: the settlers, who were aware of their growing political power, refused to recognize the company's claim to the unalienated lands in Rhodesia.

Milner was correct when in 1897 he wrote, "land was alienated in the most reckless manner to Companies and individuals."[35] Earlier, Lord Albert Grey, the third administrator in Rhodesia, had commented of Southern Rhodesia: "Land is our great difficulty. It has all been given away. I will not give away another acre until the Native Question has been settled."[36] Most of the companies to which Milner referred were subsidiaries of the British South Africa Company. By March 1899, a total of 15,762,364 acres had been alienated to Europeans and 9,276,222 acres were in the hands of private companies.[37] By 1900, the various missionary bodies held 406,200 acres,[38] half of which was owned by the Roman Catholics. Missionaries were given land by the chartered company so that they could carry on their Christian work among the Africans. Africans were still living on this land as they had been for generations prior to the coming of the Europeans, but now they were tenants paying rent or providing labor to the conquerors.

The settlement of 1894 is important for several reasons. It marked a departure in British policy toward the Africans of Rhodesia, because for the first time the British government failed to make use of the powers it possessed under the 1889 Royal Charter. The settlement also represented a repudiation by the company of the limitations imposed on it by the Rudd Concession of 1888. It was a triumph for the unrelenting pressure of the settlers, and in this respect it foreshadowed things to come. "The settlement of 1894 [was] of capital importance, because the rights and systems under which Southern Rhodesia has been administered were in all essentials settled then."[39]

The 1894 settlement may be defended as an attempt, if a weak one, by the British government both to control the company and to protect the interests of the Africans. But, as Ranger says, "the history of Company administration in 1894 and 1895 is largely the story of how these protective provisions of the Matebeleland Order in Council were flouted and evaded with regard to both land and the cattle."[40] In 1893, the might of the Matebele had been crushed and their land and cattle had been expropriated. As a result of the 1896-7 Chimurenga, the British government became aware of the consequences of uncontrolled activities by colonials. The 1895 Jameson Raid also proved what the unchecked ambitions of Rhodes and the agents of the company could do.[41] Consequently, in 1898 the British government issued an Order in Council to redefine its position and policy in Southern Rhodesia.

In issuing the 1898 Order in Council, the British government believed that it would be better able to protect the land and political rights of the Africans. It was on this assumption that the Order in Council called upon the company to set aside land (reserves) that would be occupied exclusively by Africans. The 1889 Royal Charter, affirming the Rudd Concession of 1888, had limited the chartered company's activities to mining. Yet, nine years later, the British government gave the company powers it had earlier denied it. Though there was no longer a conspicuous African ruler in Rhodesia, the British government could conceivably have chosen the West African policy by which conquest did not deprive the indigenous population of their land rights. The adoption of such a policy would have been in consonance with the stipulations of the 1889 Charter. Yet the British took no such action. Lord Olivier, a former Colonial Office employee, wrote:

Thus British Imperialism having, in framing the Charter, shown its intention to follow the British traditions and principles which have been successful in other Colonies, that is to say, to respect native land rights, had by the year 1898, been induced in furtherance of the capitalist system of European settlement, to forsake those principles and to adopt in their stead those of the Boer *voortrekkers* in dealing with Africans.[42]

The British government allowed the 1894 settlement to stand because it was not prepared to assume the financial responsibility of administration, and because any serious intervention on behalf of the Africans would have aroused the deep hostility of the settlers and the Europeans in South Africa.[43]

Though it was the armed might of the company and the settlers that by 1897 had subdued all African resistance, this action was in fact, taken on behalf of the British government. In 1918, the Privy Council ruled that, "a conquest of territory by the arms of the British Chartered Company is made on behalf of the Crown; it rests with the advisors of the Crown to determine how the territory shall be dealt with."[44] Hence, in 1898, the British government decided against the Africans on the issue of land rights. The 1889 Charter had instructed the company to recognize African customary law, under which all land was held in trust by the chief for the entire tribe. The company, as we have seen, ignored all this, and in 1898 the British government openly and unequivocally rejected African land custom. The final blow came in 1899 with Milner's proclamation, which completely dispossessed the Africans of land. "Reserve," declared Milner, "means land and property of the British South Africa Company set apart for the purposes of native settlements exclusively."[45] This meant that the British government in 1899 had completely reversed its 1889 position and now claimed that Africans did not own any land. The Africans, by being restricted to reserves, were to be rendered incapable of living where they had lived for generations before the Europeans had arrived. However, even the land into which the Africans were now expected to move did not belong to them; they were perpetual tenants of the British South Africa Company enjoying a certain tenure guaranteed by the British government. By 1898, the company and the settlers had emerged triumphant in their economic and political struggle against the Africans as well as against the British government.

NOTES

1. Peter Gibbs, *A Flag for the Matabele: A Story of Empire-Building in Africa* (London: Frederich Muller Ltd., 1955), pp. 71–72.

2. Hugh Marshall Hole, *The Making of Rhodesia* (London: Macmillan and Co., Ltd., 1926), pp. 133–134.

3. Stanlake Samkange, *Origins of Rhodesia* (London: William Heinemann, Ltd., 1968) chap. 9–11.

4. Hole, *The Making of Rhodesia*, p. 187.

5. Gibbs, *A Flag for the Matabele*, p. 72.

6. C. O. to Foreign Office, December 4, 1891, C. 7171. Copies and Extracts of Correspondence Relating to the British South Africa Company in Mashonaland and Matabeleland, p. 1.

7. Moffat to the Deputy High Commissioner, May 27, 1892, C. 7171, p. 31.

8. See p. 197 below. In 1918 the privy Council ruled that the Concession was binding only between Lobengula and Lippert but not his (Lobengula) successors.

9. C.O. to British South Africa Company, March 5, 1892, C. 7171. p. 10.

10. See Article 3 of the charter in C. 8773. British South Africa Company's Territories, p. 4.

11. Basil Williams, *Cecil Rhodes*, new ed. (London: Constable and Company Ltd., 1938), p. 172.

12. William Harvey Brown, *On The South African Frontier* (London: Sampson Low, Marston & Company, Ltd., 1899), pp. 348-49.

13. Williams, *Cecil Rhodes*, p. 145.

14. For details see Samkange, *Origins of Rhodesia*, chap. 19.

15. Quoted in John H. Harris, *Slavery or Sacred Trust* (London: Williams and Norgate, Ltd., 1926), pp. 76-77.

16. C. O. to B.S.A. Co., October 26, 1893, C. 7290. "Further Correspondence Relating to Affairs in Matabeleland, Mashonaland and the Bechuanaland Protectorate," p. 2.

17. B.S.A. Company to C.O., October 24, 1893, C. 7290, p. 2.

18. Samkange, *Origins of Rhodesia*, p. 262.

19. See British South Africa Company, *Report on the Company's Proceedings and the Condition of the Territories Within the Sphere of Its Operations: 1889-92*, 1892, p. 25.

20. C.O. 879/484, 1894.

21. Cf. M. R. Dilley, *British Policy in Kenya Colony*, 2nd. ed. (London: Cass, 1966), p. 248.

22. John H. Harris, *The Chartered Millions: Rhodesia and the Challenge to the British Commonwealth* (London: Swarthmore Press, Ltd., 1920,) p. 178.

23. A. Vindex, ed. *Speeches of Cecil Rhodes* (London: Chapman and Hall, Ltd., 1900) p. 271.

24. Sir H. B. Loch to the Marquess of Ripon, November 19, 1894. C. C. 879/482: South Africa: "Further Correspondance Relating to Affairs in Mashonaland, Matabeleland, and the Bechuanaland Protectorate," p. 97.

25. C. O. 879/484, 1894.

26. Cd. 8674. Southern Rhodesia Native Reserves Commission, Interim Report 1914, pp. 5-6.

27. C. O. 417/392, July 30, 1904.

28. C. O. 417/392, July 30, 1904.

29. See Chapter 6.

30. British South Africa Company Report, 1889-92, p. 25.

31. Cd. 8674, Interim Report 1914, p. 5.

32. Cd. 8674, Interim Report 1914, p. 6.

33. British South Africa Company Report 1889-92, p. 25.

34. Cd. 8674, 1914, Interim Report, pp. 6-7.

35. Milner to Chamberlain, December 1, 1897, in Cecil Headlam, ed., *The Milner Papers 1897-1899*, vol. 1 (London: Cassell & Co., Ltd., 1931), p. 140.

36. Quoted in Terence Ranger, *Revolt in Southern Rhodesia 1896-7* (London: Heinemann, 1967), p. 104.

37. Figures quoted in Robin H. Palmer, "The Making and Implementation of Land Policy in Rhodesia: 1890-1936," Ph.D. diss. London University, 1968).

38. Figures quoted in Harris, *Slavery or Sacred Trust*, p. 79.

39. Privy Council Judgment, *A. C. 1919 Law Reports: Appeal cases in Re. Southern Rhodesia*, p. 225.

40. Ranger, *Revolt in Southern Rhodesia, 1896-7*, p. 101.

41. Ibid., p. 335.

42. Lord Olivier, "Imperial Trusteeship," *Fabian Tract* no. 230, 1929, p. 7.

43. See Milner's letter to Chamberlain, December 1, 1897, Headlam vol. 1., *The Milner Papers*, p. 118.

44. *A. C. 1919 Law Reports Appeal Cases, In re., S.R.* p. 211.

45. C. O. 417/321. 1902.

4

The South African Filter

Rhodes, Chamberlain, and Milner all played important roles in shaping the early history of Southern Rhodesia. All three men approached Rhodesian affairs from the context of South Africa.

Rhodes's power in South Africa did not rest solely on his financial resources and his control of the British South Africa Company. In 1890 he became prime minister of the Cape Colony. As prime minister, Rhodes could easily influence the high commissioner who in his position as governor of the Cape was constitutionally the titular head of the Cape government. It was from the Cape and through its government and resources that Rhodes hoped to achieve his dreams of empire. Addressing the Cape Town Branch of the Afrikander Bond on April 17, 1891, Rhodes said: " . . . in providing for these northern developments [Mashonaland and Matebeleland] you have the most certain guarantee through me that that development is Cape Colony development. . . . I think we shall gradually go from the Cape to the Zambesi."[1] And again: "If there was anything that induced me to take the position of Prime Minister, it was the fact that I was resolved in my mind that we should extend to the Zambesi."[2] Rhodes undertook expansion into Rhodesia as a Cape colonist. He maintained "that his main object in securing the North was to redress the balance of South Africa and make it predominantly British. . . ."[3]

As far as Rhodes was concerned Rhodesia was an expansion of the Cape; the Cape, he hoped, would be the political center and Rhodesia the financial capital of South Africa. With the Cape and Rhodesia as his political and financial bases, Rhodes hoped that he could achieve what nineteenth-century British imperial policy

51

had failed to achieve—a union or federation of South Africa. On September 6, 1890, describing the policy to be pursued by his Cape government, Rhodes said: "The Government's policy will be a South African policy. What we mean is that we will do all in our power, whilst looking after the interests of the Cape Colony, to draw closer and closer the ties between us and the neighbouring States."[4]

In addition to the premiership of the Cape, Rhodes was also secretary for native affairs. He took this office because he believed that the "African Question" was very important. In 1894, Rhodes sponsored the Glen Grey Act, which was his statement of policy toward Africans. The Act stipulated the conditions under which Africans could get the vote.[5] During the second reading of the bill, on July 30, 1894, Rhodes claimed that he was also responsible for the Africans of Rhodesia. On the question of the franchise, he argued that Africans were still children who were just emerging from barbarism and were, therefore, not qualified to be responsible voters. However, Rhodes thought that those Africans who could meet the Cape Franchise qualifications, the ability to write one's name and address, a yearly income of fifty pounds, and immovable property valued at seventy-five pounds, could vote.[6] It is, therefore, not surprising that the same qualifications were adopted in Rhodesia. Rhodes also spoke, as did the Rhodesian settlers later, against liberal education for Africans, arguing that it would produce political agitators. Rhodes preferred industrial training and he advocated the establishment of African district councils in which Africans could discuss such local matters as building roads and bridges.

Rhodes was the first spokesman for self-government in Rhodesia. He believed that self-government for Rhodesia would be followed by union with the Cape and later by a federation of South Africa. But all this was predicated upon the belief that Rhodesia was rich in gold. As early as March 30, 1891 only seven months after Rhodesia's occupation, Rhodes said: "These territories [Mashonaland and Matebeleland] possess a sufficient amount of wealth to demand in time the principle of self-government. A change must then occur from the Chartered system of government to the Imperial system of union with the Cape Colony."[7] In his schemes Rhodes hoped to use the Rhodesian settlers. He believed that the British government would accede to the settlers' request for self-government as long as they used the ballot. In other words, Britain would listen to the popular "democratically" expressed wishes of the settlers. On December 19, 1893, at Bulawayo, Rhodes told the settlers that they had a right to self-government: "Now, what I want you to see is that really the mode of final settlement will not be with Her Majesty's Government, Dr. Jameson, or myself, but with you, the first settlers, and your representatives. . . ."[8]

Progress in Rhodesia was slow and this made Rhodes impatient. He tried other means to achieve his goals in South Africa. In 1895, Rhodes, Chamberlain, and Jameson entered into a conspiracy by which Jameson, heading troops from Rhodesia, would come to the aid of the Uitlanders (who were mostly British) at the Witwatersrand to topple the Boer government in the Transvaal.[9] The Jameson Raid was a complete failure; Jameson himself was arrested. Jameson survived the raid and later became prime minister of the Cape and a director of the B.S.A. Company.

The final attempt by the British to impose their will on the Boers culminated in the Boer War of 1899-1902. The consequences to the Africans of the Boer War and all the earlier unsuccessful attempts by the British to dominate the Boers in South Africa were disastrous. Aware of the small number of Europeans as compared to the African population, and aware of the Boers' racial attitudes toward the blacks and the readiness of the Boers to resist, the British government after 1902 pursued policies that were aimed at winning the friendship of the Boers at the expense of the Africans. One result of the Boer War was that "Great Britain abandoned the effort to exercise a control over the vital relations between white and black. Downing Street had surrendered to the frontier. . . . To insist upon a higher place for the natives was to offend the white communities. . . . Humanity and liberty became opposites which for long years had paralyzed action."[10]

The British government always considered Southern Rhodesia as a part of South Africa. Unlike Northern Rhodesia (now Zambia) and Nyasaland (now Malawi), the occupation of Southern Rhodesia by the B.S.A. Company was accepted by the British because it seemed likely to help them to achieve their policies in

South Africa. In the Colonial Office, Southern Rhodesia records were filed under the title of South Africa, whereas Northern Rhodesia and Nyasaland came under the title of Central Africa. Even the Rhodesian settlers considered themselves as South Africans. Rhodesian delegates attended several conferences that considered South African problems, including one in March 1903 to discuss a South African Customs Union.[11] A Rhodesian sat on the 1903–1905 South African Native Affairs Commission that sought to develop a uniform policy toward the Africans in the four South African provinces and Rhodesia.[12] Commenting on the commission, William Milton, the Rhodesian administrator, said: "During the year a further advance has been made in the direction of community of action among the several Colonies in South Africa."[13] In 1909, Rhodesians attended the conference that discussed the formation of the Union.[14] And in 1910, Rhodesian delegates attended the Inter-Colonial Agricultural Union meeting in Cape Town.[15] Even though Rhodesia refused to enter into the Union in 1910, the Union Constitution had a clause that clearly invited Rhodesia to join South Africa in the future.

Chamberlain as the colonial secretary and Milner as the high commissioner played important roles in determining British policy in South Africa at the turn of the century. Both were ardent believers in the British Empire, and both devoted their lives to consolidating the empire. Chamberlain regarded himself as "the missionary of empire" and Milner once referred to himself as "a civilian soldier of the empire." Chamberlain maintained that the racial problem between the Boers and the British was the result of deficient British policies in South Africa. He considered the British defeat at Majuba in 1881 as a tragedy. On May 14, 1888, seven years before he became colonial secretary, Chamberlain said of British policy in South Africa that: "The policy of successive Governments for a long period of time has been the policy of shirking. . . . It has been the avowed policy . . . to get rid of responsibilities and burdensome obligations, and everything we have done has been directed to this end."[16] The difficulties in South Africa, Chamberlain argued, had been caused by the fact that Britain had been pursuing a colonial policy in which the wishes of the settlers had been the decisive factor. The answer was an imperial policy in which the interests of the empire would come first. And because Britain was the guardian of the empire, she should be the paramount power in South Africa, a view that Milner wholeheartedly supported.

Milner came to South Africa when the clouds of the Boer War were gathering. He saw the Transvaal as a challenge to British preponderance in South Africa over the Boers. At one time Milner, like Rhodes, thought that Southern Rhodesia would solve the South African problem. If Rhodesia turned out to be the El Dorado everybody expected it to be, then Rhodesia would dominate South Africa financially and the Cape politically. A rich Rhodesia, Milner argued, would attract many British immigrants and in due course the British would outnumber the Boers in South Africa. However, his visit to Rhodesia in 1897 disillusioned him.

Upon his return to the Cape, Milner again turned his efforts to the Transvaal. He thought that reform there would give the English the vote and this would attract British immigrants and, in the long run through sheer voting strength, the problem of who would be dominant in South Africa would be solved. But this was not to be. The Boer War broke out in 1899. In a letter to Lord Selbourne, Milner wrote: "Certainly, unless we had asserted ourselves—with war as an almost certain result—we should have lost South Africa."[17] And in the House of Commons Chamberlain said, "The war is just and necessary, speaking for the Government, I say, that . . . there shall be no second Majuba. . . . Never again shall the Boers be able to treat an Englishman as if he belonged to an inferior race."[18]

When the war ended in 1902, Milner and Chamberlain made it the major aim of their efforts to reconcile the Boers and the British. Nothing was to be done that would create friction between the two white populations. Chamberlain visited South Africa toward the end of 1902. During his stay in South Africa, Chamberlain listened sympathetically to the many Boers and Britons who came to see him. The theme of his speeches was that all had erred in the past, but that all must now look to the future. He tried as hard as he could to win the confidence of the Boers. On December 30, 1902, Chamberlain made this plea: "I appeal to [the] Dutch and to [the] English . . . and I say, do everything in your power to bring about the union of the people . . . this union is

. . . necessary . . . and I believe is to be desired, not only in the interests of South Africa, but in the interests of the Empire as a whole. This is my message to South Africa; forget all the animosities of the past, look forward to the promise of the future."[19] And, again, in a speech, on January 8, 1903, to a deputation of one hundred Boers, Chamberlain said: "The hope of South Africa lies in closer contact between the races. We British and you Dutch are not separated either in interest or character. . . . I believe that . . . before many years are over, probably sooner than any of us can now anticipate, we shall be one free people under one flag."[20]

Milner was the chief architect of British policy in South Africa. He had confidence in eventual British supremacy. He wrote:

On the political side, I attach the greatest importance of all to the increase of the British population . . . If ten years hence, there are three men of British race to two of Dutch, the country will be safe and prosperous. If there are three of Dutch to two of British, we shall have perpetual difficulty. . . . We not only want a majority of British, but we want a fair margin. . . . It is only to be done by bringing British settlers, through Government agency. . . .[21]

After the war, Milner proposed a policy of cultural imperialism to anglicize the Boers. English was to be the medium of instruction in the schools, and English and world history were to be taught to give the Boers a world view. "If we keep it '[South Africa],' wrote Milner, "we shall have kept it by developing here a spirit of wider British patriotism."[22] In particular, Milner did not want to arouse antagonism on broader racial policy. He therefore argued successfully against Chamberlain who had at one point insisted that the franchise in the Transvaal and Free State be extended to nonwhites. Commenting on the Boer-British relationship after 1902, De Kiewiet observed that "South Africa quarrelled about everything but its native policy. Even the Home Government joined in the conspiracy of neglect. Aware of the explosive character of native policy, it forebore to speak or act lest there be added to the sum total of quarrelsomeness the outcry that had once been raised against Dr. Philip and Exeter Hall."[23] In a confidential letter, Milner, warning Chamberlain about liberalizing the franchise, wrote: "There are only two things that can placate extreme Boers, one is the restoration of their absolute independence, the other the enslavement of the native. The one thing which might possibly reconcile them to British rule, would be a native policy, the direct opposite of any we could adopt."[24] Even in Rhodesia, Milner was unwilling to intervene strongly on behalf of African rights for fear of arousing European hostility throughout South Africa. In a letter to Chamberlain he wrote:

I should feel quite confident of being able to get over the Dutch-English difficulty if it were not so horribly complicated by the Native question. . . . Rhodesia is a case in point. The blacks have been so scandalously used. Even now . . . I am not at all confident that many bad things will not happen. I am doing my best . . . but I have to walk with extreme caution for . . . if the Imperial Government were to be seen taking a strong line for the protection of the blacks . . . you might indeed unite Dutch and English against yourself and your policy of protection. There is the whole crux of the South African position.[25]

The high commissioner did not trust the Boers. When he left South Africa in 1905, he wrote to his successor warning him that the Boers could not be relied on. The Boers, he wrote, were deceitful and thought only of creating a South Africa in which they were preponderant. Leonard Thompson has made the brilliant observation that:

Milnerism became to the Afrikaner the epitome of British oppression and sowed [the] seed for a nationalism more bitterly anti-British than anything that had existed before the war. On balance, therefore, there can be little doubt that Lord Milner and the Unionist Government wrought harm in South Africa. Encouraging unattainable aspirations among British South Africans, increasing anglophobia among Afrikaners, and doing little to improve the prospects of the non-whites. . . . [were the results of Milners' policies].[26]

The editor of *The Central African Examiner*, in a review of Thompson's book, advanced the following reasons to explain why Milner's policy failed:

For, viewed in South African terms alone, Milner's policy was perfectly feasible—despite the strength of Afrikaner nationalism—provided only that Milner was given a free hand and enough troops. Two British divisions permanently stationed in South Africa might well have changed the future of the Continent. But these troops were never available; the Liberals disliked military expenditure; they were frightened of what they would have regarded as another Ireland; and their position was made even more difficult by the threatening war clouds in the diplomatic sky of Europe. Reform required strength, and the necessary link between liberal policy and physical force might well have been further stressed.[27]

Milner believed in the superiority of the British race. The implications for Rhodesia, where the British were in the majority vis-a-vis the Boers but a minority vis-a-vis the Africans, was white supremacy. Nor were these feelings confined to Milner; Chamberlain saw British rule and conquest of African tribes as conducive to the spread of civilization. Attacking the Anti-Slavery and Aborigines Protection Society and philanthropists, Chamberlain said:

There are, of course, among us—there always are among us, I think—a very small minority of men who are ready to be the advocates of the most detestable tyrants, provided their skin is black—men who sympathize with the sorrows of . . . Lobengula, and who denounce as murderers those of their countrymen who have gone forth at the command of the Queen, and have redeemed districts . . . from barbarism and the superstition in which they have been steeped for centuries.[28]

He continued:

I remember a picture by Mr. Selous of a philanthropist . . . sitting cozily by his fireside and denouncing the methods by which British civilization was promoted. This philanthropist complained of the use of the Maxim guns and other instruments of warfare, and asked why we could not proceed by more conciliatory methods, and why the impis of Lobengula could not be brought before a magistrate, and fined five shillings and bound over to keep the peace. . . . You cannot have omelettes without breaking eggs; you cannot destroy the practices of barbarism, of slavery, of superstition, which for centuries have desolated the interior of Africa, without the use of force. . . . The cause of civilization and the prosperity will in the long run be eminencly advanced.[29]

What role was the African to play in Milner's South Africa? "The ultimate end," he wrote, "is a self-governing white community, supported by well-treated and justly governed black labour from Cape Town to Zambesi."[30] Milner believed that the British government should, particularly in Rhodesia, secure adequate and sufficient protection for the Africans against oppression from the settlers. This was to be achieved by reserving legislation that affected Africans to the British government. Another way was to remind the settlers who came to Rhodesia that they had a duty to "educate" and "civilize" the Africans, but the settlers had only one interest and that was to get rich as quickly as they could even if it meant forcing Africans to work and paying them almost nothing. For instance, in March 1900 the resident commissioner, complaining to the administrator about forced labor, wrote: "The Native Commissioner, N'dangu, reports complaints have been made as to violence and irregularities committed by the Messengers of Mr. Posselt. . . . The Native Commissioner, Gutu, reports the exercise of a degree of pressure, on behalf of Mr. Posselt, to induce Natives to work . . . which in my opinion, amounts to compulsion."[31] To "civilize" and educate the Africans was detrimental to their interests since educated Africans would eventually compete with the European settlers economically and politically. This eventuality was objectionable to Milner because the unqualified opening of the social, political, educational, and economic gates to the Africans would result in the swamping of the Europeans—thus undermining Milner's cherished ideal of British preponderance in South Africa.

The role of the high commissioner was to be that of a watchdog. Milner publicly admitted that he would not intervene directly on behalf of the African to improve his condition socially and politically, when he said:

I am the man on the watch-tower, and the man on the watch-tower may see further than the men on the veld, not in the least because he is a better man, but because of the mere accident of his topographical position. . . . I hope the effect of what I say may be at any rate to mitigate what I may call the savagery of the opposition which exists in certain quarters with certain sections of our fellow creatures. It may be, or may not be, right to give them certain privileges; it must be wrong to refuse them in a way which leaves an enduring sense of injury or oppression.[32]

Curiously enough it was Milner's and his successors' refusal to intervene that has resulted in the unmitigated and savage oppression of the blacks that exists today in both South Africa and Rhodesia.[33]

So absorbed was Milner in South Africa that he did not pay as much attention as he should have to Southern Rhodesia. He believed that to appoint a governor in Rhodesia would weaken the authority of the high commissioner in South Africa.[34] The need for the Transvaal, to go through the high commissioner to get laborers from Rhodesia, and the fact that the high commissioner's authority extended over a large area enhanced his position and influence:

> I own that I do not like the idea of an independent Governor and that while I think it very desirable to relieve the High Commissioner of responsibility for many details of Rhodesian Administration, I should view with alarm the injury to his position and prestige, if Rhodesia were taken out of the sphere of his authority. . . . And in my view the influence of H. M. Government in South Africa, under present circumstances and for many years to come . . . depends very largely on the strength of the H. C.'s position. To weaken him in anyway is to weaken the most powerful factor, in fact the only factor worth mentioning, on the Imperial side.[35]

Clearly Milner did not want to risk the chance of having a governor in Rhodesia whose policies might endanger his overall South African policy. In fact, when, in 1904, Milner clashed with Marshall Clarke, the resident commissioner in Salisbury, over the issue of Chinese labor, Milner suggested that the office of resident commissioner in Rhodesia be closed at the expiration of Clarke's tenure.[36] The British government turned down Milner's suggestion arguing that:

The reasons for having a Resident Commissioner are as strong today as they were six years ago; and we can say that experience has shown that some such officer is, if not essential very useful . . . it [is] desirable to have an officer on the spot to watch developments and give warnings before anything is done which might land the territory in financial embarrassment and possibly involve H.M.G. in some pecuniary liability.[37]

Even when Milner in 1897 had felt that a rich Rhodesia could solve the South African problem, it could only do so, he believed, if it solved the African problem first, that is, make certain that there would be no recurrence of African revolts. In Rhodesia, "peace and order are absolutely essential." Milner wrote: "It [Rhodesia] must settle down now," he continued, "for another couple of years wasted over native troubles will retard development, make the Company bankrupt and throw an impecunious undeveloped country bigger than France upon your hands."[38] Once it was evident that Rhodesia could not solve the South African problem, Milner believed that any experiment in new and better white-black relationship in Rhodesia could create more difficulties for him in South Africa. Wrong though this attitude was, British policy toward the Africans in Rhodesia was allowed to follow the South African pattern.

NOTES

1. A. Vindex, ed., *Speeches of Cecil Rhodes* (London: Chapman and Hall Limited, 1900), p. 7.

2. Ibid., p. 272.

3. Ian D. Colvin, "The Future of Rhodesia," *The Quarterly Review* (April 1914): 524.

4. Vindex, ed., *Speeches of Cecil Rhodes*, p. 242.

5. Ibid. Also see Eric A. Walker, *A History of Southern Africa*, 3rd ed. (London: Longmans, Green and Co., Ltd., 1964), pp. 431-32.

6. Vindex, ed., *Speeches of Cecil Rhodes*, p. 272.

7. Ibid., p. 270.

8. Ibid., pp. 333-34.

9. See J. S. Marais, *The Fall of Kruger's Republic* (Oxford: The Clarendon Press, 1961), Chap. IV.

62 / THE RISE OF SETTLER POWER

10. Cornelius De Kiewiet, *A History of South Africa: Social and Economic* (Oxford: The Clarendon Press, 1941), pp. 143-44.

11. Cd. 1599, Report on Bloemfontein Customs Conference, p. 2.

12. Cd. 2399, Report of the South African Native Affairs Commission, 1903-1905, p. 2.

13. Southern Rhodesian Debates, April 26, 1905, p. 1.

14. Cd. 4525, Report by Delegates to S. A. National Convention, 1909, p. 2.

15. *The Rhodesia Journal* 13, no. 159 (November 3, 1910): 5.

16. Joseph Chamberlain, *Foreign & Colonial Speeches* (London: George Routledge & Sons, Ltd., 1897), p. 197.

17. Cecil Headlam, *The Milner Papers* ed. vol. 2 (London: Cassell & Co., Ltd., 1933), p. 550.

18. Quoted in N. Murrell Marris, *Joseph Chamberlain: Imperialist* (London: George Routledge & Sons Ltd., 1905), p. 116.

19. Quoted in Charles W. Boyd, ed., *Mr. Chamberlain's Speeches*, vol. 2 (London: Constable and Company Ltd., 1914), pp. 88-89.

20. Headlam, vol. 2, *The Milner Papers*, p. 433.

21. Milner to Major Hanbury Williams, December 27, 1900, ibid., pp. 242-43.

22. Milner to Spenser Wilkinson, April 27, 1903, ibid., p. 449.

23. De Kiewiet, *A History of South Africa*, p. 141.

24. Milner to Chamberlain, December 20, 1901, Headlam, vol. 2, *The Milner Papers*, p. 291.

25. Milner to Chamberlain, December 1, 1897, *Headlam*, vol. 1, *The Milner Papers*, p. 118.

26. L. M. Thompson, *The Unification of South Africa 1902-1910* (London: The Clarendon Press, 1960), pp. 16-17.

27. *The Central African Examiner* 3, no. 25 (May 7, 1960): 22.

28. Quoted in Boyd, *Mr. Chamberlain's Speeches*, p. 3.

29. Ibid., pp. 3-4.

30. Milner to Sir Percy Fitzpatrick, November 28, 1899, Headlam, vol. 2, *The Milner Papers*, p. 35.

31. Resident Commissioner to Administrator March 26, 1900. C. O. 417/284.

32. Headlam, vol. 2, *The Milner Papers*, p. 470.

33. See article by African Nationalist leader Joshua Nkomo, "Rhodesia: The Case for Majority rule," in Wilfred Cartey and Martin Kilson, eds., *The African Reader: Independent Africa* (New York: Random House, Inc., 1970), pp. 263-71. And also in Ndabaningi Sithole, *African Nationalism* (Cape Town: Oxford University Press, 1961), chap. III "White Supremacy and African Nationalism," and chap. IV "White Supremacy in Action."

34. Headlam, vol. 1, *The Milner Papers*, p. 120.

35. Milner to Chamberlain October 5, 1897, ibid., p. 119.

36. C. O. 417/391, 1904.

37. Minute by Grindle August 12, 1904. C. O. 417/392.

38. Milner to Chamberlain, December 1, 1897, Headlam, vol. 1, *The Milner Papers*, p. 140.

5
Political, Social, and Economic Development: 1898-1906

By 1898 the relationship between the Africans and the Europeans had changed and the British government issued an Order in Council to redefine its position. The 1898 Order in Council formed the basis of the country's governing machinery.[1] A resident commissioner, subordinate to the high commissioner in South Africa, was posted in Rhodesia to watch and report on the Company's activities. Milner believed that the presence of a British official in Rhodesia was very important. "It is evident to my mind," he wrote to Chamberlain, "that the only effective control over the proceedings of the Company is a local control, that it must be exercised by your Agents in South Africa, and that anything that may be done at home in the way of influencing the Board of Directors is secondary in importance to the maintenance of a guiding hand on the legislation and administration at Bulawayo and Salisbury."[2] And Lord Selbourne, who later succeeded Milner as high commissioner in South Africa, reported that: "Public opinion inside and outside Parliament insists on more control; and yet we must at all costs steer clear of saddling on H. M. Government any responsibility in the public mind, direct or indirect. . . ."[3]

But as Milner asked: "The question is, how to exercise this control in a manner which (1) shall be based on full information and therefore really useful; (2) shall not cause intolerable friction with the Company; and (3) shall satisfy public opinion at home?"[4] The composition of the Rhodesian administration ensured the company that its views would always prevail. At the head of the company government was an administrator, who in turn was assisted by an executive council, which consisted of the admin-

63

istrator himself, the resident commissioner, and five members nominated by the company.[5] Although the administrator usually acted on the advice of the Executive Council, he could if he wished ignore its advice. In such cases the administrator was required to report to the directors in London and explain why he had ignored the council's advice. The directors could reverse any action of the administrator and the colonial secretary could nullify the directors' decisions. In addition to the executive council there was a Legislative Council that consisted of five nominated members and four members elected by the settlers.[6] Both the administrator and the resident commissioner could take part in the Legislative Council debates although they could not vote. The administrator took precedence over the resident commissioner as did the nominated members over the elected members.

The power of the resident commissioner was limited to control over the military and the police, whose responsibilities were surrendered to the company in 1904 and 1909, respectively. Since the resident commissioner had neither voting nor vetoing power his control over the company was indeed very limited. In addition, he had a very limited number of independent sources of information, such as men working directly for him and paid by the British government to report from various areas of the country, particularly about the condition and grievances of the African people.[7] The resident commissioner was dependent upon native commissioners who were appointed and paid by the company and who reported to the administrator. And although the company submitted all its official documents to the Colonial Office, "important communications which the Company wished to keep out of Imperial hands simply found their way into private letters between Directors and the Administrator on the spot. Safeguards by remote control thus never worked well, and much more important than these outside watch-dogs was the local Legislature."[8]

In 1897, the Matebeleland Debating (European) Society wrote to the colonial secretary requesting representation in the Legislative Council, and, as we have seen, the 1898 Order in Council permitted the settlers to elect four representatives. The British government acquiesced in the demand for European representation for two reasons. First, settler representation would force the Company to concentrate its activities in Rhodesia. It was one of the ways to prevent future Jameson Raids. Many settlers argued that the 1896–97 African uprising took place because the Company police had left Rhodesia to take part in the raid.[9] "After the suppression of the Mashona rising of 1896 Her Majesty's Government took up the question of rendering more effective the machinery for the control of the Company's administration by the Crown. . . ."[10] Second, according to Ranger, "the importance of the effects of the rebellion were . . . that they predisposed the Company and the imperial government to accept the idea [of settler representation]. The Company did so because it believed that it was the least price which it could pay in the circumstances to satisfy the settlers and also offer to the British public the appearance of significant reform."[11] Chamberlain saw settler representation as a restraint upon Rhodes's schemes. "The sooner some kind of local government of a popular kind can be established in Rhodesia the better."[12]

Milner thought that settler representation was a progressive step toward self-government. If Rhodesia were rich in minerals, he believed, a large influx of British settlers would follow. These were Rhodes's hopes as well. Describing Rhodes's plans in a letter to Lord Selbourne in 1897, Milner wrote: "He [Rhodes] looks to making the territory of the B.S.A.C. into a separate Colony ultimately self-governed. The Colony he means to unite with the Cape and Natal, and then the three combined will bring peaceful pressure upon the Republics to drive them into a S. African Federation. . . . In my opinion the policy, in the main, is good. . . ."[13] Settler representation, it was hoped, would eventually help to achieve overall British policy in South Africa. "The success or failure of our policy in this country as a whole [South Africa]," wrote Milner, "depends largely upon getting the development of the North [Southern Rhodesia] onto the right lines."[14]

Self-government for the Rhodesian settlers was considered by the British government long before the settlers asked for it, and was apparently delayed only because of lack of sufficient economic progress to warrant it. It was the lack of sufficient economic progress that set the stage for the struggle between the settlers and the company.

The men, back in England, who had purchased shares in the company were primarily interested in the financial returns the Rhodesian venture was expected to produce. The company's activities were therefore directed at securing these returns at the earliest possible time. Herein lay one source of the economic and political misunderstandings between the company and the settlers. The settlers had come into the country in search of riches, but they also wanted to make Rhodesia their home, and were, therefore, interested in the rapid economic development of the country. The company was also interested in the rapid development of the country, but it sought to tie this development to the needs of the shareholders first and those of the settlers second.

Life for the early settlers was extremely difficult. Some, as Hole reported, had the clothes they wore as their only belongings.[15] All their requirements and their farming and mining equipment came from South Africa by road and rail.[16] The company had a monopoly on the railways and the rates it charged were very high. "Markets were few and far between. Transport was expensive."[17] Transporting goods from South Africa was also very slow. In the wet season the wagons were often bogged down in the mud, so that deliveries of mail and sometimes urgently needed medicines were delayed.[18] The company had imposed a 50 percent tax on the profits of each mining claim and expected, without spending a penny in the cost of production, to share in the profits of every mine.[19] The settlers were further annoyed by the fact that some claims were turned down in areas that the company suspected to be rich in gold.[20]

Many of the settlers felt that the company was insensitive to their problems. Adrian Darter, one of the 1890 pioneers, wrote. "Curse the money-grabbing . . . of the Company promoters who run this country. What is the life of man or horse to them?"[21]

The settlers' economic grievances against the company were justified. The settlers found out that the aims of the commercial company that ruled them were prejudicial to their own economic well-being. Both the settlers and the company wanted to be rich but the company wanted to be rich at the expense of the settlers. The settlers readily blamed the company for all their economic difficulties. By 1902, some settlers were arguing that the chartered company may have been needed during the occupation period, but that the pioneer stage of the country had ended and the company was no longer necessary. Others even claimed that company rule stood in the way of Union of Rhodesia with the other South African colonies, their argument being that in order to enter into the Union Rhodesia would have to have political status equal to the other colonies. "The continuation of the Charter," editorialized the *Bulawayo Observer*, "is a bar to the unification or federation of South Africa; and it prevents Rhodesia from taking her proper place amongst the States of South Africa."[22]

The settlers thought that a political solution would reduce their economic distress, and between 1902 and 1904 they clamored for the abrogation of the charter.[23] The following excerpt from the editorial of the *Bulawayo Observer* of September 12, 1902, is typical of the settlers' complaints. The title of the editorial, in heavy black print, was "What the People Want and What They Don't Want."

We want to stay in the country . . .
We want only what we have a right to ask for . . .
We want the Chartered Co. removed
From a false position for which
The Home Government is primarily responsible . . .
We want reduced railway rates . . .
We want a Crown colony as a first step.
We want a reasonable hope of responsible Government . . .
We don't want Charter Government any longer.[24]

The unpopularity of the Company in England was matched by a sympathy for the settlers as the "little men." The wars the company had fought with the Africans and the part it had played in the Jameson Raid were seen as clear examples of what could be expected from uncontrolled and rampant capitalism. The fact that the settlers had supported the Jameson Raid was overlooked.

There were, however, reasons why a change in company rule was impossible at the time. First, the company had a twenty-five year charter that would expire in 1914, and the company's shareholders needed time to make profits on their investment.[25] Crown Colony government would have involved Britain more directly in the affairs of Rhodesia, and the British government was not keen to do this since such an action would involve it financially in a country whose economic situation was gloomy. Responsible government was out of the question because Rhodesia's economic future was unknown and the European population, whose growth was dependent on the country's economic progress, was very small. The number of Europeans in Southern Rhodesia grew slowly; in 1909, the estimated total was only 14,007.[26]

In response to the agitation of the settlers, the board of directors sent Sir George Goldie, chairman of the board, to Rhodesia in 1904. In April of that year, Goldie suggested that the company raise a loan for £7,500,000 at 4 per cent interest, of which £2,500,000 would be spent in Rhodesia and £5,000,000 was to be paid as dividends to the shareholders of the company.[27] The proposal showed the eagerness of the board of directors to compensate the shareholders and justified the accusations of the settlers that the Company put their interests after those of the shareholders, especially when only £2,500,000 was to be spent in Rhodesia and £5,000,000 paid to the Company—and this at a time when Rhodesia was in dire need for capital. Goldie suggested the £5,000,000 amount because he claimed that that was what the company had spent in occupying the country, defeating the Africans, building the railways, and establishing the administration. His proposal led to a bitter dispute between the company and the settlers about who was responsible for the country's deficit. Even the editor of *The Bulawayo Chronicle,* who was generally sympathetic to the company, commented: "The interests of the people and of the commercial body which governs them are, far from being identical, widely opposed. The Chartered Company desires to retain its position as the grestest landed proprietor in Rhodesia; but in asking the settlers to defray the whole costs of administration it wishes to evade the payment of . . . the ordinary taxes of the country. Instances of other and widely diverging interests could be multiplied. . . ."[28] The 1905 election proved that the settlers were against the idea of a loan and that they did not consider themselves responsible for the company's deficits. The settlers were, however, prepared to pay for the expenses the company had incurred in public works.[29]

The violent agitation for the abrogation of the charter by the majority of the settlers was part of their search for a cure to the grave economic difficulties they faced at the turn of the century.

These difficulties, inevitable in a new country, had been worsened by the Chimurenga of 1896–97 and by the Boer War, which sent prices of goods soaring. The depression that followed the end of the war had not helped matters. Most Rhodesians were aware that they still needed the company to develop the country—the small European population could not raise enough revenue to run and develop the country nor could it find anyone willing to lend it money. The settlers needed to continually prod the company to develop the country rapidly. Although their political and economic problems remained unsolved, the settlers in the period beginning 1906–7 increased their efforts to improve their economic position.

This period was very important in the political development of the country. The settler community learned to organize itself into a cohesive political unit. They formed political organizations like the Matebeleland Political Association and the Mashonaland Political Association in 1904, and the Mashonaland Progressive Association and the Rhodesian Constitutional League in 1907. The settlers held public meetings in the towns throughout the country and wrote many letters to the press. Their united voice was not only heard in Whitehall but also carried weight there. By January 1907, Lord Selbourne, the high commissioner, described the principles guiding British policies toward the settlers in South Africa as a whole. He wrote: "It is a modern axiom of British policy that any attempt to manage the domestic affairs of a white population by a continuous exercise of . . . direct authority . . . in which the people concerned are not represented, is . . . a certain path to failure."[30] In 1907, Lord Selbourne visited Rhodesia to check the settlers' grievances. There is no doubt that these early exchanges between the company and the settlers put the former in a defensive position and throughout the remainder of its tenure the company felt the need to apologize for its administration. The settlers were clearly becoming the dominant political force in the country.

While the settlers aggressively asserted themselves, the political position of the Africans gradually weakened. In 1897 the power of the Africans to resist was broken. "In his [Milners'] day," commented Walker, "the Native Question was not pressing; the machine gun, Rhodes's little thing . . . had disposed of it as a military problem. . . ."[31] The Matebele were left without a king around which opposition to company control could be rallied. Until long after 1897, Matebele politics were directed mainly at the restoration of the King. In Mashonaland, the chiefs who had taken part in the uprising were punished and removed from office and replaced by loyal appointees of the company.

The political relationship between the Africans on the one hand and the company and settlers on the other had to be restructured after 1897. In a letter to Milner, Chamberlain explained why:

> The control (over the Co.) provided by the old system, adequate in theory, had not, in practice been sufficiently exercised by the High Commissioner or the Secretary of State . . . to prevent . . . abuses in the administration in connnection with the treatment of natives. It would, therefore, be necessary to satisfy public opinion [in Britain] that a new and more effective plan of control had been devised.[32]

Milner concurred with Lord Selbourne's observation. But how was this to be done? Milner wished for the Africans to be protected from oppression but he lacked the will to see it done. "We should secure for the Natives," he wrote, "particularly in the part of Africa called Rhodesia adequate and sufficient protection— against oppression and wrong . . ."[33] Milner knew that he could not depend on the settlers to redress African grievances. "We cannot," Milner wrote in 1897, "rely on the representative [settler] element . . . to cure . . . defects especially where native legislation is concerned. Rather the contrary."[34] Milner's solution was that legislation involving Africans would only become law with the approval of the British government. But the British government was not prepared to intervene positively on the Africans' behalf. Rather it hoped to use its influence to mitigate company and settler policies toward the Africans. In a letter to Asquith, Milner expressed the dilemma he faced when he wrote: "I have a strong conviction of what policy I ought to pursue, having regard at once to Colonial rights of self-government and to the plighted faith of Great Britain to the Natives. . . . I can only use personal influence . . . to restrain the [Europeans]. . . ."[35] In Rhodesia this influence was to be exercised by an appointed British resident commissioner who would periodically report to the high commissioner in South Africa.[36] Usually influence without the power and willingness to use it to back up causes or principles is ineffective.

Toward the end of 1897 Milner said this of the company's African administration:

> A lot of unfit people were allowed to exercise power, or at any rate did exercise it, especially with regard to the natives, in a manner which cannot be defended. I know the difficulties were enormous. Perhaps they explain the future, but failure it was, and the rebellion was largely due to it. . . . The number of competent men available is small, and the amount of riff-raff having some sort of claim on the Company . . . is considerable. . . . The danger comes in, when they are sent to important administrative posts, especially Native Commissioners. In the present state of the country the government of the natives must be largely personal government.[37]

The Native Department was reorganized in 1898. Milner was convinced that the best way to safeguard African interests was to ensure the appointment of able whites in the Native Department. He wrote: "The great thing here [Rhodesia] is to secure the appointment of honourable and capable men as magistrates and Native Commissioners. If that can be done, I think the lot of the Natives may be a very tolerable one. . . ."[38] In 1899, Milner empowered the administrator to appoint and remove chiefs from office.[39] Several chiefs whose actions went against the directives of the administrator were dismissed. The role and function of the chiefs was defined by Milner in 1899. A chief's duties, he proclaimed, were to assure the good conduct of his constituency and to report crimes and deaths. The chief was assisted by headmen whom he appointed; the headmen, according to Milner, were to be considered and act as constables. Above the chief was the native commissioner, who was responsible for the good behavior of the chief and the Africans in his district. The high commissioner wanted the chiefs to act as law enforcers,[40] which represented a significant change. The role of the chief prior to the advent of the European had been positive; as judge he was more corrective than punitive.

As discussed in a later chapter, the Native Department saw

reserves as areas where Africans would be easily controlled economically, religiously, and politically. The reserves were also areas where labor could be easily solicited.

The main consideration in British policy toward the Africans, ever mindful of the Chimurenga of 1896–97, was to ensure that African advancement should not present the Europeans with a challenge that might erupt into violence.[41] British policy sought to consolidate company control over the Africans while, by introducing settler representation in 1898, it strengthened the position of the settler vis-a-vis the company. The administrator, as secretary for African affairs, was the sole representative of nearly three quarters of a million Africans in the Legislative and Executive councils. But the administrator was first and foremost the representative and agent of the company—a capitalist organization interested above all else in making profit.

The ugly role that native commissioners played in their attempts to provide the farming and mining communities with labor is shown in the discussion of the labor shortage in Rhodesia. When the native commissioners were later barred from labor recruiting the majority faithfully complied.[42] In other respects, however, the work of the native commissioners was primarily concerned with controlling Africans—and they therefore worked indirectly for the benefit of the settlers. "The Native Commissioners [were] appointed by the Government to control the native population. . . ."[43] Every native commissioners' report from 1899 to 1923 reported on the African attitude toward Europeans, clearly stipulating whether it was friendly or hostile. In 1904, native commissioners' reports abound with warnings of African unrest and imminent uprising.[44] Thus, the zeal of the native commissioners was not motivated by their humanitarian disposition—rather it was primarily motivated by a desire to control Africans. It was the effectiveness of this control that made the Native Department seem so efficient in the eyes of the British government.[45]

Yet we must ask what the lot of the African was between 1897 and 1906. After 1897, any uprising by the Africans could have been easily put down. The violence and brutality of the 1896–97 encounter with the Europeans had been such that no African leader any longer thought of violence as a means to make his views known. Although the Africans had no organized or united leadership to speak for them, they nevertheless, at least until 1904, had considerable indirect influence on the thinking of both the company and the settlers. The Africans' brave and heroic efforts in the 1896–97 war left the Europeans filled with fear of similar eruptions.

During the years following their defeat in 1897, the leadership of the Africans was decimated, unorganized on a national level, and did not have articulate spokesmen to present a united political viewpoint. The old traditional African leadership had valiantly failed to stem the tide of European expansion, but it was no longer at the helm. New leadership, which was less aggressive and more acceptable to the company, had been installed. Even the new leaders' authority and control over the masses was undermined by the restrictions imposed on the leaders by the 1899 high commissioners' proclamation.[46] The native commissioners further encouraged the undermining of that authority. In 1909, the chief native commissioner of Matebeleland reported: "Chiefs. . . . [and] parents no longer have that control over their children which they formerly exercised. The natives are in a transition state, and are becoming more enlightened as each year goes by. It would be a mistaken policy to attempt to arrest this individualistic tendency."[47] New forces, such as Western education, contact with the Europeans in the industrial centers, and missionary activity dealt serious blows to the authority of traditional leadership.

In these altered circumstances, the chiefs, rather than assuming an aggressive role, invariably and passively cried out against the change that was taking place in their societies. The chiefs failed to master change—hence new spokesmen had to emerge. In every year from 1899 onward the native commissioners reported that the chiefs complained of the loss of authority over their people.

The new leadership required a knowledge and understanding of the ways of the foreigner. This had to come from Africans who were in contact with the Europeans and their ways—whether through formal or informal education. This knowledge did not arise during the first two decades of European rule because time was necessary for the educative process to produce the required leadership. What was needed was a new leadership that would meet the new situation, the kind of leadership that would operate modern political organizations, transcend tribal loyalty, and solicit the support of all Africans in order to effectively challenge the settlers. Ranger was therefore right when, in writing of the period after 1897, he said: "It was difficult for new forms of political protest or action to grow up. . . . There had been virtually no Shona converts to Christianity before the risings and so there were now very few literate Shona in touch with the new world. The educational break-through was a slow process; Shona leaders were not really produced by it for twenty or thirty years after the risings."[48] The attempts by the Ethiopian movement, led by dissatisfied Methodist African ministers, to establish a base for an effective opposition against European control was a failure. In 1906 the chief native commissioner of Matebeleland reported:

> The influence of the Ethiopian movement, which has been in a small way established here for four years, has not made itself felt. It would appear that the objective of this particular order in the first instance is to impress on the uncivilized and uneducated native that the sect is conducted quite independently of any European control, and is supported entirely by people of their own color. The dissemination of such propaganda would convey to the native mind some political meaning. A close observance of this movement is kept.[49]

It was not until the end of World War I that a new political consciousness among the "educated" Africans began to make its voice heard in Rhodesian politics.

At the kraal schools the missionaries did their best to drive a wedge between the students and the Africans who remained in the village.[50] Though they had arrived in Rhodesia before 1890, the missionaries failed to make Christianity take a hold in the country. Later the missionaries were blamed by the Matebele for having tricked Lobengula into signing the Moffat Treaty and the Rudd Concessions. Kapenzi writes: "Christianity marched into Mashonaland [and Matebeleland] on the heels of the invading Pioneer Column and found itself in close identification with the whites at the inception of its activities in the area."[51] The spirit mediums played a very important role in the Chimurenga of 1896–97 and in the early stages of the fighting Africans attacked and destroyed mission stations at Chishawasha and at St. Bernard's (now Bernard Mzike) where Mzike, an African preacher, was killed. Molele, another African preacher, was killed near Waddilove, another mission station.

It is not, therefore, surprising that the missionaries hated the ngangas (whom the whites called witchdoctors) very much. Ngangas were primarily people who specialized in detecting witches who were believed by many Africans at the time to be evildoers who either caused death or brought disaster to the people. Many Africans thought that witches did their evil work at night and that they were naked, and they were also thought to have extraordinary and magical powers such as the power to enter houses through keyholes and to open graves, and to bring the dead to life. The task of the nganga was to detect witches and to have them destroyed or banished from the village. The method of witch detection was, at times, abused by chiefs who used it to destroy potential rivals. The missionaries hated the ngangas because of the hold they had on the Africans, and they saw this hold as a threat to their Christianizing efforts.[52] The Africans thought that the missionaries used magic to counteract the influence of the ngangas. Africans feared witches because they believed that witches used magic. In their eagerness to awe and convert the Africans, the missionaries spoke of the death and resurrection of Christ. They preached that Jesus could turn water into wine, feed thousands of people on five fishes and loaves of bread, command the wind to obey him, walk on water, and raise Lazarus from the grave. It is easy to see why Africans thought that the missionaries used magic. Very often before going to a missionary hospital Africans consulted ngangas for their advice and opinions. The method of diagnosis used by the missionary often seemed magical to the ordinary villager. "The witchdoctors," wrote Kidd, "are often consulted by relations who wish to get some medicine which will counteract the influence of the missionary, who is supposed often to act on the people by magic. The only objection to medical missions is the way the people at first think the missionary is using powerful magic."[53]

The missionaries, perhaps unconsciously, compared themselves to ngangas. They were at pains to distinguish between their ceremonies at the altar and the bone throwing of the ngangas.

Rev. A. Burbridge clearly made the contrast when he emphatically wrote that the nganga "is not a priest; he knowns no altar; he never prays. He is the antithesis of religion, the personification of magic."[54] The missionary saw the nganga as the priest of heathenism.

This discussion is important because in order to succeed in his efforts at conversion or even establish a foothold, the missionary had depended, and later still continued to depend on, the European administration. Had the missionaries been successful prior to 1890, they could very well have been in a better position to oppose settler policies of coercion. Their base of operation would not have been tied down to the settler presence in the country. And, therefore, the success of the missionaries' efforts would not have been dependent on settler power. But as it was, the missionaries received land and money grants from the administration that stipulated conditions upon which money grants could be made. Because of their dependence on the Europeans, the missionaries were never able to provide effective opposition to European policies. Beyond being subject to conditions imposed by a white-dominated society, many missionaries believed that their cause was tied to the success of colonialism. The missionary effort could only continue and succeed if European presence in the country was assured. Rev. Burbridge wrote: "The crowning horror of all sickening horrors that would ensue on the whiteman's exit would be the supremacy of the witchdoctor. Though under direct civilized rule his power is not yet broken, it can never be supreme."[55]

Missionary activity among the Africans played an important role in the political development of the Africans. In the field of education the missionary emphasized the study of the scriptures and industrial work; the latter because it was one of the conditions under which government grants could be made. Discipline, complete obedience to authority, was to be rigorously cultivated in African students. The missionaries were one with the settlers in their wish to destroy tribal society and its norms. They supported the major changes that European pressure brought to bear on tribal society. Those changes that would encourage individualism would help the missionary to convince the African that his salvation could only be attained through his individual repentance. Only after the individual villager had broken his bond with the past could he be able to accept and be accepted by the new religion. For instance, many Africans who had more than one wife upon their conversion were told to keep one wife and abandon their other wives—but many chose their wives rather than Christianity. Part of the missionary's dilemma was the result of the fact that, because of his European cultural background, he shared the racial attitudes of the settlers toward tribal society— hence, his overzealousness to impose a European ideology on the African. According to Professor Gann, the Bible instructed the missionaries that, "No man putteth a piece of new cloth unto an old garment. . . . Neither do men put new wine into old bottles; else the bottles break, and the wine runneth out and the bottles perish: but they put new wine into new bottles, and both are preserved."[56] And Gann further observed: "Late Victorian and Edwardian missionaries took this injunction very seriously, and interpreted their Saviour's words in such a fashion as to try and bring about a complete change in the old Africa. The tribesmen's ways must change in root and branch and what the white preachers aimed for was not reformism, but a complete ideological revolution."[57] Ranger tells us that a Roman Catholic priest, frustrated by the conservatism of tribal society, suggested that all Africans above the age of fourteen be killed.[58] Resolutions unanimously passed by the clergy of the Anglican Diocese of Mashonaland in 1902 are interesting. The missionaries resolved:

under a deep sense of responsibility to the native races. . . . We offer as a humble contribution to the solution of a great question affecting . . . the whole political, social, and industrial future of South Africa . . . 1) . . . We believe that the Christain Faith . . . recognizes the inequalities existing in individuals and races arising from the fact, that neither individuals nor races are born with equal faculties or opportunities. . . . 5) We believe that the only way to fit the natives of Africa to fill the place intended for them in the Commonwealth is by the disciplinary influences of the Christian Gospel. This Gospel . . . involves the training of the native in a sense of responsibility to himself to his neighbour, and to the State.

. . . 8) the Church and the State should introduce . . . a universal system of industrial training and education.[59]

The missionary was apparently aware of the fact that he identified his culture with Christianity. In other words, to be a Christian one had to be "Europeanized." At a Pan Anglican Congress in London in 1909, Bishop James Johnson of Nigeria argued that Christianity was a religion not of one race but of the whole world, and that it should embrace the cultures of other races.

It [Christianity] should have in Europe a European type; in Africa an African type;—different formulae of Faith and different ceremonies of worship. . . . The Christian missionary has commonly been a European, a foreigner. . . . Whatever his excellence and however liberal-minded he may be, he must be less than human if he should be altogether free from the weakness which leads every nation or every tribe to account its own language and customs better than those of others, and indeed the best in the world, and to speak of those of others as barbarous. But the foreign missionary's order from his Divine Master is to preach the Gospel, and not European customs or form of civilization, or the Gospel and this civilization together. His attitude, however, towards African customs of all kinds has not shown him to have been entirely unaffected by European prejudice.[60]

Furthermore, the missionaries and their involvement with the African were "generally looked at askance [by the settlers], for the popular impression was that they laid too much emphasis on the 'man-and-brother' theory, and overlooked the necessity for starting at the bottom and gradually inculcating ideas of discipline, hygiene and thrift, with the result that the black man . . . became uppish and troublesome."[61]

An important consideration in the political development of the Africans was the attitude of the white settlers to African aspirations. At the turn of the century most if not all Europeans in Rhodesia believed that the Africans were savages. The *Bulawayo Observer* in its editorial of September 12, 1902, expressed this typical settler attitude when it said:

The fundamental principle which must underlie legislation and which must be understood in Britain is that an overwhelming [number] of the millions of natives under British rule ... are in practically the same position to-day that they occupied a hundred years ago, that is in regard to their moral and mental equipment, and the physical conditions of their daily life; in other words they are barbarians, and are likely to continue so for many years to come. .... The natives must be treated by the Government as being what they are, that is a people still in its childhood.[62]

Three years later *The Bulawayo Express* echoed these sentiments. "There is a wide gulf fixed between the black and the white which cannot be bridged in a country like South Africa." Its editor wrote, "No matter what Exeter Hall may say, the whites will not reckon the blacks as equals, and if they did it would simply mean the degeneration of the whites."[63] Professor I. D. Maccrone of Witwatersrand University tells us that these attitudes united the settlers and that they were "the underlying reality of social life. ...."[64] Maccrone explained: "In spite of numerous exceptions in both races, it is these images or concrete ideas strongly charged with emotion which determine the attitude of the white man both to members of his own group as well as to members of the alien group."[65]

Most settlers were in agreement that a liberal education was bad for the Africans. It was frequently argued that education would make Africans cocky and dishonest. One white woman in Salisbury once remarked that the sight of an African doing arithmetic raised visions of "educated" Africans forging checks.[66] In August 1902, *The Rhodesia Herald* reported that the aim of education should be to make the African "more respectful and obedient to the white people."[67] In May 1907 during a debate in the Legislative Council, Homan, an elected member, revealed that the government had collected £190,000 in taxes from Africans and of this only £1,500 had been given as aid to African mission schools.[68] "They had in this country," argued Homan, "a very valuable asset in the native and . . . thought that the sum voted to the missions in this country should be largely increased. Not for merely technical education but for the purpose of teaching natives such trades as carpentry, masonry and so forth. He did not want the native to be given a higher school education; they could learn the ordinary abc and the numbers but if they taught them trades it would make the natives far more useful men than they were today."[59] In the same debate, Col. Napier, another elected member, said that African taxes were used to police the country: "If there were no natives in the country there would be no police, for there would be no necessity for them. . . . £1,000 was amply sufficient for any education which they gave to the natives. Personally . . . the uneducated native was the most honest, trustworthy, and useful . . . let them teach the native industrial habits and learn that he must get his bread by hard, honest, and continuous work and not by plurality of wives."[70]

The settlers feared that once the Africans were educated they would agitate against political, social, and economic discrimination.[71] "If we are to widely and thoroughly educate the Kafir," wrote the editor of the *Rhodesian Times*, "we are signing the death warrant of the success of white posterity in South Africa. Nature and destiny have ruled that the black races are to be hewers of wood and drawers of water. . . . The lesson of the past has always shown that education cannot improve his [African] morals, though it may enlarge his intellect. . . ."[72] In June 1904, Col. Napier suggested that Africans be prevented from walking on the streets used by Europeans and, Holland, another elected member, maintained that blacks and whites were not equal socially. Educated Africans would not stand for this. "Today," editorialized the *Chronicle*, "the natives are, in the mass, uneducated and without organization; they are split up into many tribes of different habits and thoughts. . . . The native of South Africa is strong and virile; he is imitative, quick to learn, naturally vain and fond of power. His compelled submission to white rule results, at present, mainly from the fact that he is uneducated."[73]

The educational and property qualifications were theoretically color-blind but were discriminatory in practice. In 1903, there were 5,199 European voters, 52 Asiatics, and only 51 Africans.[74] Most, if not all, of the qualified Africans were South Africans who had come into the country with the 1890 settlers and had received eighty-acre land grants for their services to the company. Yet despite the fact that there were practically no Rhodesian Africans on the voters roll, Forbes, an elected member of the Legislative Council, suggested, in 1905, that Africans be suspended from the rolls until a federation of South Africa had taken place and general legislation passed.[75] "At present," Forbes argued, "Rhodesia consisted of a small white community surrounded by a very large native population; and once the natives realized the power given them by the franchise, there might not only be a jury entirely composed of natives, but they might elect every one of the representative members sitting in this House."[76]

We have discussed the attitudes of the company toward African development; we have also considered the missionary role and its limitations. The net object of the whites in Rhodeisa was to produce partially Westernized Africans who would not challenge European supremacy. The progress of the Africans, particularly in education despite their eagerness for it, was slow. Since the B.S.A. Co. submitted its records and minutes (these included native commissioner's reports, Legislative Council debates, and occasionally cuttings from Rhodesian newspapers), the British government was aware of the European attitudes and the rate of African advancement. The outstanding feature of British policy toward the Africans is the lack of clear principles about the advancement of Africans. By silence, Britain conspired with the settlers to retard African development.

NOTES

1. C 9138, Papers Relating to the British South Africa Company, 1899, pp. 1–3.

2. Milner to Chamberlain, October 5, 1897, Cecil Headlam, ed., *The Milner Papers* vol. 1, (London: Cassell & Co., Ltd., 1931), p. 118.

3. Selbourne to Milner, November 11, 1897, ibid., p. 122.

4. Milner to Chamberlain, December 1, 1897, ibid., p. 141.

5. C 9138, 1899, p. 6. The five nominated members could be removed or suspended by the company if they voted against it.

6. The franchise qualifications were similar to those of the Cape. Any male British subject over the age of twenty-one who had immovable property valued at seventy-five pounds or over or whose annual salary was fifty pounds or over and could write his name and address in English could vote. C 9138, 1899, p. 20.

7. On December 1, 1897, in a letter to Chamberlain, Milner noted that information on African administration was far from accurate. See Headlam, vol. 1,*The Milner Papers*, p. 141.

8. L. H. Gann, *A History of Southern Rhodesia: Early Days to 1934* (London: Chatto & Windus, 1965), p. 143.

9. William Harvey Brown, *On the South African Frontier* (London: Sampson Low, Marston & Company, Ltd., 1899), p. 321.

10. Privy Council Judgment, *A. C. 1919 Law Reports Appeal Cases In re.*, S.R., p. 228.

11. Terence Ranger, *Revolt in Southern Rhodesia 1896-7* (London: Wm. Heinemann, Ltd., 1967), pp. 334-35.

12. Chamberlain to Milner, July 5, 1897. Headlam, vol. 1, *The Milner Papers*, p. 9.

13. Milner to Lord Selbourne, June 2, 1897, Ibid., pp. 105-6. Similar views were also expressed by the English traveler and historian James Bryce after visiting Rhodesia and South Africa. See James Bryce *Impressions of South Africa*, 3rd, ed. (London: Macmillan and Co., Ltd., 1899), p. 277.

14. Milner to Graham, September 29, 1897, Headlam, vol. 1 *The Milner Papers*, p. 118.

15. Hugh Marshall Hole, *Old Rhodesian Days*, (London: Macmillan and Co., Ltd., 1928) p. 76. Also see Chap. X in Adrian Darter, *The Pioneers of Mashonaland: Men Who Made Rhodesia* (London: Simpkin, Marshall, Kent & Co. Ltd., 1914). Darter went to Rhodesia in 1890 with the Pioneer Column.

16. The railway line from South Africa to Bulawayo was completed in September 1897.

17. *The Rhodesia Review*, 1905-6 p. 57.

18. Hole, *Old Rhodesian Days*, p. 74.

19. Darter, *The Pioneers of Mashonaland*, p. 150.

20. Ibid., p. 149.

21. Ibid., p. 146.

22. *Bulawayo Observer*, August 20, 1902, p. 3.

23. J. D. Fage observed that "the main issues of the early years were either economic or presented themselves in economic forms because of the economic difficulties of the period. . . . There was a tendency to try to solve economic problems by legislation." J. D. Fage "The achievement of Self-government in Southern Rhodesia 1893-1923" (Ph.D. diss., Cambridge University, 1949), p. 51.

24. *Bulawayo Observer*, September 12, 1902, p. 3.

25. See H. Fox. Memorandum on Land Development 1912-13, p. 35.

26. British South Africa Company annual meeting, October 1904, p. 7.

27. Ibid., p. 7.

28. *The Bulawayo Chronicle*, September 10, 1904, p. 1.

29. C. O. 417/525, 1913.

30. Cd. 3564. A review of the present mutual relations of the British South African Colonies, January 1, 1907, p. 13.

31. Eric Walker, *Lord Milner and South Africa* (London: Humphrey Milford Amen House, E. C., 1942), p. 21.

32. Chamberlain to Milner, November 16, 1897, Headlam, vol 1. *The Milner Papers*, p. 122.

33. Milner to Asquith, December 1, 1897, ibid., p. 177.

34. Milner to Chamberlain, December 1, 1897, ibid., p. 141.

35. Milner to Chamberlain, December 1, 1897, ibid., p. 141.

36. The resident commissioner depended for his information on the reports of the native commissioner who were employees of the company.

37. Milner to Chamberlain, December 1897, Headlam, vol. 1, *The Milner Papers*, pp. 140-41.

38. Milner to Asquith, November 18, 1897, ibid., p. 179.

39. See High Commissioners' Proclamation, C.O. 417/321, 1902.

40. C. O. 417/321, 1902.

41. See Milner's letter to Chamberlain, December 1, 1897, in Headlam vol. 1, *The Milner Papers*, p. 140.

42. See telegram from Taberer, chief native commissioner of Mashonaland, to administrator C.O. 417/391, March 29, 1904.

43. Report of the C.N.C. Matabeleland, December 31, 1909, p. 1.

44. C.O. 417/391, 1904.

45. In a letter to Nyamanda, Lobengula's eldest son on October 23, 1921, Prince Arthur of Connaught, the high commissioner, described Company African administration as *Wise*. See also Terence Ranger, *The African Voice in Southern Rhodesia*, London: Heinemann, 1970), p. 84.

46. C. O. 417/321, 1902.

47. Report of the C.N.C. Matabeleland, December 31, 1909, p. 1.

48. Terence Ranger, "African Politics in Twentieth Century Southern Rhodesia," *Aspects of Central African History* (London: Wm. Heinemann, Ltd., 1968), p. 215.

49. Report of the C.N.C. Matabeleland, March 31, 1906, p. 1.

50. See (Sister) Hannah Frances Davidson, *South and South Central Africa: A Record of Fifteen Years' Missionary Labours among Primitive Peoples* (Elgin; Ill.: Brethren Public House, 1915).

51. Geoffrey Zwirikunzeno Kapenzi, "A Study of the Strategies and Methods Used by the American Methodist Missionary Society in its Religious Education Program from 1898-1967" (Ed. d. diss. Boston University, 1970), p. 12. Also see Lawrence Vambe, *An Ill-fated People* (Pittsburgh, Penn.: University of Pittsburgh Press, 1972), pp. 143-44.

52. See Rev. Burbridge in NADA: *The Southern Rhodesian Native Affairs Department Annual*, 1925, p. 23.

53. Dudley Kidd, *The Essential Kafir*, 2nd ed. (London: Adam & Charles Black, Ltd., 1925), pp. 41-42.

54. *NADA: The Southern Rhodesia Native Affairs Department Annual*, 1925, p. 23.

55. Ibid., p. 23.

56. Gann, *A History of Southern Rhodesia*, p. 201.

57. Ibid., p. 201.

58. Ranger, *Revolt in Southern Rhodesia 1896-7*, p. 3.

59. Quoted in *The Rhodesian Times*, October 11, 1902, p. 9.

60. Bishop James Johnson "Political and Social Conditions of Missionary work: The Relations of Mission Work to Native Customs," in *Pan Anglican Congress*, 1909, p. 1.

61. Hole, *Old Rhodesian Days*, p. 45.

62. *Bulawayo Observer*, September 12, 1902, p. 1.

63. *The Bulawayo Express*, January 14, 1905, p. 2.

64. I. D. Maccrone, *Race Attitudes in South Africa* (London: Oxford University Press, 1937), p. 1.

65. Ibid., p. 263.

66. *The Rhodesia Herald*, February 15, 1902, p. 7.

67. Ibid., August 28, 1902, p. 9.

68. Southern Rhodesia Debates, May 10, 1907, pp. 56-57.

69. Ibid., pp. 56-57.

70. Ibid, p. 57.

71. *Rhodesian Times*, August 11, 1904, p. 1.

72. Ibid.

73. *The Bulawayo Chronicle*, September 17, 1904, p. 1.
74. Cd. 2399. 1905, p. 67.
75. In the Transvaal the constitution excluded Africans from the franchise.
76. Southern Rhodesia Debates, May 2, 1905, p. 33.

6
The Labor Problem

The Europeans who came to Rhodesia in search of gold expected to make quick returns from their venture. The early settlers, if they were to succeed, had to depend on an abundant supply of cheap labor. The Africans were expected to supply the mining, railway construction, agricultural, and domestic labor requirements of the settlers. The settlers' efforts to secure cheap labor met with great difficulties, despite a relatively large number of able-bodied African men, because in the first place Africans did not expect the settlers to remain long in the country.[1] More important, however, was the fact that African life—economic, political, and social—revolved around tribal organization. So deep was the African's attachment to tribal society that the new political and economic forces of the settlers failed, initially at least, to tear the African from it.

So little did the Europeans understand this deep attachment of the African to the tribe that their attempts at forced labor met with resistance, which culminated in the 1896–97 Chimurenga. Forced labor was prohibited by the British government. Nevertheless, the British government encouraged any legal means the company administration might employ to secure African labor. But the settlers very often used distasteful measures to secure labor; their aggressive methods, as in the violent land expropriation that resulted in the protective policy of reserves, forced Britain to adopt a policy of restraint.[2] The guiding principle of British policy in regard to labor relations between whites and blacks was one of prevention or at least containment of white excess.

Before we explore the difficulties in recruiting labor and how

British policy evolved, a brief discussion of the social and economic functions of tribal organization is necessary. In Western
society, dominated by bourgeois economic ideas, the individual is
motivated to do what he does because he wishes, primarily, to
acquire material things for himself. To acquire the material
possessions the individual must work. The African society into
which the settlers moved had totally different conceptions of
economic activity. The African, unlike his European counterpart,
lived not unto himself but for the tribal group. The life of the
individual African revolved around his tribe.

The tribe was a social, economic, religious, and political unit.
The chief was the main moving spirit in the tribe; he was the ruler,
the court of appeals, the leader in war, and the provider in times of
scarcity. If called upon to perform a task by the chief, the
tribesman willingly did it even if he considered the task to be
beneath his dignity. The ordinary tribesman was prepared to do
anything that was asked of him by the chief not because he feared
the chief but because he believed that whatever the chief asked
him to do was for the good of the whole tribe.[3]

In times of hunger, the chief fed his tribesmen; therefore, tribal
society provided for all its members. To use a modern term, tribal
society had its own welfare scheme. The chief was usually the
richest man in the tribe and was generally hostile to any member
of the tribe who became rich. The chief's possessions were the
measure of the wealth of the tribe. To put it differently, the tribe
was rich if the chief was rich. The economic endeavors of the
tribesmen were not aimed at a market—for none existed or was
thought necessary. The tribesman aimed at self-sufficiency, that
is, he produced enough for his family for one year and hoped to do
the same thing the following year. If his crops failed he could
always look to the chief for relief.

The fundamental difference between the Europeans and the
Africans was that the Africans were basically communalistic,
whereas the Europeans were individualistic. From this fact followed the major labor and, therefore, economic problems that
Rhodesia faced in the first two decades of the twentieth century.
Ethel Jollie crystallized the difference when she wrote: "the
culture of Europe is based on individualism and capitalism, that of
the Abantu on communal possession, collective responsibility and

sometimes hereditary jurisdiction. . . ."[4] Capitalism thrives on the individual's efforts. Because the individual seeks to gain personal advantages, he is thought to have greater incentive to work than one who does not seek direct personal gain in his work.

The tribesman whenever he worked, either as a member of a group, for his chief, at a *nhimbe*,[5] or on his land, did not receive any payment for his services. If a tribesman went to someone's *nhimbe* either to help in ploughing the field, harvesting the crops, or building a hut, he would in return receive similar services from the members of his group when he needed them through his own *nhimbe*.

Whatever economic activity the African engaged in, it was not aimed at producing profit; it was simply to achieve self-sufficiency. In the African's economy, money was nonexistent. The tribe, through its chief, provided all that was needed or would be needed for its comfort and happiness. If the settlers were to succeed in their attempts to lure the African from his tribal society and to enroll him in the new industrial empire they dreamed of, the settlers should have created favorable conditions—both in the reserves and in the burgeoning centers of industrial activity—that would be conducive to changing the economic attitudes of tribal life. "The true inducement to labour, and the only one," wrote Marshall Clarke, the resident commissioner in Salisbury, "I submit, calculated to benefit the natives, is a development of legitimate wants, which money can satisfy. . . ."[6] But the fortune-seeking settlers, eager to get rich quickly and ignorant of the aims and functions of tribal society, were angered by tribal custom and the African's refusal to break away from it, and often clamored that the African be forced to work.

The labor problem was extremely serious for the Europeans at the beginning of their occupation as is reflected in the violent methods the settlers used to secure labor and the acrimonious debates in which they engaged on how to find a solution to the problem. Without cheap labor (no matter where it came from) European enterprise in Rhodesia was bound to fail. In the period following occupation, the settlers simply forced Africans to work. One of the reasons given for destroying Lobengula's power was that his raids in Mashonaland disrupted the labor supply of the Europeans who lived in the areas that were raided. The Africans not only found forced labor objectionable but considered the very idea of working for Europeans humiliating. W. H. Brown, an American who accompanied the Pioneer Column and not only traveled throughout Rhodesia but lived with Africans in their villages, recorded the following sentiments expressed by Africans:

> The laws established by these newcomers were decidedly distasteful . . . these white baases [masters] are among us continually; they seem never satisfied to rest as rational beings should . . . They [whites] are ever asking us to dig their munda (fields), work in their magodi (mines), help build their houses, and herd their cattle . . . what unreasonable beings these contemptible makewa (Europeans) are, anyway . . . they wander like madmen over the country in their search for darama (gold). . . .[7]

Brown, like many of the settlers at the time, saw nothing wrong with forced labor. The views and feelings of the Africans, although they may have been observed by the settlers, were irrelevant to the settlers. Brown maintained that the Africans had been conquered and should do what their conquerors asked them to do or else they would be extinguished as a race. "Unless a primitive people," he wrote, "can be made useful to their conquerors, the latter will inevitably crowd them to the wall."[8] Brown thought that the conquerors would "preserve" the conquered only if the conquered were useful. The conquered could make themselves of use by becoming laborers and servants of the conquerors. It was argued that through work (forced or voluntary) the African would, in the process, learn something that would improve him and raise him in the "scale of civilization." Many Europeans felt that the company should have legalized forced labor. Again, Brown wrote: "The enforcement . . . of state regulations which will compel the Africans to toil for a compensation will almost certainly result to his benefit."[9]

Professor Ranger has described in detail the various methods the company used between 1891 and 1897 to force Africans to work for the Europeans. Armed police were used to extract labor from reluctant villagers. Failure, on the part of a chief or village headman, to produce the required laborers could and did result in the confiscation of some of the chief's or headman's cattle, sheep,

and goats. The following account, as told by Ranger, was typical of
the police methods:

In March 1893, for instance, sub-inspector Bodle took a police
patrol out to Amanda's Kraal because the headman had replied
to a message ordering him to send some boys to work by saying
that his men were not going to work for white men and that if
Police came he would fire on them. The headman was arrested;
fined six goats and three head of cattle; and given 50 lashes
administered in the presence of his men, beside people belonging to other Kraals.[10]

Even after the British government had prohibited the use of
armed police in 1897 to use force the practice continued. In 1898
and 1899, a Labour Board and a Labour Bureau were established in
Mashonaland and Matebeleland, respectively, to reorganize the
labor-recruiting machinery. Each regional agency was headed by a
chief labour agent and was assisted by five (European) agents all
of whom were salaried officials of the Chamber of Mines. Their
appointment to the board or bureau was approved by the administrator and their activities were watched carefully over by the
native commissioners.[11] The European labor agents were supposed to know the language and customs of the Africans. All of
them employed armed Africans as labor recruiters. In his minutes
of March 14, 1901, reviewing the labor recruiting practices in
Rhodesia, Milner recorded that four African labor recruiting
agents employed by Mr. Acutt and Mr. Crewe, European labor
agents in Rhodesia, used violence in their attempts to recruit
laborers on the banks of the Zambezi. After their arrival at a
Batonga village the African agents, armed with guns, sat down to
drink with the villagers. And then all of a sudden the four agents
surrounded the villagers and demanded that the villagers go with
them. Shots were fired, and three villagers (one later died) and
one agent were injured. The agents left without laborers but took
some goats and sheep.[12] In 1900 reports such as this one by A.
Lawley, the administrator of Matebeleland were common. "I
regret to say that quite recently a case has occurred where native
messengers sent by one to the [white] labour agents to collect
boys, used force."[13]

Forced labor conditions in Rhodesia came to the attention of the British government only after a commission of inquiry (set up by the British government) had reported that the 1896–97 Chimurenga had been partly caused by forced labor. The enemies of the company, like Labouchere and the Anti-Slavery and Aborigines Protection Society, found good reason to renew their attack on the company's activities in Rhodesia. The British government ordered the company to prohibit forced labor.[14]

General European behavior toward Africans, forced labor, the 1896–97 Chimurenga, and its aftermath left a great impact on the Africans of Southern Rhodesia. The Africans had been forcibly separated from their families to work long hours for people they despised and considered mad.[15] They had fought valiantly and had been ruthlessly suppressed. In the early part of Chimurenga, Europeans, taken by surprise, suffered many casualties. Within the first two weeks of the fighting, over two hundred white men, women, and children had been killed. The settlers, in retreat, had been forced to abandon their mines and farms to build *laagers* (forts) to defend themselves. When in the end the Europeans emerged victorious and the fighting had ended, they lost their sense of proportion, and in revenge, they put many innocent Africans to death.[16] Long after the fighting, Europeans continued to mistreat the Africans and not infrequently they punctuated their orders to the Africans with shouts and slaps. The Africans had fought partly to extricate themselves from forced labor and to regain their independence. For this, not only were they defeated but they were brutally treated. The Africans remembered the excesses of the revengeful Europeans; they associated working for Europeans with their loss of independence. It is therefore not surprising that the Africans were reluctant to leave their villages and go to work for Europeans.

When the British government ordered the company to stop forced labor the company sought other means to induce or to force Africans to work for Europeans. In 1898 the company introduced a hut tax of ten shillings, primarily to force Africans to go to work and earn money to pay the tax rather than to raise revenue. The Africans were well aware of this, as indicated in a popular folk song that describes how the Africans lost their independence:

First came forced labor
Then came taxes
Then came roads
And now our cattle are finished.[17]

Some Africans paid their taxes in alluvial gold.[18] The Rhodesian Chamber of Mines asked the company to stop Africans from paying their taxes in gold for two reasons. First, because the chamber believed that to allow Africans to trade in gold would place European traders at a disadvantage since Europeans were required to have a license, which cost fifty pounds, in order to carry on the gold trade. Second, the chamber argued that if Africans paid their taxes in coins, they could obtain such coins from Europeans and could only do so if they worked for the Europeans. "It would greatly facilitate," wrote the executive committee of the Chamber of Mines, "the settlement of the labour question if the Hut-Tax had to be paid in current coin for in order to obtain the same, the native would have to more frequently enter into the service of the settler."[19]

The company had hoped that the taxation of Africans would solve the labor problems. It did not. "The necessity of providing means to pay taxes," wrote the resident commissioner "is but a temporary expedient, and does not work out satisfactorily. . . ."[20] Africans living on the border between Mozambique and Rhodesia often slipped into Mozambique whenever tax collectors appeared in their villages.[21] In the Fort Victoria district of Ndanga, Africans even killed their own cattle because they feared that the cattle would be confiscated if they refused to work for Europeans. "The conclusion I came to," the resident commissioner wrote, "was that the action [killing cattle] taken by the natives was the result of apprehension that their cattle would be forcibly seized, either by the Boers . . . or by the Administration of Southern Rhodesia as a punishment for their not furnishing labour for the mines."[22]

The company administration, arguing that the tribesmen usually obeyed their chief's commands, sought to use the chiefs as recruiting agents.[23] Native commissioners toured the districts under their jurisdiction and appealed to the chiefs to encourage their followers to go to work for the Europeans. The native commissioners argued that they were friends of the Africans and knew what was good for them. With his traditional authority the chief could be certain that his orders would be followed. But the members of the tribe had obeyed the chief because they believed that what he asked them to do was good for the tribe. In former times the tribe members were prepared to work for the chief and the tribe, but now they were being addressed by foreigners who had usurped the powers of the chief and were being asked not to work in the village and work for the good of outsiders who had recently conquered them. Furthermore, although the chiefs and *indunas* were under heavy pressure from the native commissioners, many of them were reluctant to antagonize their followers, particularly since many of the chiefs (mostly in Mashonaland) realized that their legitimacy in traditional terms was compromised. After the 1896–97 Chimurenga, chiefs were appointed and paid by the company.

Chamberlain, as colonial secretary, objected to the method of securing labor through chiefs and *indunas*. He argued that since *indunas* were paid by the company there would be a tendency for the company to expect returns from those who were employed by it. "Undoubtedly the receipt of a salary by an Induna implies a responsibility on his part to uphold the authority to promote the policy of the Government."[24] Pressure on chiefs, Chamberlain believed, was tantamount to indirect forced labor. He, therefore, asked the high commissioner to make sure that no pressure was brought to bear on the chiefs to secure labor. "The Indunas," Chamberlain wrote, "whilst they were clearly informed . . . that the government would not allow forced labour, were at the same time led to understand that they were expected to supply the necessary number of labourers, and that as government officials with stipends, they were to carry out the wishes of the government. The system of obtaining a supply of labour through the Indunas . . . appears to be liable to a form of compulsory labour. . . ."[25]

When persuasion failed, some native commissioners openly used threats to get Africans to leave the villages and go to work. H. J. Taylor, who then was chief native commissioner for Matebeleland, toured the area in 1899 addressing the Matebele and their *indunas*. At the end of every meeting to "prove" his friendliness to the Matebele, an ox would be killed or blankets or beef would be distributed to all those who attended the meeting. Anyone who dared to oppose him would be severely reprimanded. On July 31, Taylor visited Inungu; his report was typical of the many he made:

Sipo, a native who was continually interrupting, and who is a reputed agitator, was silenced by the C.N.C. Before the conclusion of the Indaba the C.N.C. said that there was one thing that prevented them going to work, that was the Ndaga [War] dance. At the mention of this there was a general titter. The C.N.C. said that whatever they might think, it was not a laughing matter, and anyone found attending it would certainly get himself into trouble . . . they must not be surprised if the originators were punished. The C.N.C. then broke up the Indaba, after telling those present that there was a beast to be killed for their supper.[26]

Taylor also tried to use competition to induce the Africans into going to work for the Europeans. Often he told the Matebele that if they did not go to work he would get alien Africans, Fingoes, from South Africa, to do the work. Taylor argued that the government did not want to do this as this would be enriching foreigners. "Fingoes were other natives," Taylor argued, "who were anxious to come and work in this country, but . . . the government had no desire to have any other natives in this country, if they could avoid it . . . it all depended on the natives of this country themselves, whether or not other tribes were brought in from elsewhere. They would not like to see strangers brought in to live alongside them."[27]

Fingoes came to Rhodesia with the Pioneer Column; in 1893 they helped the Company to suppress the Matebele. In 1899, a total of 300 male Fingoes were brought into Rhodesia to be laborers.[28] Arable allotments of ten acres were given to each head of the family. Title to the land could be obtained on condition that the Fingoes spent at least three months every year working for Europeans. The title could be claimed after three years full service or on the production of a certificate showing that the holder had worked for a total of 36 months. Failure to fulfill these conditions would result in the payment of a fine of three pounds annually in addition to the poll tax. By 1905 there were about 1,291 Fingoes in

Rhodesia; their number thereafter remained small.[29] Some returned to South Africa, and by 1923 there were about 1,700 of them left in Rhodesia. The B.S.A. Co. reports of 1898-1900, as well as the 1903-1905 South African Native Affairs Commission and the 1915 Southern Rhodesia Native Reserves Commission, described the Fingoes as unsatisfactory workers. In its final report the commission wrote: "We believe they [Fingoes] were not a success as workers. . . . They are gradually drifting back to the South. . . ."[30]

Taylor was accompanied on all his tours by an agent of the Labour Bureau. Because of Taylor's threats, it is easy to see why the Matebele did not trust the agents of the Matebeleland Labour Bureau and later of the Rhodesian Native Labour Bureau.

Chamberlain found Taylor's methods to be particularly objectionable. The British government felt that since native commissioners were paid officials of the Company it was only natural that they were eager to please their employer. The British government came to the conclusion that native commissioners should not act as labor-recruiting agents.[31] The Native Department had been established so that it could look after African interests. "The object of . . . the N.C.s [Native Commissioners] was to secure the protection of the interests of the natives and to enable them to look to these officers for the redress of any wrongs they might suffer at the hands of mining companies and others . . . if this object is . . . defeated . . . the peace of the country [will be] endangered. . . ."[32] It was the duty of the Department to see that African rights and interests were not impinged upon by either the company or the settlers. If the native commissioners acted as recruiting agents there was bound to be a conflict of interests and loyalties. The British government maintained that the loyalty of the native commissioners should be to the Africans. Whatever grievances Africans had they took to the native commissioners who would try or were expected to see that the reasons for the grievances were removed. But if native commissioners were the recruiting agents, it would be difficult for Africans to report any cases of ill treatment by employers to native commissioners. Africans found it difficult to distinguish between recruiting agents and employers since both mistreated them. There were many instances of the ill treatment of Africans on their way to farm or to work in the mines by agents of the Labour Bureau.

With native commissioners acting as labor agents it would be impracticable to expect them to redress grievances arising out of their own acts and embarrassing for them to deal with the illegal or injudicious acts of others. The British government felt that if native commissioners were disengaged from labor recruiting they would be in a better position to check on the abuse of African laborers both by the recruiting agent and by the employers. This the government hoped would also increase the confidence of the Africans in the native commissioners. Lord Milner, however, believed that the Africans would have been better off with native commissioners as recruiting agents than with private recruiting agents, if only the commissioners were not subjected to company and settler pressure. Milner wrote:

> it may be argued that the interests of the natives are best guarded if they are engaged to work directly by officials of the Government instead of by private contractors, who will proba-bly try to bully or cheat them and will to some extent succeed in spite of all remedies the law can devise. Practically, however . . . it will be found that this disadvantage is more than cancelled by the disadvantage which arises from using Government officials as agents for the supply of labour. There is an inevitable tendency for the officials so employed to be pressed by the wants of employers into using the influence and authority of the Government as a means for inducing a plentiful supply of labourers to come forward . . . but if recruiting is left in the hands of private contractors, the native, when he thinks agri-eved, can go to an official for redress. If, on the other hand, it is officials who recruit, the native is rarely able to distinguish between the two functions of the Government. He may think himself agrieved but he sees no person to appeal to except the very authority of which he wishes to complain.[33]

Native commissioners were banned from recruiting laborers so that they would act in a supervisory capacity over all the activities of the private recruiting agents and report any cases of ill treatment by either the agents or employers. The British govern-ment instructed the Company:

> The proper system for dealing with indigenous labour is for the actual recruiting and distribution of the labourers to be carried

out by an unofficial association acting through licensed agents, while the Government through its own officers, confines itself to what is necessary for the protection of the labourers, e.g., ensuring that the contract entered into by the native is regular, contains no false representation and is understood by the native, and that proper treatment is given to the native both before and after he is handed to the actual employer.[34]

Although they were prohibited from acting as labor recruiters, native commissioners could inform Africans who came to them in search of employment where employment could be secured and what the conditions of service were.

The decision by the British government to bar native commissioners from acting as recruiting agents angered European farmers and miners throughout the country. The settlers argued that they would be ruined financially if they did not have sufficient labor. They argued that unless the native commissioners told Africans to go to work they (Africans) would not seek work on their own accord. The farmers of the Charter district even petitioned the high commissioner, pleading that the orders prohibiting native commissioners to act as labor recruiters be suspended. The Mashonaland Farmers Association expressed its strong disapproval of the new regulations, arguing that such a policy was detrimental to the agricultural development of the country. The association further argued that the Africans would misunderstand the change in policy, and would see it as a sign of weakness in the government. The association resolved: "That recent instructions . . . are in the opinion of the Association both unjust to the settler on the land . . . and unwise with regard to the natives themselves, who, before understanding so sudden a change in the policy of the Government, will interpret such policy as actuated by weakness and dictated by fear of the consequences."[35]

The Chamber of Mines wrote a similar letter to the administrator warning of the dangers to the mining industry upon which, it argued, the country's whole future depended if the new regulations were not rescinded.[36] Not only had Taylor's methods failed to secure labor, they had resulted in Britain's prohibiting the native commissioners from acting as recruiting agents.

In Mashonaland, Taberer, the chief native commissioner, used different methods. Taberer appealed to the Africans to realize the importance of money. Throughout his tours in Mashonaland, Taberer persuaded the old men to insist on demanding the payment of lobola from their would be sons-in-law before giving their daughters away. Because the number of cattle had been greatly reduced, and many African cattle had been confiscated by the company during the 1896–97 Chimurenga, many Africans could not pay the customary lobola in cattle. They would instead marry and pay later. Taberer told the old men that any young men who wanted to get married could go to work for Europeans, and with the money he received he could buy the necessary cattle to fulfill the lobola requirement.[37]

In Matebeleland, Taylor also urged that the custom of lobola be upheld. Without lobola, Taylor argued, the Matebele would live in a state of prostitution. "By decreasing prostitution," he wrote, "the young men have a stronger inducement to work and so place themselves in a position to become husbands."[38] Taylor advocated the legalizing of lobola. In 1900 the company arranged for the importation of cattle and their sale to Africans at a bare margin over cost price so that Africans might be induced to go to work and to buy cattle for lobola purposes.[39]

The missionaries opposed lobola because they thought that it was wife buying, which left the wife a virtual slave. This belief that a married African woman was a slave was shared by the native commissioners. They supported lobola not for ethical reasons but because they hoped that it might solve the shortage of labor.

All these efforts did not succeed. The logic of the arguments used by Taberer to persuade chiefs to encourage their followers to go to work was appealing and reasonable. But both Taberer and Taylor made their tours in 1898 and 1899, just after the terrible fighting of 1896–97. It was unreasonable for them to expect that their endeavors to secure labor would succeed so long as the memories of the suffering and brutalities of the recent war were still so fresh in the minds of the Africans.

Very often the activities of the private recruiting agents and their messengers convinced many villagers of the physical dangers to which they might expose themselves if they went to work for Europeans. It was very common for agents to round up men in a village, at gunpoint, and beat up those men who were unwilling to go to work. Even those men who "consented" to go were not spared this treatment on the way to the places of employment. "The Administration and the Company," wrote Milner in 1902, "have had a wholesome fright which will prevent them displaying so much energy in beating up recruits."[40]

The few Africans who dared to leave their villages did so in winter, the dry season; in summer, the rainy season, they returned to their villages to work their fields. The living conditions in most mine compounds were so bad that the compounds were literally death traps. Most mines were on the high plateau where the weather gets cold in winter. During the nights the compounds would get very cold. Mine managements did not allow the African laborers to have fires in the compounds. Many laborers had very little clothing and were usually given a thin blanket of very poor material. Medical facilities were very poor and in most cases nonexistent. Many African laborers died of pneumonia.[41]

The quality of the food was usually bad. "The natives complain [that] some of the mealie-meal provided at the mines is very badly ground, which accounts for the large number of cases of diarrhea amongst them."[42] Figures provided by the company show that during the quarter ending December 31, 1898, in Matebeleland, forty (Rhodesian) Africans died on the mines and twenty died on their way to the mines.[43] It is very likely that the real figures were higher. These statistics are significant because only a very small number of Rhodesian Africans went to work on the mines. Moreover, because of the lack of adequate precautions, there were in this early period a few mine disasters, and those who had remained in the villages heard of these disasters. Those who managed to return from the mines told of terrible cold nights, poor food, poor medical facilities, and cruel employers. How then could others have been expected to leave the comfortable life of the village for the horrible life on the mines? In 1899, thirteen chiefs complained to Taberer about the deaths that had occurred at one mine at Selukwe. Taberer recorded that the chiefs told him that "they [chiefs' followers] wished to work at places at which they did not die in such numbers . . . that the compounds were cold and that they were not allowed to have fires in them, that the air in the mines was very warm . . . that they disliked the hospital."[44]

To combat the negligence of the employers, the British government asked the company to set up a scheme under which African mine compounds would be inspected every month to check the working and living conditions of the African laborers. Every month beginning in January 1903, Inspectors of African Compounds reported on the quality of the food, the housing, the treatment of the laborers, the deaths and their causes, and the desertions from the mines. Despite the conscientious work of some inspectors, the conditions in the mines changed little.[45]

Another complaint made by Africans working in some of the mines and the farms was that their employers did not pay them regularly.[46] There were usually two reasons for this. The main reason was that as long as laborers were not paid, they would be forced to remain in the mine or farm long after their contracts had expired, thus compelling them to continue working while they were waiting to be paid. If a European farmer could detain his workers until October or November he would ensure himself of a labor force to work his fields when the first rains came. The second reason was that some of the employers simply claimed that they had no money to pay their employees. Chamberlain asked Milner to check this abuse. "In some cases," wrote Chamberlain, "the natives asserted that they were not paid regularly."[47]

But despite Chamberlain's instructions that African laborers be paid regularly, either at the end of a week or month, the practice of withholding pay was not stopped. Almost a year later the resident commissioner reported: "There seems to me no sufficient reason why employees . . . should be kept waiting ten days for their wages. . . . In the special instance . . . boys have been kept waiting a year— considering this I think it is natural that Mr. Pauling's Company should at times find it difficult to get labour."[48]

Africans who got employment through labor agents were not as well paid as those who found employment on their own. With the demand for labor so high, those who acted as their own agents had greater bargaining power than those who were recruited by agents under contract.[49] Those employers who were reported to pay more than others had more laborers coming to them than those who relied on recruiting agents.

Recruiting agents and employers often did not tell Africans the truth about the pay, the job, or the working conditions. "From time to time complaints have been made by the natives that the inducements offered them to work by irresponsible recruiters, who extended their operations all over the territory, were evaded and that many [were] cheated out of their dues. . . ."[50] In the mining industries, most Rhodesian Africans refused to work underground, preferring to work on the surface. Africans from Mozambique, Northern Rhodesia, and Nyasaland did the underground work. "Neither the Matebele nor other Rhodesian tribes," wrote the resident commissioner, "take kindly to labour in the mines. . . . They work in the mines either from direct pressure brought to bear on them by the administrator, a pressure only short of force, or the necessity of earning enough to pay their taxes. . . ."[51] When, as often happened, the Africans upon reaching the mine discovered that the work they were asked to do was different from what they had been earlier led to believe it would be, they either refused to work or deserted. In 1901, the company administration passed a Masters' and Servants' Ordinance that bound the laborer to keep his agreement to work for the stipulated time in the contract. However, the agreement did not bind the employer to give the laborer the exact kind of job he had promised. Sir Marshall Clarke, the resident commissioner, complained about the unfairness of the ordinance when he wrote: "This [Ordinance], while it protects the employer against repudiation of an agreement entered into in good faith does away with the existing safeguard to a servant who finds that through ignorance he or she has agreed to conditions of service which . . . are duly irksome or otherwise objectionable."[52] Despite Clarke's objection nothing was done to rectify the unfairness in the ordinance.

The labor problem was further complicated by the fact that during this early period the political situation in the country was not stable. From 1897 until 1904, as already pointed out, there were wild rumors of an imminent African uprising. In 1900, the administrator of Matebeleland wrote:

Chilimanzi and his tribe, who it should be remembered, have been loyal to the whites, showed an evident reluctance to pay his hut-tax when called upon to do so. A large and important meeting of Indunas took place at Chilimanzi's, at which one of his wives who is reputed to be the mouthpiece of the M'limo, urged those present to decline to pay the hut-tax. The attitude of the Natives was interpreted by the Native Commissioner . . . as being of so threatening a nature as to warrant him assuming that there was about to be an organized rising.[53]

In Mashonaland, Chief Mapondera was still resisting European control. Mapondera moved from place to place and between 1900 and 1904 his followers often beat up Mozambique Africans (and confiscated their money and belongings) returning to their homes from Rhodesia.[54] The unstable conditions were not conducive to indigenous Africans leaving their villages for mining centers.

The attempts of the company administration to exploit the indigenous labor supply were supplemented by efforts to solve the labor shortage by looking beyond the boundaries of Southern Rhodesia. In order to secure cheap labor from the neighboring countries, the company needed the permission of the British government as the instrument for conducting relations with foreign countries or even with other British colonies and protectorates. Attempts to secure laborers from Bechuanaland were not successful. Chief Segkome allowed the company to recruit labor from among his followers on the condition that his followers would not be permitted to settle in Rhodesia. In all, only about two thousand were recruited.[55]

The experiment with the Fingoes proved to be such a failure that by 1900 Lawley, the administrator of Matebeleland, reported: "If one may judge the class by the individual, the Fingoes cannot be said to be satisfactory. They apparently have no inclination to work."[56] The Fingoes like the local Africans refused to work underground. Most of them were engaged in railway construction.

The Company next turned to Ethiopia, and there too it met with failure. From Ethiopia, the company recruited Arabs, Somalis, and a few Indians, all of whom the company called Ethiopians. The first group of Ethiopians arrived in Rhodesia in February 1901. Of the original 411 Ethiopians who had left Aden, only 156 reached the Surprise Mine whose management had recruited them. At every stop that the party made some of the Ethiopians disappeared. The following entry made by R. R. Eustace of the Surprise Mine is revealing:

No. who left for Beira	411	
No. who reached Beira	385	
No. who left Beira	349	
No. who reached Salisbury and Marandellas	237	
No. who reached Do.	200	more than half
No. who deserted en route from Beira	82	disappeared
No. who deserted en route to Mine and Road Party	33	
No. who deserted from Salisbury and Marandellas	29	
No. who died at Salisbury en route to mine	4	
No. who reached Surprise Mine	156 [57]	

Of the 156 Ethiopians who finally reached the Surprise Mine, 40 were suffering from dysentery, 6 died, and 17 later deserted. Of these 156, 66 were Somalis, 26 Abyssinians, 61 Arabs, 2 Indians, and 1 was described as Swahili.[58] These figures show that the number of desertions was very high. On the boat before reaching Beira the recruited men were told by the ship's captain that they had been recruited for underground work, whereas in Ethiopia they had been told that they would work on the surface. When the ship docked, some of the laborers mutinied and refused to disembark and when armed police boarded the ship, many of the laborers jumped into the water. A few managed to evade the police and a few others were reported missing—these probably drowned. At Beira some of the men were lured away by promises of higher pay and better treatment by other labor recruiting agents. The conditions under which the Ethiopians traveled from Beira to Salisbury were very hard. In their eagerness to deliver these men to the mine, the recruiting agents often drove them too hard, giving the weak, the tired, and the sick no rest, which probably explains the disappearance of so many of them. Reports from the Surprise Mine's manager indicate that the Somalis were the poorest workers of the entire group. The Ethiopians ate rice rather than the corn mealie-meal that the local Africans (as well as the Nyasas and Northern Rhodesians) ate and were more expensive to maintain. Company figures show that in all only about 1,850 Ethiopians came to Rhodesia.[59]

The Company also looked to Mozambique for a solution to the labor shortage in Rhodesia. The Portuguese authorities there were prepared to allow the company to recruit laborers for

Rhodesia on the condition that the company did not employ its own private recruiting agents. Recruiting could be done through the Rand Native Labour Association, which was responsible for furnishing the Rand mines with labor. Most of the African laborers on the Rand came from Mozambique. In 1899 over 100,000 Africans were employed on the Rand and three quarters of them came from Mozambique.[60] Many Mozambiquan Africans also worked on European farms in Nyasaland. Although the Witwatersrand Native Labour Association agreed to recruit labor for Rhodesia, it was unable to satisfy Rhodesia's labor requirements since most of its recruits were themselves urgently needed on the Rand. A suggestion to recruit labor from the West Indies was turned down by Chamberlain.

Hardest hit by the shortage of labor was the mining industry, and several mines actually closed down. In August 1900, J. F. Jones, secretary of the company, reported "a serious situation has lately arisen in Rhodesia through the scarcity of native labour which has caused the shutting down of several of the most important mines."[61] The Boer War also, dislocated labor on the Rand. The Witwatersrand mines had done relatively well in recruiting labor from within South Africa and from the neighboring territories, Rhodesia, Mozambique, Northern Rhodesia, and Nyasaland, because they paid more than did the Rhodesian mines. In Rhodesia, the wage for a mine laborer was twenty-five shillings per month, whereas on the Rand, competition had raised the wage to forty-five shillings per month.[62] At the outbreak of the war, the Rand Native Labour Association suggested lowering wages so that the mines would save without reducing the labor supply. The plan was to increase the labor supply by making the Africans stay longer. Because of the dislocations in production caused by the war, wages on the Rand actually fell to twenty shillings.

Because of the length of the Boer War the work habits of the Africans in the mines were dislocated. To make matters worse, the war was followed by a depression and other economic difficulties. During the war, agriculture had virtually come to a standstill. When the war ended in 1902, the first year of peace saw South Africa experience a severe drought. In 1903 the economic situation worsened as a result of an industrial depression. Worse still, labor that otherwise would have been used by the mines was employed elsewhere in the work of repatriation and restoration, on the railways, and at the seaports.

With a severe shortage of labor the development of South Africa, which was dependent on the mines, was in jeopardy and with it the whole of Milner's policy in South Africa was in peril. The labor shortage could have been solved by emploping whites to do the rough work done by the blacks. But Milner did not want Europeans to do this type of work for reasons that are described later. Without an abundant supply of cheap labor the economic development of the country would be brought to a standstill. Amery commented: "The failure of the supply of native labor for the mines threatened to impose a permanent check on all development, to upset for good all the calculations of capitalists and investors, and to frustrate irretrievably the expectation on which the whole of Milner's policy was based."[63] To the capitalists' failure to resolve the labor shortage meant financial loss; to Milner it was a setback of British policy.

To introduce Europeans as laborers, though it might have resulted in increased production since the Europeans would work on a permanent basis, would have resulted in an initial raising of the costs of production. The Johannesburg Chamber of Commerce and the Rhodesian Chamber of Commerce suggested that the labor problem could be solved by the introduction of Chinese laborers.[64] The Company argued that unless the Chinese were introduced the mining industry would have to close down and that would mean the termination of European economic activity in Southern Rhodesia. The settlers, who were bitterly opposed to the idea, argued that the introduction of the Chinese would further complicate the already grave racial situation. The settlers feared that once the Chinese were introduced it would be difficult not only to control their movements but also to get them to leave the country when their work permits expired. The promise by the company to pass legislation that would enforce the departure of the Chinese did not ease the fears of the Europeans.

The Europeans' main fear was apparently that the Chinese would become dangerous economic rivals to them. The Europeans feared the possibility of the Chinese either becoming miners or entering into partnership with Europeans. Because the standard of living of the Chinese was lower than that of the European, as a trader the Chinese might undersell his European counterpart. In an editorial The *Bulawayo Observer* expressed these fears: "All men, except special-pleading partisans, admit that the Asiatic once introduced cannot be got rid of, but will wander over the country entering into injurous competition with the European . . . the foreign plant could never be entirely weeded out again."[65] The *Observer* supported the introduction into Rhodesia of cheap white labor. On the other hand, Milner argued that it would be to the advantage of the Europeans to have Chinese as traders owning small shops. He considered this occupation as debasing to the Europeans. If this kind of work were done by the Chinese, Milner believed that the Africans' respect for the Europeans would increase. "Moreover," he wrote, "the native's respect for the European, which it is, for every reason, so important to keep up is certainly far more likely to be impaired by the spectacle of Europeans engaged in the basest forms of trade than it would be if such trade was in the hands of Asiatics."[66]

Some Rhodesian settlers argued that the introduction of Chinese laborers would damage the chances of an eventual political federation of all British territories in Southern Africa. The South African situation was already complicated by the existence of four main races: the Africans, the Indians, the Boers, and the British. The antagonism between the last two had erupted into the Boer War. The Africans were always a potential source of discord in the country (in 1906 there was an African rebellion in Natal). The introduction of the Chinese would further complicate the situation. Appearing in the *Bulawayo Observer* of April 11, 1903, was an editorial whose heading was "Federation or Chinamen? Choose Ye this day." The editor commented that those who were resisting the introduction of the Chinese were "sincere in their determination not to allow Federation to be wrecked . . . by the gratuitous introduction of a new Chinese complication."[67]

Clarke, the resident commissioner, was opposed to any experimenting with Chinese labor. He believed that the local supply of indigenous labor had not been exhausted, and noted that at some mines desertions were frequent because Africans felt they could not have their grievances redressed. He advocated, as a first step to solve the labor shortage, an improvement in the treatment of laborers by employers. As long as employers were cruel, the introduction of Chinese laborers would not solve the problem. "I believe," he wrote, "in some cases, at least, it [desertion] is due to the way in which natives are treated by European miners in charge of them, and over whom it is impossible to exercise an efficient and constant control. If this is the case it will probably be found that the substitution of Chinese for natives will not relieve unpopular miners. For these reasons it appears to me that it is premature to come to an immediate decision on the introduction of Chinese."[68] Clarke argued that the Chinese had low morality and would also compete unfairly with both the Europeans and the Africans. This view was also supported by the Bishop of Mashonaland who said that he "was opposed to the introduction of Asiatics into South Africa as a citizen, on economic, social, and moral grounds. Economically, it will introduce unfair competition between them and the white men and the natives of this country."[69] To which Milner brilliantly replied:

The reason, as stated by Sir Marshall Clarke, apparently is that these Asiatics are so specially gifted with qualities of frugality, thrift and staying power as to make them formidable competitors of white men. It really seems to me that the opponents of Asiatic immigration must make up their minds which of two self-contradictory arguments they are going to rely upon. The Asiatics cannot be so bad, intellectually low and morally worse that their presence will corrupt the native community, and so good, so clever, so thrifty, so frugal and so industrious that even the white man, to say nothing of the poor native, will have a bad chance against them. I am anxious that the experiment should be made.[70]

Milner believed that Chinese competition with the Africans would be a healthy thing. He argued that if Africans were ever to become better workmen, the presence of the Chinese would be a stimulus to them. He wrote: "In the present state of affairs, while we are exclusively dependent upon natives for all the rough labour of the country, and they can be as irregular and idle as they please without any fear of the consequences, that stimulus is lacking. In my opinion a little competition is just what they want. . . . It seems to me that the native has as much to gain as anybody from the introduction into South Africa of active labourers of another race."[71] Milner supported the company's point of view, that Chinese labor be introduced into Rhodesia regardless of what happened in the Transvaal. He argued that the Rhodesian mining industry was on the verge of closing down and that Rhodesia's difficulties had increased because the Rand paid more and Rhodesian mines could not complete with the Rand. "The case of Rhodesia is most piteous," he wrote, "inasmuch as its only other resource, agriculture, has suffered. . . . Under these circumstances it does seem to me that it would be both a cruelty and an injustice, if we forbade Rhodesia making an experiment in Asiatic labour, especially as that experiment would be on a limited small scale and might be very instructive to all the rest of us."[72]

Nevertheless, the colonial secretary sided with the view of the resident commissioner who feared that the competition between the Africans and the Chinese might lead to unrest among the Africans. Any African trouble in Rhodesia immediately after the Boer War would focus unfavorable attention in Britain on South Africa. "I need hardly remind you," wrote Lyttleton, "that the attitude of the natives will have to be taken into account if and when the introduction of Chinese labourers into Southern Rhodesia is finally decided upon."[73]

The British government had two obstacles to overcome in the Chinese labor dispute: first, the vociferous opposition to the scheme of the settlers both in Rhodesia and the Transvaal and, second, opposition in Britain. "The opinion of Europeans in Southern Rhodesia," the resident commissioner wrote, "has so far been expressed as opposed to the introduction of Asiatics. . . ."[74] Rhodesian settler opinion would have mattered little if the majority of the Europeans in the Transvaal were in favor of the introduction of Chinese laborers. Chamberlain, who was aware of this said in 1903: "I consider that such action [in Rhodesia] would be extremely unpopular, and would cause a storm at home, and that such a step could not be safely taken unless the Transvaal were previously or at the same time to adopt a similar course. . . . The feelings at present all over South Africa is against such a policy, and as long as this continues, it is not likely that the Home Government would give its assent."[75] Back in Britain the labor movement expressed vague fears that the introduction of cheap Chinese labor in South Africa, if successful, would lead to the introduction of Chinese laborers in the coalfields of Wales.

Chamberlain stipulated that he would consider the introduction of Chinese laborers into Rhodesia only if the majority of South Africans favored the introduction of them into the Transvaal. The Rhodesian Chamber of Commerce appealed, in vain, to the Colonial Office to accept the majority view of the Rhodesian Legislative Council as the expression of the Europeans. The administrator informed the resident commissioner: "After full consideration of all the circumstances the Council is of the opinion that the request . . . [for the introduction of Chinese laborers] should be acceded to, and . . . that the Secretary of State may be moved to approve of China being named as a country from which immigration shall be permitted."[76] The British government, however, realized that since the company's appointed members were in the majority in the Legislative Council, the council's view only represented that of the Company.

In the Transvaal, the opposition to introducing Chinese labor was led by the White League, which argued that the development of the country would always be retarded as long as it depended on black labor. The league maintained that whites were quite capable of doing the work that hitherto had been done by Africans only. During 1902 and 1903 many well-attended settler meetings were held throughout Rhodesia and Transvaal to express opposition to the introduction of Chinese laborers. In June 1903 a deputation from the league asked Milner to solve the labor problem by employing whites. Milner flatly turned down the suggestion, arguing that to do so would involve the reduction of wages and the European standard of living. He told the deputation emphatically:

Our welfare depends upon increasing the quantity of our white population, but not at the expense of its quality. We do not want a white proletariat in this country. The position of the whites amongst the vastly more numerous black population requires that even their lowest ranks should be able to maintain a standard of living far above that of the poorest section of the population of a purely white population. But, without making them hewers of wood and drawers of water, there are scores of employments in which white men could be honorably and profitably employed, if we could at once succeed in multiplying our industries . . . However you look at the matter, you always come back to the same root principle—the urgency of that

development which alone can make this a white man's country
in the only sense in which South Africa can become one, and
that is, not a country full of poor whites, but one in which a
largely increased white population can live in decency and
comfort.[77]

It is worth noting that a deputation of Whites had on its own
offered a solution to the labor problem that involved employing
whites to do the rough work usually done by blacks. At a time of
crisis some Boers had offered to ignore the classification of work
designated for blacks. It was a British high commissioner who
surprisingly rejected this plan. Arguing that it was simply too
expensive to employ whites, Milner wrote: "The cost of living for
white men was so high, that neither farmers nor mines could
afford to employ them as manual labourers."[78] Milner further
argued that to employ whites in such jobs would create a proletariat—a class of people that would sooner or later challenge the
capitalists and agitate for higher pay and better living conditions.
Although his actions supported the capitalists, the overriding
consideration in Milner's mind was the fear that few Englishmen
would be prepared to come to South Africa as laborers. His whole
scheme was aimed at developing the mines on cheap labor and
importing Englishmen as white-collar workers to fill the man-
agerial and clerical posts that an industrial boom would generate.
Such a class of Englishmen would join hands with their fellow
English-speaking brothers in Rhodesia and the rest of South
Africa to form the dominant voice in the affairs of a future
federated South Africa.[79]

As a result, in June 1903, 500 men were brought from England
to do railway construction in South Africa.[80] The experiment was
soon abandoned as a failure because it turned out to be very
expensive. The work the Englishmen performed cost nearly four
times as much as it would have done had African laborers been
used. The work done by the unskilled Europeans was not well
done because their efficiency was affected by the fact that they
were doing "African" work.

Despite the opposition from Chamberlain and from the settlers
in both Rhodesia and Transvaal, Milner continued to press for the
introduction of Chinese laborers. (The deputy high commissioner

refused a suggestion that a referendum be held throughout South Africa on the Chinese question. In Rhodesia, settlers alleged that the mining industry was paying gangsters to break up anti-Chinese meetings.) Milner argued that the British government should concentrate on finding a way to regulate Chinese labor in such a manner that once they were introduced the Chinese would not be allowed to compete with the Europeans economically. "We should not reject Asiatics altogether," pleaded Milner, "but devote all our ingenuity to seeing how we can regulate their labour in such a manner that they will not flood us in other industries and trades than mining."[81] Milner argued that the Chinese themselves would not want to stay in the country once they fulfilled the terms of their contracts. He thought that the Chinese would want to return to their homes with the money they had earned because they would live in comparative comfort on their return. Milner was, however, opposed to Chinese settlers and traders. "I am dead against the Asiatic settler and trader," wrote Milner, "but I do not believe the identured Asiatic labourer to be uncontrollable."[82] He maintained that people confused Asiatic importation with Asiatic immigration. The former entailed Asiatic laborers coming into the country under strict contracts at whose expiration they would, by law, be forced to return to their countries, whereas the latter entailed settlers. Milner maintained that Asiatic importation was essential not only to solve the labor problem but also the financial and political problems the country was then experiencing. The Boer War, as previously noted, was followed by a depression; shortage of labor reduced production and hence led to the laying off of some Europeans. The stability of the new order that Milner hoped to build depended upon the increase of the British population—and this too could only take place if there was an industrial boom. "The failure of the supply of native labour for the mines," wrote Amery, "threatened to impose a permanent check on all development, to upset for good all the calculations of capitalists and investors, and to frustrate irretrievably the expectations on which the whole of Milners' policy was based."[83] Milner himself confessed: "Without the impetus he [Chinese laborer] would give, I do not see how we are to have that great influx of British population. . . ."[84] Again he wrote:

"Without a substratum of coloured labour, white labour cannot exist here. . . ."[85]

Milner then set up a commission to inquire into the Chinese question: Opponents of the commission denounced it as a partisan body that served the interests of the capitalists. The commission recommended that Chinese laborers be introduced into South Africa, and on February 10, 1904, the Transvaal Council approved the importation of Chinese. By the end of the year, about 23,000 Chinese were working in the mines (mostly on the Rand.)[86]

It is interesting that the beating of a Chinese laborer on the Rand, authorized by law and sanctioned by Milner, led in 1906 to his censure by the House of Commons. The censure forced Milner to disappear from the political scene for a long time until he returned as colonial secretary in 1919.

The Great Chinese debate did not solve the labor problems of Rhodesia, but it clearly pointed the way to the future of the economic relations between whites and blacks in South Africa. It revealed the policy advocated by Milner—the policy silently approved by the British government. This debate led to another, not as bitter but more important, over the economic function of the African in Rhodesia. Even before the Chinese dispute was finally settled, the debate on the role and place of the African in the economy of the country had begun in earnest.

The British government, the company, the settler, and the missionary all unanimously agreed that the economic role of the African in the development of the country was to be that of a laborer. All agreed that any form of manual labor was to be done by Africans, since it would be degrading for Europeans to do similar work. They disagreed on the methods to disengage the African from his tribal society to work for the European. In this debate various theories were advanced.

In the formative period of Rhodesian history, Europeans imposed forced labor by the right of conquest.[87] But as we have seen the British government prohibited forced labor, because of the opposition it aroused in Britain and because the British government feared another violent outbreak of African resistance. In his report of April 4, 1900, the resident commissioner wrote: "It would be a difficult matter without the employment of force to wean the natives from their fields; to do so, having regard to the increasing native population in South Africa, would be unwise."[88] Since the Africans had decided that working for Europeans was not beneficial to them, the settlers changed their tune. Forced labor, it was now argued, was "good" for the African. By working the African would not only earn money but he would also learn; to labor was to learn. As far back as 1895 the *Chronicle* had argued: "Sooner or later the native will have to be forced to work, and, though such a fact may not be palatable to a section of the English people, those who have lived longest amongst the natives and know best, are fully aware that there is no help for it."[89] The *Chronicle* maintained that without forced labor the African would bask in the sun and do nothing. There were some who argued that some things people were forced to do, though inconvenient to them, were in the final analysis of great benefit to them. "By common consent school education in Great Britain is compulsory. This is a distinct interference with the liberty of the subject in the undoubted interest of the individual, although the average school boy, in his ignorance and inexperience, holds very different views. . . . Manual labor is undoubtedly the form of education which black men stand in need of in their own interest."[90]

In its edition of September 12, 1902, the *Bulawayo Observer* argued that it was necessary for Africans to be forced to work for a political reason. This the *Observer* maintained would remove any lingering doubts that the Africans entertained as to the strength of the Europeans. If Africans were left to do what they wanted and to live unperturbed by the Europeans, it was argued, they would forget that the Europeans were in power in Rhodesia.

Although the overriding preoccupation of the missionaries who worked in Rhodesia was spreading the word of God,[91] they played an important role in creating the white society's attitude to black labor. The arguments the missionaries often used to persuade Africans to go to work were different in tone from those of the settlers. Many missionaries thought that Africans were lazy and the devil, they argued, makes tools of idle hands. If Africans went to work for the Europeans, they would be separated from the restrictions of tribal society and in the new environment they would be exposed to a new ideology—that of individualism— which would facilitate their conversion. Salvation for a Christian, as the missionaries in Rhodesia saw it, lay not in a group but in the repentence of the individual. Rev. W. G. Mitchell, a Methodist missionary, in a sermon reported by *The Rhodesia Herald* of March 1, 1902, maintained that God had placed the Africans in the hands of the Europeans and that it was the duty of the European to give the African not only the white man's religion but his civilization as well.

For the missionaries then, labor was justified on moral grounds. The Anglican Bishop of Mashonaland maintained that man should work to justify his existence. In an article in the *Rhodesian Times*, the Bishop wrote: "Everyman is bound to justify his existence by labor. There should be no loafers in the kingdom of earth or Heaven."[92]

Some, like Father Rickortz, a priest in charge of the Catholic missions in Rhodesia, believed that the African's laziness was fostered by his parents and the tribal society. Father Rickortz maintained that the native commissioners

should have the right to call out from the different kraals as many natives as one wanted ... only the lazy native has to live in fear of being compelled ... From my experience I say that this fear will be sufficient to make most of the natives come of their own accord to work ... the native will not find such compulsion unjust, though perhaps disagreeable for the lazy ones ... We have to teach the native the obligations and reward of labour and to fight against idleness as the source of immorality.[93]

Father Rickortz strongly believed that as long as Africans remained in the village living their lives undistrubed by European intrusion, they would become useless and dangerous members of the society. He thought that the administration could prevent this by passing what he called "wise legislation," which would make the "uphill work" of the missionary easier, more effective, and lasting. Father Daignault, another Catholic priest, argued:

In my opinion, the natives of this country [Rhodesia] must be considered, and in reality are, but grown-up children. Unfortunately, they do not possess the innocence of children, but, on the contrary, are given to many vices, conspicuous among them being their strong inclination to idleness. . . . It [idleness] fosters drinking habits, and is the cause of many thefts and deadly quarrels. Consequently, men in authority, who have the true interests of the natives at heart, ought not only to treat them as children, but they ought also to do all they can to make them acquire habits of industry. As this cannot be attained by mere moral persuasion, authority must necessarily be used.[94]

And Rev. Isaac Shimmin, superintendent of Wesleyan Missions in Rhodesia, said: "No one will contend for a moment that a crowd of idle loafers, whether white or black, is as useful to the community as a company of industrious laborers. But in this country we have thousands of savages living in sloth; and thus ready for all kinds of mischief. . . ."[95]

The views of the missionaries received wide publicity because the settlers found themselves supported by the missionaries, the guardians of conscience. Company journals like the *African Commerce* often echoed the missionary's voice, arguing that the African should be "made" to realize that in working he was dispensing his moral obligation to the community, and that this moral obligation should be legally devised.

When in 1898 a hut tax of ten shillings had been imposed, its results had proved negligible. Nevertheless, almost the only weapon the company could effectively use was taxation. In 1903, the Legislative Council unanimously proposed to raise the hut tax to two pounds. The resident commissioner advised the high commissioner to turn down the proposal because he feared that such an increase would spark off an African uprising.[96] The resident commissioner also doubted that increased taxation would solve the labor problem. The British Government eventually settled for a hut tax of one pound and ten shillings for each extra wife that any man had after the first. The resident commissioner's fears were justified, for in 1904, the reports of the native commissioners generally expressed fears of an uprising. In January 1904, W. S. Taberer, then acting chief native commissioner of Mashonaland, reported on the meetings of some spirit mediums and some of the African leaders of Mashonaland. So extensive were the reports that in April the resident commissioner wrote: "From the reports I have seen there was a good deal of dissatisfaction expressed at the announcement of the increased native taxation."[97]

Although the Africans were disappointed with the increased tax they were in general able to pay it. They went to work, very often just to make enough to pay the hut tax, and usually left immediately afterwards. Not only were Africans mistreated and exposed to health hazards in the mines, but they were not allowed to come into European areas with their wives and children. Working for Europeans meant the separation of African families. The 1903–1905 South African Native Commission reported that Africans were attached to their houses and only went to work to meet their tax requirements and generally preferred to return to their homes to look after the interests of their families. The commission wrote: "Except in the case of farm labour . . . it must not be forgotten that what is known as paid labour generally means to the Native, as a rule, absence from home and family, and in some employments irksome and often hard and dangerous work, and the abandonment of the ease, comforts and pleasures of Native village life."[98] The commission found that the social life in the village was more attractive than that in the mining areas. "So long as it is impossible," the commission wrote, "for the Native to marry and make his home near the great centers of labour, so long will there be the yearning to return frequently to his distant home, and so long will the flow of labor be impeded by this really amiable trait in his character."[99] And "if . . . a proportion . . . were encouraged to bring their wives with them there would be more natives in continuous employment."[100]

To allow the African to live with his family in a European area was against the fundamental settler policy of segregation. The pure reserve or "separation" theory, as Dilley has described it, required the African to remain undisturbed in his tribal state and to develop his own institutions. But this policy had to be modified to meet the labor requirements of the Europeans. The African could come into European areas to work, but could not live there permanently. The heart of African culture and institutions was to be on the reserves, but for the purposes of serving European economic interests, the African could be allowed to stay temporarily in a European area. Dilley called this the "dual policy." However, while he was in employment, the African, by mere contact with Europeans, was expected to learn something to his advantage. This Dilley called "interpenetration theory." She wrote: "From this need for native labor, the theory of the dignity of labor has developed. . . . The theory has also developed that it is preferable for the native to have direct contact with the white race so that his advance in civilization may be more rapid than if he remained in his tribal area attending to his own affairs."[101]

General Jan Christian Smuts, the second South African prime minister, made the dual policy the cornerstone of African policy in the Union. This policy, which was also adopted by Rhodesia, called for cultural segregation of the races based on economic cooperation. In several lectures, General Smuts maintained that contact between the black and white would not necessarily lead to the destruction of black culture. "So long as there is territorial segregation," he argued, "so long as the native family home is not with the white man but in his own area, so long the native organization will not be materially affected. . . . It is not white employment of the native males that works mischief, but the abandonment of the native tribal home by the women and children."[102]

There was, therefore, an ambivalence on the part of the Europeans in their attempt to solve the labor problem; the European, despite all the talk about the dignity of labor and their "moral obligation," did not protect the family life of the people whom they wanted so badly to join their economy. The Africans were not unaware of this. "We [Africans] hate . . . being made to work in mines and on farms for Europeans. We lived without working for whites before. . . . What change has come to this land that a man, because he is white, demands that he must be worked for? . . . let them do their own work."[103] If people are to accept change freely, the new system must provide greater security, happiness, and benefits than the old. The new taxation of 1903, designed to force Africans to go to work, was not seen as a benefit, but was seen as an imposition by callous rulers. On April 6, 1904, Clarke, the resident commissioner, reported to the high commissioner about African dissatisfaction with the increased taxation.[104]

Clarke was reasonably well informed about African opinion. In 1901 he expressed the view that only the development among

Africans of a desire to improve their standard of living would induce them to work for wages.[105] Clarke saw taxation as a temporary expedient that even then did not produce satisfactory results. He cited the example of Basutoland where officials described the tax as a land tax. Because the Basutos produced crops it was easy for them to see the "beneficial" connection between tax and land. One contemporary writer boasted, "the native population, as tax payers, are helping to pay for their own conquest."[106]

Taxation, though it forced a considerable number of Africans to go to work, on the whole failed to provide a solution to the labor problem in Rhodesia. Those who went to work usually did so during the winter months and returned to plough their fields at the beginning of the rainy season. Many Africans were able to produce enough crops for sale and with the money obtained from this sale they were able to pay the required tax. The reports of the native commissioners throughout the period state that Africans of Southern Rhodesia were well off and did not see the need to go to work. In 1903 an inspector of mines commented: "A woman cultivating an extra acre or two can earn her husband more money in a month than he can at the mines in three months, notwithstanding the high rate of wages."[107]

The company was forced, once again, to look beyond the borders of Rhodesia to secure labor. With the permission of the British government it turned to Nyasaland and Northern Rhodesia. The Rhodesia Native Labour Bureau, which had replaced the old Labour Board and Labour Bureau, failed to secure sufficient local labor partly because it also recruited laborers for the Rand. The bureau was supposed to support itself financially; employers were required to pay some money to the bureau for the workers provided. It also depended on voluntary contributions. The Rand mines paid twenty-nine shillings per head.[108] In 1903, the Rhodesian Native Labour Bureau, for 1,736 laborers, received £2,534 from the Rand whereas for 5,803 workers the Rhodesian mines paid £3,322.[109] In 1904, the bureau recruited 8,953 laborers of whom 4,340 were handed over to the Rhodesian mines at twenty shillings per head and 4,613 to the Rand at 30 shillings per head.[110] Because the Transvaal could pay more, the bureau provided more laborers for the Rand. The policy of supplying labor to the Rand deprived Rhodesia of labor that otherwise would have been available for her mines. Local Africans who failed to secure employment during the dry season sometimes went to the Rand mines. In 1905 the resident commissioner observed that during the dry season only 84 Africans (from the Fort Victoria district) were able to get jobs in Rhodesia and 1,084 went to the Transvaal.[111]

In 1906 the company tried to raise money to finance the bureau by adopting a Labour Ordinance fee by which every miner employing twenty-five laborers or more paid a tax of one shilling per month per employee. This was in addition to what employers directly paid the bureau for laborers provided. In 1911 the company passed the Labour Tax Ordinance, under which all employers, whether mining or agricultural, could upon paying £5 receive laborers from the Rhodesian Labour Bureau. The farmers objected fiercely and in 1912 the colonial secretary rescinded the ordinance.

The bureau's difficulties were compounded by the fact that many Africans from Nyasaland and Northern Rhodesia preferred to get employment on their own rather than through its auspices. If the Africans got employment through the bureau, they usually were not able to bargain for "good" salaries as these were determined at the time of agreement with the recruiting agents. But if they directly sought employment they were usually able to bargain for higher salaries as competition for their services was great. As free agents they were able to seek work for those employers whose reputations were not tarnished by accusations of cruelty and ill treatment.[112] However, the main reason why many foreign laborers ignored the bureau was that those laborers who secured employment through the offices of the bureau did not receive all their pay during the period of employment. Part of the pay was held back and given to them in a lump sum at the end of the contract. They usually had to wait several weeks for all the forms to be processed before they received the money.

Laborers who came to Rhodesia on their own experienced many disadvantages. They did not have the benefit of medical examination, and on the way to Rhodesia they often ran the danger of being attacked by wild animals. Many of them, tired and sick, were often left by the wayside to die by their compatriots who had to continue the journey if they were not to run short of food supplies. Very often these men arrived in Rhodesia in no condition to work. In 1906 the British government prohibited the Rand mines from recruiting labor from Northern Rhodesia and Nyasaland because the death rate (166.3 per 1000 per annum) was very high. In 1907, J. C. Casson, superintendent of native affairs in Nyasaland, complained to the British government about the poor conditions under which Africans from Nyasaland live in Rhodesia. "I am of the opinion" he wrote " . . . that at some of the mines . . . in Southern Rhodesia . . . little attempt is made to care for native welfare generally so long as a supply of labour is forthcoming somehow and from somewhere."[113]

The most important reason why Africans from Northern Rhodesia and Nyasaland came to work in Southern Rhodesia was the high wages that were offered. In Nyasaland farm laborers received 3 or 4 shillings against 22/6 in Rhodesia a month; and in the mines they were paid between twenty shillings to forty shillings a month.[114] The influence of the local shopkeeper played a part in the Nyasa's desire to work. In 1905, Wallis, the Nyasaland acting commissioner, reported that Africans were opening up small retail shops in competition with the Indians. Wallis also noted that Africans returning from Rhodesia and Transvaal with new clothes for themselves and their wives and such items as tea, sugar, and biscuits encouraged other Africans to go South. With the money they made in Rhodesia or Transvaal many returning laborers were able to pay lobola for their brides in cash. Another reason was the fact that in their homeland the Nyasas were sometimes unable to find work because Africans from Mozambique had taken the jobs.

By 1909, 10,875 indigenous Africans worked on the Rhodesian mines against 23,433 aliens; of the latter, 6,447 came from Mozambique, 9,991 from Northern Rhodesia, 5,261 from Nyasaland, and 1,734 from Bechuanaland and other places.[115]

The shortage of labor continued to plague Rhodesian industries until toward the end of the period of this study. As time went on the agricultural industry experienced more difficulties in getting laborers than did the mining industry. Africans preferred to work in the cities and in the mines in gangs rather than in relative isolation on farms where the employers were usually very hard driving. Since many Africans sought work directly and not through the bureau, the bureau found it difficult to meet the labor demands of the farming community. So dissatisfied were the European farmers with the bureau that in 1911 they unsuccessfully demanded its abolition.

Perhaps in response to the pressures for more laborers by the European farming community, the Company administration resorted to the only "legal" means at its disposal—taxation—and introduced a dog tax much to the displeasure of the Africans. In 1913 every dog owner paid 2 shillings 6d tax per dog. "The natives," wrote the chief native commissioner, "protested against the introduction of the dog tax. . . ."[116] Still, the labor shortage was not solved, and the bureau's recruiting activities produced no satisfactory results. As time passed, the Bureau actually recruited less every year. For instance, during the first six months of 1910, the bureau recruited 11,750 mostly from Northern Rhodesia and Nyasaland. In 1914 the bureau recruited only 9,588, in 1915 it recruited 11,316, and in 1924 out of the 43,205 aliens who entered Rhodesia for employment, only 4,589 were supplied by the bureau.[117]

Because of its failure to recruit laborers the bureau confined its activities to helping immigrant laborers on their way to and from Rhodesia, by supplying medical help, blankets, and transportation whenever it could, "in the hope of popularizing the Bureau, and inducing the natives to pass through our agents' hands."[118] The hope that these efforts would give the bureau a good name was empty; it did not improve its image. However, the humanitarian role that the bureau undertook was a direct result of the pressure (applied through native commissioners and inspectors health reports) by the British government.

Throughout the period, despite the persistant pressure by the British government, African laborers were mistreated by their employers. Sometimes the abuse remained unknown to the native commissioners and inspectors of compounds because many Africans tended to report cases to the agents of the bureau who had recruited them, and these agents were not eager to make this known as it would have brought them even more unpopularity.[119] In some cases, either because they did not trust the inspector or for fear of reprisals from their employers when the inspector left, laborers did not complain to the inspectors. In such cases many

Africans simply deserted. Even when Africans gave evidence against their employers the machinery of justice sometimes failed hopelessly. Early in 1904, Andrew Dale, a native commissioner in the Wankie District, visited compounds along the railway line. He found living conditions extremely poor at every camp he visited. In one compound he found the dead body of an African who had been left to die by his employers because he had been too ill to move. The three employers, Piripiri, Melfi, and Mura, were brought to trial. Eager that these men be punished to set an example to other employers, the chief native commissioner of Matebeleland wrote: "I am particularly anxious that no loop hole of escape should be left for these persons to evade the consequences of their behavior as I feel convinced that if their punishment can be brought about it will serve as a very salutary object lesson for many others who may be inclined to follow their example."[120] Despite the testimony of eleven Africans, Piripiri, the man who had left the African to die, had his case dismissed on the grounds that a principal witness in the case had disappeared. The presiding judge did not even bother to find out why the witness had disappeared. Melfi ran away and Mura was fined five pounds.[121]

There was one sure way which, if followed, would in the long run have solved the problem. What was required was time to transform the reserves into trading centers where goods capable of improving the standard of living of the Africans would be available. "The labour question is not only economic, it is also ethical. . . . You cannot force even a native to work; what you have to do is to increase his civilization and so make it necessary for him to work in order to earn wages. Once a native begins to raise himself above the degrading life of his kraal, he immediately begins to want money to satisfy his new desires, and this want of money leads him to work."[122]

In the end, the Rhodesian economy had to rely heavily on alien labor. These foreign laborers came because they could earn money, or at any rate more money than they could earn at home. Most local Africans, on the other hand, worked for one reason only—to secure money to pay taxes. The alien laborer, once in the country, either because part of his pay was held back until his contract expired or simply because he was disinclined to desert and undertake the dangerous return journey immediately after his arrival, could generally be relied upon to work longer than six months. That is why at the end of the laborer's contract the Rhodesian Native Labour Bureau usually tried its best to make the return journey as "pleasant" as it could. For these resons the backbone of the Rhodesian industries was the foreign laborer mainly from Northern Rhodesia and Nyasaland with a few from Mozambique. By 1923, there were 89,800 alien to 49,000 indigenous laborers.

	Work Other Than Mining 1923	Mining 1923	Total 1923
Indigenous	39,000	10,000	49,000
Alien	62,000	27,800	89,00
	101,000	37,800	138,800[a]

[a.] Chief Native Commissioner's Report 1923, p. 6.

NOTES

1. See William Harvey Brown, *On the South African Frontier*, (London: Sampson Low, Marston & Company, Ltd., 1899) p. 348. Also see B. Wilson, "Rhodesia and Its Prospects," *United Empire*, vol. 2, 1911, p. 560.

2. Cd. 1200, Correspondence Relating to the Regulations and Supply of Labour in Southern Rhodesia, 1902, pp. 26-27.

3. Elizabeth Colson and Max Gluckman, eds. *Seven Tribes of Central Africa* (Manchester: Manchester University Press, 1959).

4. Ethel Tawsie Jollie, "African Dilemma," *African Observer* 6, no. 4, (November, 1936, April 1937): 35.

5. A "working beer party" where people work for no pay but at intervals drink beer.

6. Resident Commissioner to High Commissioner, April 4, 1900, Cd. 1200, p. 67. A. J. Hanna, in her book, *The Story of the Rhodesias and Nyasaland* (London: Faber and Faber, Ltd., 1960) suggested this as the policy that might have solved the shortage of labor, p. 179.

7. William Harvey Brown, *On the South African Frontier*, pp. 348-49.

8. Ibid., p. 390.

9. Ibid., p. 391. Brown justified forced labor arguing: "Through an apprenticeship of bondage, the [American] negro has been removed from a state of barbarism and superstition, and placed in possession of the language and customs, religion and useful arts of the most progressive of all races. Thus, forcibly weaned from his benighted associations, taught to labor, and kept under influence of an energetic people, he has reached a point on the high road of progress that his brother in Africa probably will not attain in a thousand years."

10. Terence Ranger, *Revolt in Southern Rhodesia 1896-7* (London: Wm. Heinemann, Ltd., 1967), p. 67. Also see Chapters 2 and 3 for a detailed description of police methods to recruit labor. Ranger also reports that to discourage African laborers from deserting the mines and farms, armed African police, employed by the company, often seized the men's wives as hostages. Also see Philip Mason, *The Birth of a Dilemma: The Conquest and Settlement of Rhodesia* (London: Oxford University Press, 1958), p. 193.

11. Cd., 1200, 1902, p. 36. Both the Labour Board and the Labour Bureau were abolished in 1901 and were replaced by the Rhodesian Native Labour Bureau which was subsidized by the company.

12. C. O. 417/319, 1901.

13. Administrator of Matebeleland to the Resident Commissioner, April 5, 1900 Cd., 1200, 1902, p. 34.

14. Cd. 1200, 1902, p. 27.

15. See William Harvey Brown, *On the South African Frontier*, p. 348-49.

16. See Mason, *The Birth of a Dilemma*, pp. 197-99; for a description of European feeling and anger aroused by the uprising and for the "chivalrous" desire to avenge the killing of white women and children. One tenth of Rhodesia's white population was killed in the revolt.

17. My translation.

18. Cd. 1200, 1902, p. 62.

19. Chamber of Mines to Government, February 28, 1899, Cd. 1200. p. 62. About 3,000 ounces of gold every year were estimated to be traded across the Zambezi by Africans.

20. Resident Commissioner to High Commissioner April 4, 1900, Cd. 1200, 1902, p. 67.

21. Report of the Chief Native Commissioner, Mashonaland, March 31, 1903, p. 1.

22. Resident Commissioner to High Commissioner, September 3, 1900. C. O. 417/284.

23. Cd. 1200, 1902, pp. 27-28.

24. B.S.A. Co., to C. O. February 22, 1900, Cd. 1200. 1902, p. 28.

25. Chamberlain to Milner, December 23, 1899, Cd. 1200, 1902, p. 27.

26. Cd. 1200, 1902, pp. 2-4.

27. Cd. 1200, 1902, p. 10.

28. Cd. 2399, 1905, p. 18.

29. Ibid., p. 19.

30. Cd. 8674: The Southern Rhodesia Native Reserves Commission Final Report 1915, p. 21.

31. Cd. 1200, 1902, p. 83.

32. C. O. to B.S.A. Co., October 3, 1901, Cd. 1200, 1902, p. 83.

33. Milner to Chamberlain, October 4, 1901, Cd. 1200, p. 88.

34. C. O. to B.S.A. Co., October 3, 1901, Cd. 1200, p. 83.

35. Mashonaland Farmers' Association to the Administrator, November 6, 1901, C. O. 417/343.

36. C. O. 417/343.

37. Cd. 1200, 1902, p. 42.

38. Cd. 1200, 1902, p. 45.

39. Cd. 1200, 1902, p. 29.

40. Milner to Graham, an official at the Colonial Office, January 17, 1902, C. O. 417/343.

41. Cd. 1200, 1902, p. 18.

42. Taberer, Report to the Labour Board, September 2, 1899, Cd. 1200, 1902, p. 18.

43. Cd. 1200, 1902, p. 18. Cd. 3993, pp. 30-35 (1906) and C. O. 417/539 (1914).

44. Taberer, Report to Labour Board, August 12, 1899, Cd. 1200, 1902, p. 17.

45. Cd. 3933, 1906, pp. 30-35.

46. Cd. 1200, 1902, p. 26.

47. Chamberlain to Milner, December 23, 1899, Cd. 1200, p. 26.

48. Resident Commissioner to Imperial Secretary, October 29, 1900, O. 417/284.

49. See Report of the Rhodesian Native Labour Bureau, April 23, 1915.

50. Resident Commissioner to High Commissioner, March 24, 1904, C. O. 417/391.

51. Resident Commissioner to High Commissioner April 4, 1900. Cd. 1200, 1902, p. 67.

52. Resident Commissioner to High Commissioner, August 17, 1901, C. O. 417/321.

53. "Report by The Administrator of Matabeleland for the Year Ending March 31st, 1900," in *The British South Africa Company Reports on the Administration of Rhodesia 1898-1900*, pp. 22-23.

54. Resident Commissioner to High Commissioner, March 23, 1901, C. O. 417/319.

55. C. O. 417/284, 1900.

56. B.S.A. Co., Reports, 1898-1900, p. 28.

57. C. O. 417/321, October 19, 1901.

58. C. O. 417/321, October 19, 1901.

59. Cd. 1200, 1902, p. 91.

60. L. S. Amery, ed., *The Times History of the War in South Africa* (London: Sampson Low, Marston and Co., 1900-1909), vol. 4 p. 105.

61. B.S.A. Co., to C. O. August 18, 1900. Cd. 1200, 1902, p. 46.

62. Amery, *The Times History* vol. 4, p. 105.

63. Ibid., p. 101.

64. Cd. 2028. "Correspondence Relating to the Proposed Introduction of Indentured Asiatic (Chinese) Labour into Southern Rhodesia 1904," p. 13.

65. *Bulawayo Observer*, April 11, 1903, p. 3.

66. Milner to Lyttleton, January 25, 1904, C. O. 417/391.

67. *Bulawayo Observer*, April 11, 1903, p. 4.

68. Resident Commissioner to High Commissioner, December 11, 1903, Cd. 2028, p. 12.

69. *Rhodesian Times*, December 26, 1903, p. 7.

70. Milner to Lyttleton, January 25, 1904, C. O. 417/391.

71. C. O. 417/391.

72. Milner to Chamberlain, April 6, 1903, in C. Headlam, *The Milner Papers*, vol. 2, p. 462.

73. Lyttleton to Milner, June 8, 1904, C. O. 417/391.

74. Resident Commissioner to High Commissioner December 11, 1903. Cd. 2028, p. 11.

75. Headlam, *The Milner Papers* vol. 2, p. 438.

76. Administrator to Resident Commissioner, December 7, 1903, Cd. 2028, p. 16.

77. C. Headlam, *The Milner Papers* vol. 2, p. 459.

78. Ibid., p. 477.

79. Ibid., p. 477.

80. Ibid., pp. 458-59.

81. Milner to Chamberlain April 6, 1903, ibid., p. 461.

82. Milner to Sir E. Walton, April 8, 1903, ibid., p. 461.

83. L. S. Amery, *The Times History* vol. 6, p. 101.

84. Milner to Sir E. H. Walton, April 8, 1903, Headlam, vol. 2., p. 461.

85. Milner to Bishop Hamilton Baynes, March 3, 1904, ibid., p. 488.

86. Ibid., p. 488.

87. Rhodesian history begins in 1890—African history of the country dates back centuries earlier.

88. Resident Commissioner to High Commissioner, April 4, 1900. Cd. 1200, p. 67.

89. *The Bulawayo Chronicle*, February 1, 1895, p. 2.

90. *African Commerce* 2, no. 2 (April, 1901): 123.

91. Most of the missionary magazines I checked, such as *The Rhodesia Missionary Advocate* of the American Methodists, and *Southern Rhodesia Quarterly*, of the Anglicans, exclusively concerned themselves with the problems of spreading Christianity among the Africans.

92. Quoted in the *Bulawayo Observer*, December 26, 1903, p. 7.

93. *The Rhodesia Herald*, March 1, 1902, p. 6. The South African Native Affairs Commission of 1905 denied that the African was lazy.

94. Quoted in Brown, *On the South African Frontier*, p. 394.

95. Quoted in ibid., p. 393.

96. C. O. 417/391.

97. Resident Commissioner to High Commissioner, April 6, 1904, C. O. 417/391.

98. Cd. 2399, 1905, p. 58.

99. Ibid., p. 38.

100. Frank H. Witts, "The Native Labour Question in Southern Rhodesia," *The Empire Review* 22 (1911,): 337.

101. Marjorie Ruth Dilley, *British Policy in Kenya Colony*, 2nd ed. (London: Cass, 1966) p. 214. What Miss Dilley says of Kenyan policy of reserves is applicable to Rhodesia.

102. Quoted in W. Benson, "The African Labourer," *The Nineteenth Century and After: 1877-1930* 108, no. 641 (July 1930): 67.

103. T. V. Bulpin, *The White Whirlwind* (Cape Town, South Africa: Cape Times Limited, 1961), pp. 305-6.

104. Resident Commissioner to High Commissioner, April 6, 1904. C.O. 417/391.

105. Cd. 1200, 1902, p. 67.

106. Ethel Tawsie Jollie, *The Real Rhodesia* (London: Hutchinson and Co. Paternoster Row, 1924), p. 45.

107. Southern Rhodesia Reports of the Inspectors of Native Compounds for the Year Ended 31st March, 1903, p. 2.

108. Report of Native Labour Enquiry Committee, 1906, p. 3.

109. Ibid., p. 3.

110. Ibid., p. 3.

111. C. O. 417/409, July 4, 1905.

112. Cd. 1200, 1902, p. 67.

113. Report and Suggestions Relating to Nyasaland Natives at work in, and proceeding to, Southern Rhodesia, November, 1907, Cd. 3993, p. 82.

114. Cd. 3729, British Central Africa Protectorate: Report for 1906-7, p. 24.

115. Rhodesia Native Labour Bureau, 1910, p. 4.

116. Report of the C.N.C. For the Year 1913, p. 1.

117. The British South Africa Company Reports, 1915-1940, p. 7.

118. V. Giegland, of the Rhodesian Native Labour Bureau, to Sir Marshall Clarke, December 22, 1904, C. O. 417/407.

119. C. O. 417/407, 1904.

120. C.N.C. to Andrew Dale, January 28, 1904, C. O. 417/391.

121. C. O. 417/391, 1904.

122. Witts, "The Native Labour Question", p. 337.

7
Reserves: Protection or Control

Between 1898 and 1900, the Company, under orders from the British government, set aside reserves.[1] In terms of land occupancy, there were four classes of Africans in 1900. The first class lived on expropriated land; they were said to be living on native locations. Such Africans lived by an agreement with the landlord. The provisions for native locations were issued by Lord Rosmead on October 14, 1896.[2] The Rosmead Proclamation stipulated that each private farm should have not less than seven families living as tenants. The second group of Africans lived on unalienated lands belonging to the company. The third consisted of those who lived as squatters, on private farms without any agreement. The last group was composed of those who lived in reserves specifically allocated for African occupation.[3]

In 1898 there were two reserves, totaling six thousand five hundred square miles, in Matebeleland. These reserves had been set up in 1895, after the 1893 Matebele War, because European land expropriation had threatened to make the Matebele completely landless. In Mashonaland, on the other hand, no reserves had been set up before 1898 because,

At that time [between 1890 and 1898] it was felt that no hardship would be inflicted upon the natives by the absence of a Proclamation formally constituting the reserves, as in the majority of cases they were residing on land which would ultimately be set apart as such, and the Administration considered that their interests would be safeguarded by a rule prohibiting the alienation of any land until the Native Commissioner of the District had furnished a statement that it was not situated within a provisional reserve and was not likely to be required for that purpose.[4]

With the exception of those living in the reserves, Africans had no secure tenure. Those who lived on private farms without any agreement could be evicted at any time. Africans on locations enjoyed insecure tenure; they signed a two-year contract which the owner, if he wished, could refuse to renew.[5] Those Africans living on chartered company land were at the mercy of any European who might buy the land.

Reserves, it was thought, could provide perpetual land tenure for the Africans. The Africans could not be moved from the reserves except for valid reasons and then only after a commission of inquiry had ascertained the validity of the reasons, and on the condition that an exact amount of suitable land would be provided for their needs. "No natives shall be removed from any kraal or from any land assigned to them for occupation, except after full inquiry by . . . the Administrator in Executive Council [and] approved by the High Commissioner."[6] The primary aim in establishing reserves was to provide Africans with land from which Europeans would be excluded.[7] European economic and educational activities would be confined to building roads, schools, and churches. But African land tenure in the reserves was not completely secure; the discovery of minerals constituted a "valid" reason for their removal. The company would then look for an adequate amount of suitable land elsewhere to give the dispossessed,

The Company shall retain the mineral rights in all land assigned to natives. . . . The Administrator in Executive Council . . . with the approval of the High Commissioner [can] order the natives to remove from such land or any portion thereof, and shall assign to them just and liberal compensation in land elsewhere, situate in as convenient a position as possible, sufficient and suitable for their agricultural and pastoral requirements, containing a fair and equitable proportion of springs or permanent water, and as far as possible, equally suitable for their requirements in all respects as the land from which they are ordered to remove.[8]

The interests of the company were always paramount, and those of the Africans, were secondary. Whenever there was a conflict between African and company interests, company officials always argued that removal of the Africans was in their (African) best interests. Although the 1898 Order in Council stated that Africans could only be removed to areas as fertile and well watered as the previous ones, this condition was not always fulfilled.

The Nyakwanyeskwa Kraal, which was situated near the Penhalonga Proprietary Mines, serves as a case in point. The Africans lived near a stream that provided both themselves and the owners of the mines with water. The manager of the mines did not wish to share the water with the Africans, arguing that it was unhealthy for him and for his employees. He therefore requested the administration to remove the Africans from the area. The administrator, without investigation or any attempt to reach a compromise between the Africans and the manager, wrote to the high commissioner seeking permission to remove the Africans. In fact, the administrator moved the Africans even before writing to the high commissioner.

> It has been represented to the Administrator by the Proprietors of the Mines that the Kraal is situated near the source of the stream upon which they are dependent for their water supply and that the health of their employees is endangered through its pollution by the Natives of the Kraal in question.
> . . . it is desirable in the interests of the natives that they should be removed from close proximity to the mines, to which course they have assented. In the meantime, Nyakwanyeskwa has voluntarily removed to a site one mile distant from his old kraal, which, while not so suitable [for agriculture] as the site first proposed, removes the chief objection raised by the Manager of the mine.[9]

This letter indicates that the high commissioner was presented with a *fait accompli*, which was supposed to be a request for permission to remove the Africans from their old village. In this case, Africans did not even live in the mining area where they would have been in the way of the Company. It is doubtful that any potential health hazard was either caused by the Africans or was solved by their removal. The manager of the Penhalonga

Proprietary Mines simply did not want to drink from the same well with the Africans. It was the duty of the high commissioner to inquire fully into all the details and problems that involved the people of the Nyakwanyeskwa Kraal. Africans were generally reluctant to leave the villages in which they had lived for many generations.[10] It is difficult to imagine that the people of Nyakwanyeskwa voluntarily left their village for a place that was not as suitable for their needs. Even though one of the requirements laid down by the Order in Council was that the reserves should be suitable for agriculture and should have a sufficient supply of water, the administrator admitted that the people of Nyakwanyeskwa village were moved into unsuitable land,[11] but the high commissioner raised no objections, and the case demonstrates the weakness of such safeguards.

Very often the British government approved recommendations made by company officials without checking their accuracy or validity, knowing that there was an insufficient number of British officials in Rhodesia to carry out on-the-spot checking. In 1897 the British government denounced the report of the 1894 Land Commission that it had approved in 1895. In response to the requirement of the 1898 Order in Council to set up reserves, the administrator in December, 1899, submitted his suggestions. He proposed sixteen reserves for Matebeleland and eighty for Mashonaland, totaling 24,877,440 acres.[12] The secretary of state for the Colonies approved this allocation. In December 1902 the secretary of state, to his surprise, was presented with another allocation that was substantially different from the one in 1899. "These discrepancies," wrote the British resident commissioner, "are owing for the most part to the completion of the surveys of lands adjoining several of the reserves."[13] By 1900, Europeans had laid claim to the best lands in the country so that it was difficult to find suitable land for the needs of the Africans. In a dispatch dated December 2, 1902, Milner noted: "In some parts a difficulty in finding suitable land has been experienced . . . owing to the large portion of the territory alienated to companies and individuals before the justice of making provision for natives had the consideration which it has since received."[14]

In 1914 the company wanted to reduce the size of the Sabi Reserve.[15] Most of the land that the company wanted was good for agriculture. The company argued not only that the reserve was sparsely populated[16] but also that it wanted to build a railway on that location. It promised to resettle the Africans on suitable land elsewhere. Rev. S. Cripps, an Anglican priest, argued that the company's estimation of the population was wrong. "It appears to be very likely," wrote Rev. Cripps, "that the native population on the reserves of the district had made a large increase since the Commission sat. Also it would appear that a considerable number of natives have moved from private lands onto our reserves since then."[17] He also argued that if the company were only interested in constructing a railway line, it merely needed a fifty-yard strip and not a twelve-mile belt.

The recommendation for reducing the area of the Sabi reserve rested mainly on the report of a special agent who represented and was paid by the company and not on the recommendations of the local native commissioner, who although paid by the company would have been in a better position to know the needs of the Africans. The British government's willingness to allow the company to cut the size of the Sabi Reserve suggests that African tenure was only secure as long as the company had no interest in their land. Even after the reserves had supposedly been definitively delimited in 1917, the company could still remove Africans from any land if minerals were discovered on it. The Aborigines Protection Society protested against this lack of secure land tenure. The society proposed "that once native reserves have been officially alloted to indigenous tribes the title to them should be a secure one, and that portions of reserves should only be alienated from the natives for indisputable public works, and then only upon the same conditions as those applying to the alienation of lands occupied by white settlers."[18]

Alfred Milner, the British high commissioner in South Africa, was opposed to the policy of reserves. He argued that reserves would keep Africans from contact with the new economic methods of European production, and would also encourage tribalism. "The reserve," wrote Milner, "is of course an oasis of barbarism, while location brings the native into contact with civilization under more favorable conditions than at a mining centre."[19] By 1905, 151,503 Africans were living in locations on private lands.[20] The landlord usually made an agreement with tenants as to the amount of land they were to cultivate, the amount of rent due, or the amount of labor required in payment of the required rent. This contract was to be made in writing and in the presence of a native commissioner.

> The landlord is forbidden to enforce compulsory labour upon his Native tenants, nor can he call them for payment under agreement until after the expiration of the first year of their tenancy the amount of rent to be approved by the Chief Native Commissioner, or failing any agreement, to be fixed by that officer. . . . Once located on the land, such Natives cannot be removed against their consent.[21]

To the Africans, the idea of living as tenants and paying rent to a landlord was new. Africans had previously worked the land primarily at a subsistence level. Payment of rent, no matter what the amount, was an innovation that could have had great possibilities if tenure had been assured for longer periods of time. But, the tenant was not assured a secure tenure. One year the African tenant might break up a new piece of land, only to be moved elsewhere in the following year.[22] Some landlords saw their tenants only as sources of labor. In such cases the landlords charged no rent but signed contracts with their tenants by which the Africans would work for a stipulated length of time at a certain period of the year, usually during the time when the tenants should have been working in their own fields.

Milner was convinced that the location system would be good for both Africans and settlers. It would be good for the settlers by providing them with labor. The Europeans would be in a position of constant supervision over the Africans; hence, it would be easy for the Europeans to know what the Africans thought and what grievances they might have. Mere contact with the Europeans, Milner thought, would lead Africans to change their way of living. Milner wrote:

> My hope is that the number of natives who may be provided with land under the terms of that [the Rosmead] Proclamation will be large and constantly increasing, for it seems to me that this method of settlement is more promising for the development of the country and the maintenance of peace, as well as for

the progress and well-being of the natives themselves, than the reserves themselves.[23]

The British government rejected the policy of locations mainly on the grounds that tenure was insecure. "The weak point in the location system is of course the insecurity of tenure, as the agreement is renewable year by year. We read occasionally of land that will have to be cleared of natives."[24] The Rosmead Proclamation had been intended to encourage Africans to return to the lands they had inhabited prior to the 1896–97 war[26] even if it now "belonged" to the Europeans. In Matebeleland, where land alienation had been ruthlessly carried out, in 1898 there were 35,000 people living on locations and 27,000 living on private farms; in 1902 the combined totals had increased to 70,000.[29] By 1909, 78,000 were living in the reserves; 60,000 on unalienated land of the chartered company; 84,000 in the locations, and about 4,000 were living on mission stations.[27] These figures suggest that in 1914 close to 150,000 Africans lived on land from which they could be evicted, should the owners so desire. In 1903 the South African Native Affairs Commission was set up, on which one Rhodesian sat, to look into and determine what the political, social, and economic position of the Africans should be in South Africa. From its findings we can deduce the attitude of the settlers toward the locations. It resolved; "That the unrestricted squatting of Natives on private farms, whether as tenants or otherwise, is an evil and against the best interests of the country."[28]

Throughout most of this period, both the Europeans and the company allowed a considerable number of Africans to live on "their" land. The previous discussion of the labor problem noted that as long as Africans lived on European land it was much easier to persuade them to work than it would have been had they all been living in the reserves. This does not suggest that the location system solved the labor problem, because it did not. In the decade 1915–25, Africans began to feel the full effect of European settlement, and began to move in large numbers into the reserves. In 1915, Africans living in the reserves numbered 405,376, and those living outside the reserves were 327,777. By 1924, 508,270 Africans were living in the reserves and 304,307 lived outside the reserves.[29] As time went on, European farmers no longer wanted

Africans to live on their farms as tenants. All these Africans would eventually have to move to the reserves.

The first tendency of the settler was to encourage the Matabele to remain on the farms for the sake of their labour. The natives were regarded as tenants, and in many cases they were glad to enter into arrangements. . . . Whereby, in consideration of a small annual rental or of an undertaking to furnish labor for their landlords at stated seasons, they should enjoy un-disturbed possession of their old village sites and lands. It was found impossible, however, to provide for all the natives in this manner. Some refused to settle on land occupied by white men while they exhibited strong objection against migrating to the Shangani and Gwaii Reserves the former of which they declared was unhealthy and the latter waterless.[30]

Before 1910 European farmers, in general, had preferred to have African tenants. Although their attitude began to change and from time to time some Europeans forced Africans off their lands, a considerable number of Africans continued to live on alienated European lands as tenants. In 1913 the African population was estimated at 712,783, more than 400,000 of whom lived in re-serves and about 312,000 lived on European-owned or unalienated land.[31]

By 1913, Africans owned 377,000 cattle and 893,000 sheep and goats as compared to the 1902 estimates of 55,000 cattle and 257,000 goats.[32] It is easy to see the pressure that Africans (and their livestock) could cause on locations or on private farms. This period also saw European farmers increase their production and stock. Africans thus began to be an economic challenge to the Europeans on whose "land" they were living. As their stock increased, some European farmers simply gave their African tenants notice to quit. "Stock farmers in Matebeleland par-ticularly have begun to find that the pasturage on their land is insufficient to maintain both their own cattle and those of their native tenants. . . . The consequence has been that in many instances farmers have been compelled to give their tenants notice to quit. . . ."[33] The 1915–16 drought, particularly in Matebeleland, made the situation even more difficult.

Some European farmers and some land companies imposed

grazing fees on their tenants and raised the rents. In 1913, Taylor, the chief native commissioner for Matebeleland, reported that there were "grazing fees for both large and small stock. . . . This innovation has given rise to a great deal of dissatisfaction, and has had a disturbing effect on natives concerned, who naturally enquire how long they are to be subjected to these increasing demands. . . . The natives hate the idea of having to give up their old kraals and associations, but the fresh demands made upon them, which are now becoming more general have made them uneasy in regard to their land tenure on private property."[34] The imposition of grazing fees and the raising of rents usually forced Africans to sell part of their stock in order to meet the new financial demands of their landlords. In some cases the Africans were forced to sell their stock at prices that suited their European landlords. European farmers in these instances virtually expropriated African cattle.

Unfortunately for the Africans, in 1912 there was an outbreak of East African coast fever. To prevent their cattle from catching the disease, European farmers further restricted the movement of African cattle on their farms. The Europeans refused to erect dipping tanks although dipping could have cured the disease; they simply asked their tenants to leave. In order to move their stock, the Africans needed the permission of the European farmers through whose lands they would pass on their way to the reserves. Some farmers refused to allow Africans to move their cattle through their farms. Consequently, the Africans had no alternative but to sell their stock at whatever price they could get.[35] Robinson, a native commissioner in the Nyamandlovu district, believed that with dipping, the danger of the disease spreading would be removed, and that it then would be unnecessary for the Africans to ask for the landowners' permission to cross their farms.

At this time the settlers, in particular the farmers, were opposing the company's land settlement scheme. The company, eager to win the support of the settlers at this crucial time, paid little attention to the pressures that European farmers were putting on their tenants. The high commissioner asked the administrator to inquire into the reports of European pressure on African tenants, and particularly into the incidents mentioned by Robinson.[36]

Later on, the administrator wrote to the high commissioner that Robinson could not cite specific cases to substantiate his allegations. Yet the details of his report suggest that his story was more than mere speculation or rumor. Robinson's "failure" to cite specific cases may well have been the result of pressure from the administrator, who being the top company official in the country, was eager not to antagonize the farmers who had to be persuaded to accept the land settlement scheme.

Native commissioners' reports until 1923 show that European pressure on African tenants did not cease. Europeans imposed heavy fines on Africans whose cattle wandered beyond their stipulated grazing area and in some cases Europeans impounded cattle that were not even trespassing and imposed fines on their owners. Africans sometimes retaliated by burning the farms in question. After reading a native commissioner's report, in a letter to the resident commissioner, the high commissioner observed:

> A case showing how natives are imposed upon by a certain class of European is reported from Insizwa. A farmer named B. L. Whyte captured 70 herd of cattle . . . trespassing on his farm (not cultivated land) and charged the owners of the cattle an ox valued at £5: and £4: in cash. The Native Commissioner adds:—when farmers descend to such methods of enriching themselves at the expense of ignorant natives, it is not surprising if the native retaliates by burning farms out.[37]

To prevent such incidents, the native commissioner warned all Africans that if their cattle were impounded, they should go to the native commissioner who would see that justice was served.

Whereas land tenure on locations was insecure for the African tenants, the reserves were established so that Africans could be provided with secure tenure. When the reserves were first set up, the British government argued that the Africans could not afford to buy land as the Europeans could and did. The British goverment, by setting up the reserves, did not intend to exclude Africans from the unalienated lands. The reserves were a protective measure to ensure that Africans should always have land available to them for their needs. In theory, Africans, if they had had the money, could also have bought land on the same basis as the Europeans anywhere in the country. Article 80 of the 1898

Order in Council stipulated: "No conditions, disabilities, or restrictions shall, without the previous consent of a Secretary of State, be imposed upon natives by Ordinances which do not equally apply to persons of European descent, save in respect of the supply of arms, ammunition, and liquor."[38] Clause 83 was more specific: "A native may acquire, hold, encumber, and dispose of land on the same conditions as a person who is not a native, but no contract for encumbering or alienating land the property of a native shall be valid unless the contract is made in the presence of a Magistrate."[39] This actually meant that Africans, if they wanted to "own" land, had to buy back the land on which they had lived for many years before the settlers had come.

The settlers were opposed, for economic, social, and political reasons, to Africans' owning land on an equal basis with them. They feared economic competition from the Africans. If Africans could have purchased land anywhere, Europeans would have occupied scattered islands, physically and socially, in "seas" of African-owned land. The 1905 South African Native Affairs Commission wrote:

Where the circumstances are exceptional, and the numerical disproportion between the races is so great as in South Africa, the question is: what effects are to be expected if Natives are allowed free traffic in land? No emphasis is required in stating that, wherever, Europeans are living, repugnance is shown to the invasion of their neighborhood by Natives for residential purposes.[40]

Settlers were opposed to the Africans holding land on an individual basis. Yet by 1899 there were in Matebeleland seventy-eight farms totaling 7,810[41] acres that belonged to the "Cape Boys," Africans and Coloureds who had come from South Africa and had helped to suppress the 1896–97 Chimurenga. In spite of their help to the Europeans in this conflict, they were subsequently forced to sell their farms to Europeans.[42] In 1903 the application by William Lincoln, an American (black), for a farm, was turned down by the company. A year later the application of a Fingo minister of religion, Rev. John N'gono, was also turned down. The company argued that selling land to blacks, especially land adjoining European farms, would be a bad policy because the value of the land would decrease. Europeans would never buy land near an African farm. The company advanced the usual argument used to justify segregation, namely, that the best interests of the Africans would be served by keeping them and the Europeans apart. In its final report the 1915 Native Reserves Commission wrote: "In confirming the white man in possession of a certain area we are securing the truest benefit of the native by moving him therefrom."[43] In 1919 the chief native commissioner wrote: "If natives are permitted to purchase farms surrounded by or contiguous to land owned by Europeans, friction will probably occur."[44] And in 1920 he wrote: "In the interests of all alike it is not desirable that natives should acquire land indiscriminately, owing to the inevitable friction which will arise with their European neighbors."[45] To have allowed Africans to own land, especially after 1907, would have undermined the ascendant position of the settlers by opening the way to African entry into their social and economic class.

The Agricultural Union formed in 1902 to look after the interests of white farmers led the fight to prohibit Africans from buying land in Rhodesia. R. A. Fletcher, the president of the Union and member of the Legislative Council, in 1908 appealed to the company not to sell any land to Africans pending the determination of a uniform policy for the whole of South Africa.[46] In 1913 the Union government promulgated the South African Native Land Act, which prohibited Africans from buying land in European areas and vice versa. This was the policy that Fletcher had been waiting for, but in 1913 the British government refused to approve the extension of the South African policy to Rhodesia. The British government's policy, in this case as in many others, was inactive. It upheld the principle of equality between blacks and whites with regard to land ownership, but was unwilling to take action to make the principle effective. The drift to territorial separation continued. While the settlers were actively opposed to Africans buying the land, particularly land adjacent to their farms, native commissioners and missionaries favored the idea of Africans holding land on an individual basis, but only on land adjoining the reserves.[47]

With the successively harsher discrimination against Africans on the land elsewhere, the reserves came to have greater and greater significance. The managment of the reserves came under the Native Department, headed by the chief native commissioners for both Matebeleland and Mashonaland who every year submitted reports of the educational, political, economic, and social condition of the Africans in the country. The primary concern of the Native Department was the maintenance of peace. Reserves, to the department, were primarily centers of control. The 1898 Order in Council gave the administrator power to apportion reserves to the Africans either as tribes or portions of tribes; in other words, the administrator was empowered to divide a tribe into one or two groups if he thought it was necessary for good government, that is, to maintain peace.[48]

In the early period of European occupation, the Native Department saw reserves as places where Africans could be grouped together, prevented from moving from place to place, taxed, and generally brought more "effectively and efficiently" under European rule. Toward the end of the period of this study, Africans were starting to become politically aware in the modern sense. They were beginning to organize themselves first into labor organizations and then into political associations for specific economic, social, and political goals. The Native Department saw the reserves as centers through which African political development could be harnessed, guided, and controlled so that it would not threaten European supremacy. It was suggested that African councils be set up in the reserves in which the political energies of the Africans would be expended. "As a vent for the psychological necessity of the native to express himself politically," wrote Wilson, a former native commissioner, "native councils founded and developed from the present existing system are preferable to any exotic political growth not based upon an interest in the soil."[49]

In 1903 the administrator sought permission from the high commissioner to move Chief Mkota, of Mtoko area on the border with Mozambique, from his kraal to an area nearer a police station where he and his tribe would be more easily controlled. Whenever native commissioners and tax collectors went into the area to collect taxes, the Africans would slip into Mozambique.[50] They openly defied the government and refused to acknowledge the authority of the company. Several patrols were sent to subdue them, but without success. The high commissioner refused to give permission, but only because he felt that to move Mkota and his people would leave a vacuum on the border that might lead to border trouble with the Portuguese in the future.[51]

In 1904, for two reasons, the British government refused to approve, as the final settlement, the reserves as they existed at that time. First, the British government had in 1895 approved the Gwaai and Shangani reserves only to learn later that these areas had not been thoroughly surveyed and that they did not fulfill the conditions the government had stipulated. The reserves were considered unhealthy in some parts and in other parts they were without water. Any proposed reserves needed the final approval of the secretary of state, and this approval would not be given until surveys had shown that they were suitable and met the agricultural and pastoral needs of the Africans. "We must wait," wrote Grindle,

> for the final report, and when it comes approve on the understanding that the area of suitable land will be increased, if necessary, and that the present reserves are not to be regarded as a solution of the native problem for the future, and we had better take occasion to observe that the S of S has no means of judging how far some of the areas proposed are suitable for their purpose, and reserves the right to withdraw his approval if they turn out to be unsuitable.[52]

The second reason for the lack of approval was the fact that not all Africans lived in the reserves. The South African Native Affairs Commission of 1903–1905 estimated that 416,121 Africans lived in the reserves, 264,618 on unalienated lands, that is, land belonging to the company, whereas 151,503 lived on locations and private farms.[53] Most of the Africans living on locations were in Matebeleland. By 1905 about half of the African population lived in the reserves and another half lived on European land. The British government believed that the reserves would be able to accommodate these people when they moved or were removed from European land. "The natives living on reserves form only a part of the whole population. We cannot therefore deal properly with the question of the reserves without taking into account the natives elsewhere who may have to be provided for on reserves in the future."[54]

Another difficulty was the inaccuracy of the estimates of the African population. In 1905 it was estimated at 832,242[55] but in 1914 the figure was put at 712,783.[56] These estimates vary according to the purpose of the different commissions. In 1905 it is probable that the estimate was set that high in order to prove that European occupation benefited the Africans by supposedly buying peace and stopping internecine tribal wars. The 1914 Southern Rhodesia Native Reserves Commission proposed a reduction of the total area by 3,000,000 acres. It is, therefore, likely that a smaller African population would have justified reducing the area of the reserves.

The British government proposed that a final determination of the reserves should be made only after a commission had inquired into all the problems and had learned all the facts about the areas concerned, including the number of cattle, sheep, and goats owned by the Africans. Such a commission was set up in 1914.

Between 1905 and 1914 two crucial factors, which played an important part in determining the political, economic, and social path that the country later followed, intervened. The first was the realization on the part of both the company and settlers that the fortune in minerals that they had sought in Rhodesia did not exist. The second was the rise of European agriculture and the increasing pressure by both the company and settlers to reduce the size of the reserves. The company proposed an extensive land settlement scheme to encourage immigration and to raise money to pay the shareholders. The scheme elicited bitter opposition from the settlers who argued that any money made from land sales should be used for the benefit of Rhodesia and not for the shareholders in London.[57]

The 1914 Southern Rhodesia Native Reserves Commission was composed of three men. R. T. Coryndon, who had worked in Swaziland and for the Company in Rhodesia, was the chairman the other members were E.F.C. Garraway, formerly a member of the Bechuanaland Protectorate Police and the South African Constabulory, and F. J. Newton of the Native Department. The chairman was nominated by the high commissioner and the two members were appointed by the company. The British government had demanded that a member of the Native Department be appointed by the company to sit on the commission but Newton, because of ill health, sat on the commission for only a few weeks. The commission held its first sitting on June 14, 1914, and on July 14, 1914, Newton resigned. He was replaced by W. J. Atherstone, an employee of the company. In appointing Atherstone, the company flagrantly disregarded the British government's suggestion that the third member be an official of the Native Deparment. The Aborigines Protection Society claimed that Newton had been appointed by the company knowing that he was ill and could not withstand the strain of traveling throughout the reserves.[59] The British government raised no objections to this disregard of its stipulation. Atherstone had blatant conflicts of interest in that he not only worked for the Land Department of the company but also had since 1908 advocated the reduction of the size of the reserves.[60] In 1910 Atherstone specifically called for the reduction of the Sabi Reserve.

From 1908 onward, various native commissioners resisted company encroachment on African Reserves.[61] The native commissioners feared that any land taken from Africans might lead to rebellion. The company could not trust anyone from the Native Department to further its land interests. The company was opposed to a commission because it feared that such a commission, depending on its composition, might pay too much attention to African interests. Since the company paid the expenses of the commission and could decide who sat on it, it sought to use the commission to obtain as much good land from the reserves as possible. It is not surprising that the commission's attitude toward the reserves was similar to that of the company's.[52] The Aborigines Protection Society bitterly complained to the British government about the government's failure to insist on the appointment of a member of the Native Department to replace Newton.

For the ommission to do this is another striking illustration of the Company's determination to ignore the suggestion of His Majesty's Government. Thenceforth it can hardly be a matter for surprise that, by reason of his position and access to information, the Company's chief land agent became the dominating influence on the Commission. These are the principal reasons which gave rise to the sanguine belief held locally that a report issued by a Commission so heavily weighted against the natives could hardly be accepted as an impartial document.[63]

When the membership of the commission was revealed, a Rhodesian settler wrote: "The three Commissioners might just as well have been three Chartered Company's directors. . . ."[54] And the Rev. S. Cripps observed, "It was a Commission imperially constituted, but its personnel was allowed to consist, without an exception whatsoever, of past or present British South Africa Company servants."[65]

In 1914 there were 104 reserves ranging in size from under 5,000 acres to 3,475,170 acres. The reserves totaled 21,783,222 acres, about 3,000,000 acres less than calculated in 1902.[66] The African population was estimated in 1914 at 712,783. From the outset the commission took the position that Africans had no inalienable rights to land by virtue of the fact that they were Africans. The commission foresaw that if African land requirements had been tied to the rate of population increase, this would have eventually denied Europeans the right to land. "The Commission is of the opinion that it cannot be assumed that every unborn native is to enjoy an indefeasible right to live on the soil under tribal conditions. . . ."[67] Under tribal customs, every adult male African had an inalienable right to the use of land. In 1915 the Commission concluded: "The native of the country must not assume that he can demand as a right the immense areas of land which would be necessary if he were increasing. If that right was granted he would soon come to need the whole of the territory for his scattered improvident lands and his small kraals miles apart."[68] The commission's statements on land had nothing to do with its purpose for existing, namely to investigate the size, suitablity, and sufficiency of the reserves at that time and to report on its findings. By overstepping its terms of reference, the commission showed its own commitments on the question of land ownership in which the Africans, the settlers, and the company had divergent interests. Behind the commission's arguments one can discern the fear that if the British government decided that reserves, as then constituted, were insufficient, the government might assign some of the unalienated lands to the Africans.

In all, the commission interviewed forty-four chiefs and head-men, forty-seven officials of the Native Department, twelve European farmers, seven missionaries, and seven employees of the company.[69] The commission openly admitted that it had wholly ignored the evidence of the chiefs. It wrote:

The evidence given by the officials of the Native Department was relevant and valuable. We did not, as a rule, examine native chiefs unless there was some point to be elucidated or some definite information to be gained . . . in some other cases the direction which our recommendations must take was so ob-vious that the local chiefs were not examined. We felt that we might do more harm than good by questioning the natives upon a matter of which they were very likely to misunderstand the real scope, and which also no effect could be given for a year or more.[70]

The commission's recommendations, by its own admission, must take a definite direction and this direction was contrary to African wishes.

A brief look at the evidence given by the African chiefs and headmen clearly indicates that, in general, they believed that the African reserves were inadequate. On June 16, 1914, Chief Magawu gave evidence as to the inadequacy of the Ramagubane Reserve. On the same day Boriwong told the commission that Raditladi Reserve did not have an adequate supply of water. On June 17 and 19, Chiefs Sipako and Gambo both complained about the lack of water in their reserves. Magina, an *Induna* in the Matopo Reserve, testified on July 8 that there was an insufficient amount of land and water in his reserve. On July 28 the Chiefs of Wedza and Bellingwe Reserves complained of the inadequacy of their reserves and of the shortage of water.[71] These examples show the general nature of the evidence given by the African chiefs and headmen; in fact, of all those who gave evidence only one chief expressed satisfaction with his reserve and merely implored the commission not to reduce its size. The commission's specific purpose was to determine if the reserves were adequate in size and had sufficient water. It did not bother to travel through the reserves or to survey even a single one to refute the evidence given by the chiefs.

Most of the missionaries who were interviewed gave evidence that indicated that the reserves were adequate. They complained about the wasteful methods of African farming.[72] Only in one case did a missionary advocate the increase of a reserve. The Rev. E. H. Etheridge requested an increase in Mtasa's reserve, because a large part of it was mountainous. T. B. Hulley, the native commissioner of Umtali, supported this request. The majority of the officials of the Native Department were satisfied with the reserves as they were then constituted. Nevertheless several felt that some reserves should be reduced. All the settlers and employees of the company emphatically urged the commission to reduce the size of the reserves. The views of the European farmers and the company's employees had more influence on the commission than those of the Native Department officials and missionaries, who were supposed to be the knowledgeable representatives of African opinions and wishes.

Whereas the Africans wanted more land and generally complained about the shortage of water, Europeans generally agreed that the reserves were adequate; the majority of the settlers thought that the reserves were more than adequate and should even be reduced. The commission observed:

Whatever influence has been brought to bear in favor of the settler has been balanced by the influence of the Missions and the Native Department on behalf of the native interests. We have not found it to be intolerant or excessive in either case. While missionaries and clergy who are closely in touch with the natives have shown as a rule a broad point of view, and though there may be some conflict between their attitude and that of the settler and that of the Administration, the differences have never become acute.[73]

Whereas the settlers wanted to change the status quo, the missionaries wanted to preserve it. When the commission made its recommendations, it ignored the views of the missionaries and the native commissioners. When the British government approved the commission's proposals, many native commissioners attacked them. The commission advocated a reduction of 3,000,000 acres and the British government, afraid of the opposition this would raise from the Aborigines Protection Society, refused to allow a reduction on that scale, eventually settling for a 1,000,000-acre reduction.[74] The commission believed that its recommendations were very generous, and to illustrate its point it compared the area of the reserves in Rhodesia with that in the rest of South Africa. The table (on page 147) shows that, except for Basutoland, which had very few Europeans, Africans in Rhodesia had the highest average acreage per head. The 1915 estimation of the size of the reserves, as given by the commission, was 20,491,151 acres.[75] This figure suggests that between 1914 and 1915 the area of the reserves had been reduced by 1,241,071 acres. In its final report, the commission, and then only because of the British government's opposition, recommended a reduction of 1,062,460 acres, thus leaving 19,428,691 acres for African reserves.[76] While the commission was sitting, supposedly to determine the adequacy and sufficiency of the reserves, the company actually reduced them by over 1,000,000 acres. In 1919 the Aborigines Protection Society quoted a letter from a white Rhodesian settler: "In response to the call of the British South Africa Company, not a few of these local natives went to German East [Africa in 1914] to serve their country, and they come back to find about 1,000,000 acres of land have been filched away."[77] It is not clear how this reduction took place. Had the commission been impartial, it would have asked the company to await its recommendations. It is also likely that the commission falsified the 1915 reserve estimate to minimize opposition to its proposed reduction.

The recommendation by the Reserves Commission to reduce the Sabi Reserve by 291,800 acres, the mistreatment of the Africans on locations, and the acquiescence of the British government deeply moved and brought the Rev. Arthur Shirley Cripps to the forefront of opposition to the Reserves Commission's recommendations. These events reminded Cripps of the Enclosure Movement in England. Convinced that the Enclosure Movement had been an evil, Cripps recalled for his audiences the valiant struggles of the suffering peasants to retain their land. Cripps felt that it was his duty to speak against, and to stop, a movement that he believed would cause similar suffering on the part of the African people. The peasants, during the Enclosure Movement, had had no spokesman with the result that their suffering was only to be exposed later by history. Cripps became the spokesman

1914
Area and Population of Native Reserves in Various Parts of South Africa

Country	Area of Native Reserve	Total Native Population	Population on Reserve	Area on Reserves per head of total Population	Acres on Reserves per head of Population therein
Basutoland [a]	6,587,520	400,058	400,058	16.4	16.4
Swaziland	1,601,179	108,733	84,000	14.7	19.
Bechuanaland Protectorate	56,640,000	123,308	117,000	459.	484.
Pondoland Transkei	12,608,050	1,519,939	1,145,645	8.3	11.
Remainder of Cape Province Zululand	3,905,610	214,969	430,528	6.6	14.7
Remainder of Natal Province	2,425,698	738,429			
Transvaal Province	1,861,026	1,219,845	436,846	1.5	4.2
Orange Free State	156,750	325,824	69,184	0.5	2.3
Southern Rhodesia	21,732,222	712,783	400,000	30.49	54.

[a] Almost all Basutoland is reserve.
Table cited in Cd. 8674 Interim Report, 1914, p. 11.

for the African population that was only on the verge of political awareness in modern terms. In his writings, Cripps inveighed against the wrongs committed by the Europeans against the Africans.

In the Southern and Eastern Africa of my own day I seem to have seen history repeating itself on the deplorable lines of that now long accomplished divorce in Old England. As we puzzle over our problems about land and labourers in Britain overseas, it would be well if we attended to the warnings which that ancient transaction, recorded in our Mother Country's domestic history, has bequeathed to us. I for one am glad to have had certain lessons in Old English rural history afforded by my own experiences, as well as by books. Such lessons have I hope, helped to intensify my protest against the thing that has been in old Britain repeating itself, and reproducing itself, before my very eyes in the new Britain of my adoption.[78]

Cripps wrote many articles denouncing the commission's recommendations. He argued that the recommendation to reduce the Sabi Reserve was not made on the basis of the evidence of the local native commissioner. He further contended that the population of the reserve was larger than had been estimated by the commission. Cripps revealed that the land the company desired to obtain was fertile. In 1919 he went to England to furnish information to the Anti-Slavery and Aborigines Protection Society, themselves also champions of the African cause, and to protest to the British government. When toward the end of 1919, Lord Buxton, then high commissioner in South Africa, visited Rhodesia, Cripps, and Rev. John White, a Wesleyan missionary, met with him. They told Buxton that the reserves, as approved by the British government in 1917, were inadequate. Buxton complained bitterly about Cripps' articles on the land issue and even requested that he delete certain "offensive" words from his memorandum.[79]

The Aborigines Protection Society appealed to the British government to delay implementing their approval of the commission's recommendations on the reserves arguing that the commission was not impartial and that the government should set up another Commission of inquiry. Lord Milner, who was now the colonial secretary, replied that he was "not prepared to question the competence of, or recommendations made by the Southern Rhodesia Natives Reserves Commission of 1915, which had been appointed by one of his predecessors, and the report of which had been examined and approved by the High Commissioner for South Africa and adopted by another of Lord Milner's predecessors."[80] The society also appealed to the good common sense of the British people, citing at one point a Rhodesian settler who wrote: "I am convinced that the wrong done to the natives will be righted when the full facts are in the hands of the Home Parliament; for with all our faults real injustice is always righted by our people."[71] The Society further argued that the Rhodesian settlers and the Company had, as long ago as 1908, talked about reducing the size of the reserves.

Lord Olivier wrote extensively on the subject of land alienation. He maintained, as did John Harris of the Aborigines Protection Society, that the British government had neglected its responsibility to the Africans. Olivier believed that the terms of the charter were explicit in excluding Europeans from holding land. He maintained that it was the responsibility of the Colonial Office "to make operative its original stipulation that native land rights should be honoured. . . ."[82]

The unflagging efforts of the Aborigines Protection Society, Lord Olivier, and Rev. Cripps did not produce any positive results. The British government approved the recommendations of the Reserves Commission in 1917, but because of the vociferous criticism waited until November 1920 to promulgate the necessary Order in Council to make the Commission's recommendation official.

In establishing reserves the primary purpose of the British government was to prevent competition between the Europeans and Africans in buying land which the African would have lost. The reserves would prevent Africans from becoming landless. The missionary viewpoint went beyond that. Walter Aidan Cotton, an Anglican priest of St. Augustine's Mission Penhalonga, wrote a book in which he recorded his observations on the relations between whites and blacks in South Africa.[83] At the time, Southern Rhodesia was still considered a part of South Africa. Cotton noted that the blacks had been scandalously treated by the whites. He denounced this action and prayed for better treatment of the Africans, attributing the main cause of segregation to the fear on the part of the Europeans that an open society would result in the Europeans being swamped by the larger African population. Cotton's view of the future was dour. He feared that if the Africans should come to power in the future, they would seek revenge and would in turn segregate the Europeans and expropriate "their" land. The only solution, as Cotton saw the problem, was separate development. Only by separate development, he thought, would the black and white races in South Africa live peaceably.

Separate development became a vogue among missionaries. Maurice Evans, a member of the 1906 Natal Native Affairs Commission, wrote a book, *Black and White in South East Africa*, in which he described how tribal life was being destroyed by Europeans who saw no moral attributes in this way of life.[84] Evans maintained that some aspects of tribal life were worth preserving. He called upon his fellow white men to do the only honorable thing possible; namely, to leave Africans alone in their own areas to live according to their customs. This book was to become Cripps' second Bible; he referred to it many times in his crusade for the reserves.

Cripps came to view reserves in idealistic terms. He cried out against the destruction of tribal life by Europeans caused by land alienation. "I was to see," he wrote, "that life of theirs [Africans] threatened with encroachments, if not suppression, as the advancing tide of colonists' land settlement made its way into this part of Africa, and the consequent expropriation of African's mother soil proceeded."[85] Cripps came to believe that all the positive aspects of tribal life should be preserved and could, only be safeguarded on the reserves. He thought that on the reserves Africans would be able to realize their highest potential as human beings. Cripps pleaded with the Europeans to allow Africans to develop along their own way in the reserves. He wrote passionately: "Let the blessed institution of native reserves be safeguarded wherever it be found in our Empire, as our best makeshift harbour of refuge for the very natural and legitimate instincts of the African's race consciousness."[89] Cripps also wrote:

> I want a racially self-conscious African not to feel himself homeless in a colonized Africa; I want a miniature Africa of the Africans, free as far as may be from exploitation, and free as far as may be for self-development to exist within the borders of every one of our native reserves. . . . I want African native reserves to be properly safeguarded, so that on them Africans may be free to go about their proper business of preparing Africa's own distinctive contribution to the city of God, and of bringing Africa's own unique "glory and honour" into it.[87]

At the turn of the century, native commissioners generally had welcomed the disintegrating effects of European occupation on tribal society. At that time it had been thought that this disintegration would tend to destroy the communalistic tendencies of tribal society. This, it was thought, would individualize Africans and thus eventually lead to the solution of the country's labor problem because, they argued, individualism was a necessary incentive to work. By the end of the period of this study, the bonds in tribal society had been loosened and the native commissioners began to warn about the danger of loosening these bonds too quickly. "The reserves," wrote the C.N.C. in 1920, "will for a long time uphold tribalism. . . . The tribal system will . . . gradually disappear, but no sudden breaking down of such a system should be attempted."[88] The native commissioners began to realize that a completely detribalized African would not only enter or be drawn into the economic sphere of the European as laborer but would also soon challenge the European economically and politically. The Native Department came to the conclusion that if European supremacy was to remain unchallenged, Africans would have to live on the reserves. It was possible, Wilson, a former native commissioner, argued to create a modified African institution so as to ensure their development along lines satisfactory to, and safe for, Europeans. Wilson foresaw the kraals evolving into towns with headmen as their mayors. His words eloquently speak for themselves.

> These towns (kraal towns) will be industrial and trading centers, places for schools of craft and mission schools. In them, as a natural development of the kraal headman and the elders, there will be headmen (i.e., mayors) and Councils. Every effort should be made to vivify this civic life. It will do both a training and an outlet for energy, and the political instinct.[89]

Wilson also advocated road building to facilitate communication and to vitalize the reserves. Britain was prepared, in 1923, to grant self-rule to Rhodesia, but demanded that it remain, nominally at least, in charge of African affairs. Control over reserves was to be vested in the high commissioner; that is, reserves could not be altered without his approval. The 1914 Reserves Commission was intended to finalize the allocation of reserves. In 1923, the British government was not at all sure whether or not the reserves could be altered in the future depending on the country's political future. Buxton wrote:

> But in the event of responsible government or entry of Union security so effectively safeguarded. . . . Presumably [it will be] impossible so to draw any Order in Council as to protect its provision against amendment by local legislature under self-government. Some stipulations might perhaps be insisted on by Crown in granting responsible government but this might not be practicable in the event of entry of Union.[90]

Despite the British government's belief that it was aiding the Africans by securing reserves for them, the reserves were not centers of freedom. The settlers who were soon to assume power viewed the reserves as centers of paternalistic control, where the social, educational, economic, and political ambitions of the Africans were curbed in order to eliminate any threat to European supremacy.

NOTES

1. See C. 9138 Southern Rhodesia Order in Council, 1899, p. 15.
2. Cd. 2399, Report of the South African Native Affairs Commission 1903–1905, p. 18.
3. C. 9138, 1899, p. 17.
4. Cd. 8674, Interim Report, 1914, p. 8.
5. C. O. 417/391, 1904.
6. C. O. 417/391, 1904.
7. Ibid., p. 15.
8. Ibid., p. 15.
9. Administrator to High Commissioner, March 4, 1902, C. O. 417/343.
10. Cd. 8674, Interim Report, 1914, pp. 6–7.
11. Administrator to High Commissioner, March 4, 1902, C. O. 417/343.
12. Cd. 2399, 1905, p. 18. But the 1914 Reserves Commission estimated reserves to be 21,732,222 acres. Cd. 8674 Interim Report 1914, p. 10. The Company and settlers controlled over 70,000,000 acres.
13. Resident Commissioner to High Commissioner, December 27, 1902, C. O. 417/392.
14. C. O. 417/392.
15. Cd. 8674, Final Report, 1915, p. 24.
16. Population was calculated on the basis of the annual tax returns. The number of adult male tax payers was arbitrarily multiplied by 3.5 and the result was then given as the estimated African population. The accuracy of this method is questionable. First, it presupposes that all adult male Africans paid tax and, second, that the average family size was about four; this does not take into account polygamous marriages. Cd. 8674. S. R. Native Commissioners Interim Report 1914, p. 11.
17. Cmd. 547, Correspondence with the Anti-Slavery and Aborigines Protection Society Relating to the Native Reserves in Southern Rhodesia, 1914, p. 12.
18. The Anti-Slavery and Aborigines Protection Society to C. O. April 4, 1919, p. 9. Cmd. 547.
19. C. O. 417/392, July 30, 1904.
20. Cd. 2399, 1905, p. 18.
21. Cd. 2399, 1905, p. 118.
22. W. M. Onslow-Carleton, *Land Settlement Scheme for the Matebele* (Cape Town, South Africa: Townshend, Taylor and Snashall, 1910), p. 10.
23. C. O. 417/392, July 30, 1904.
24. Minute by Grindle, C. O. 417/392, July 30, 1904.

25. C. O. 417/392, July 30, 1904.

26. C. O. 417/392, July 30, 1904.

27. Cd. 8674, Interim Report, 1914.

28. Cd. 2399, 905, p. 24.

29. C.N.C. Report, 1924, p. 3.

30. Cd. 8674 S. R. Native Reserves Commission, Interim Report 1914, pp. 6-7.

31. Cd. 8674, Interim Report, 1914, p. 10.

32. Ibid., Interim Report, 1914, p. 10.

33. Ibid., Interim Report, 1914, p. 9.

34. Report of the Chief Native Commissioner of Matebeleland for the Year Ending 1913, pp. 1-2.

35. C. O. 417/538, 1914.

36. C. O. 417/538, 1914.

37. High Commissioner to Resident Commissioner, November 10, 1919, C. O. 417/623.

38. Cd. 2399, 1905, p. 21.

39. Ibid., p. 21.

40. Ibid., p. 25.

41. Quoted in Robin Henry Palmer, "The Making and Implementation of Land Policy in Rhodesia: 1890-1936" (Ph.d. diss., London University, 1968).

42. Ibid., p. 46.

43. Cd. 8674, Final Report, 1915, p. 25.

44. C.N.C. Report 1919, p. 2.

45. C.N.C. Report 1920, p. 20.

46. *The Bulawayo Chronicle,* June 12, 1908, p. 1.

47. See Chief Native Commissioner's Report for the Year 1922 and Proceedings of the Southern Rhodesia Missionary Conference, 1922.

48. C. 9138, 1899, pp. 17-18.

49. *NADA: The Southern Rhodeisa Native Affairs Department Annual* 1923, p. 14.

50. C. O. 417/374, 1903.

51. Ibid.

52. Minuted by Grindle, C. O. 417/392, July 30, 1904.

53. Cd. 2399, 1905, p. 18.

54. Minute by Grindle, C. O. 417/392, July 30, 1904.

55. Cd. 2399, p. 18.

56. Cd. 8674, Interim Report, p. 10.

57. See Petition by Rhodesian Farmers to Harcourt, Colonial Secretary, December 1913, C. O. 417/538.

58. Coryndon had fought in the Matebele War of 1893 and had selected 6,000 acres as had been provided for by the Victoria Agreement. Cmd. 547, 1919, p. 23.

59. Cmd. 547, 1919, p. 7.

60. Cmd. 547, 1919, p. 7.

61. See L. H. Gann, *A History of Southern Rhodesia: Early Days to 1934* (London: Chatto and Windus, 1965), p. 186.

62. As Gann says, "Their [commission's] recommendations were influenced to a considerable extent by pressure from the Company's own Land Department." Ibid., p. 188.

63. Aborigines Protection Society to C. O. March 17, 1919, Cmd. 547, p. 7.

64. Cmd. 547, 1919, p. 23.

65. A. S. Cripps, "The Dispossession of the African," *East and West* 20 (1922): 218.

66. Cd. 8674. Interim Report, 1914, p. 8.

67. Ibid., p. 12.

68. Ibid., Final Report, 1915, p. 26.

69. Ibid., pp. 60–63.

70. Ibid. Interim Report, 1914, p. 14. In 1920 the Rev. John White maintained that African chiefs did not understand the purpose of the Commission. See, Proceedings of the Southern Rhodesia Missionary Conference, 1920.

71. Cd. 8674. Final Report, 1915, p. 60.

72. In 1920 the Rev. E. H. Etheridge, president of the S. Rhodesia Missionary Conference, said it was not good politics to attack the personnel and recommendations of the 1914 Native Reserve Commission. See: Proceedings of the Southern Rhodesia Missionary Conference, 1920.

73. Cd. 8674, Final Report, 1915, p. 21.

74. Ibid., p. 67.

75. Cd. 8674, Final Report, 1915, p. 67.

76. Ibid., p. 67.

77. The Anti-Slavery and Aborigines Society to C. O. October 21, 1919, CMD. 547, p. 24.

78. Cripps, "The Dispossession of the African," op. cit., p. 212.

79. C. O. 417/617, 1919.

80. C. O. to A.B.S. May 29, 1919. Cmd. 547, p. 13.

81. The A.B.S. to C. O. October 21, 1919, Cmd. 547, p. 24.

82. Lord Olivier, "Native Land Rights in Rhodesia," *The Contemporary Review* (1926): no. 728 150.

83. Walter Aidan Cotton, *The Race Problem in South Africa* (Edingburgh: Turnbull & Spears, 1926).

84. Maurice S. Evans, *Black and White in South East Africa* (London: Longmans, Green and Co., Ltd., 1911).

85. Cripps, "The Dispossession of the African," p. 214.

86. A. S. Cripps, "An Africa of the Africans," *The International Review of Missions* 10 (1921): 105.

87. Ibid., p. 109.

88. Report of the C.N.C. for the Year 1920, p. 2.

89. N. H. Wilson, "The Future of the Native Races in Southern Rhodesia," *South African Journal of Science* 17 (1921): 148.

90. High Commissioner to Secretary of State, May 4, 1920. C. O. 417/637.

8
The Rise of European Agriculture 1907-1914

Land alienation was initially regarded by both the settlers and the Company as of secondary importance, a source of marginal income with perhaps future economic possibilities. The fact that the company, after 1907, earnestly encouraged European agricultural settlements does not imply that prior to this date the Europeans had completely ignored farming. From time to time between 1890 and 1907 the company had issued detailed reports on the nature of the soil and on the favorable climate for agriculture. The company also stressed that new settlers did not need large capital outlays to begin farming. In 1898 M. Lingrad, the company's secretary for Agriculture, wrote: "Anyone who has travelled through Rhodesia and regarded it from the point of view of a practical farmer, cannot fail to recognize that whatever attractions it may possess in the shape of its minerals, it has undoubtedly vast possibilities in the way of agricultural industries. . . ."[1] And in 1900 Lawley, the acting administrator of Mashonaland, wrote: "There has been a considerable growth of the agricultural industry, especially in Mashonaland, where many farms are being occupied and worked by Europeans."[2] Nevertheless, despite this optimistic statement, European agriculture had not taken root. According to Mrs. Ethel Tawse Jollie, "the first fifteen years [of European settlement] were almost lost from the farming point of view. . . ."[3] By April, 1904, there were still only 948 land holdings (about 3,000 acres apiece) of which only 32,000 acres were under cultivation, most of which were in Mashonaland.[4]

Many difficulties tended to discourage the early settlers from going into large-scale farming. Political conditions in this early

155

period were unstable. In 1893 the Matebele War broke out and the 1896–97 war forced Europeans to abandon their farms. The historian Percy Hone observed that after the 1896–97 fighting "[European] farming in Southern Rhodesia was practically non-existent. . . ."[5] Not until the end of 1904 did the fear of further African uprising abate. Natural disasters also affected the development of agriculture. In 1896, rinderpest killed many cattle belonging to both the white and black farmers. Rinderpest and the east coast fever, if they had recurred, could only, at that time, be contained by killing all the infected stock. According to Hone, the outbreak of east coast fever in 1901 killed between 98 percent and 99 percent of European cattle.[6] But these difficulties were soon overcome by the importation of a serum from South Africa with which the cattle were innoculated. The company administration distributed articles on the causes, symptoms, and treatment of various animal diseases to all the white farmers. Crops in the early years of settlement were destroyed by locusts and other pests, but by 1898–99 locusts had, according to the administrator's report, been eliminated by the use of an antitoxin.[7]

These difficulties were experienced by both the African peasantry and the European farmers. Yet European agriculture not only recovered at a far greater pace than African agriculture but improved tremendously, particularly after 1907, because of the efforts made by the Company to help the European farmers. A Department of European Agriculture established in 1900 administratively controlled the movement of cattle and thus the spread of cattle or horse diseases.[8] The Department also registered all the different brands of cattle owned by European farmers.[9] It examined all imported fruit and inspected fruit nurseries to prevent disease from spreading. The Department also advised European farmers on what implements and machinery to use, and on the best methods of stock breeding, dairying methods, and on how to purchase stock from South Africa or Europe. The Department provided an agricultural chemist to analyze soils and to give advice on the use of fertilizers. An entomologist gave advice on matters connected with pests and livestock, crops, and fruit trees. By 1908, tobacco had been recognized as a good commercial prospect, and experts traveled throughout the country advising tobacco growers. An irrigation engineer was available if needed by any white farmer to help in surveys or selections of suitable sites for boring. Department officials were available to give lectures to groups of farmers who needed advice. *The Rhodesia Agricultural Journal* was published six times a year and copies were distributed to the farmers for their information.[10] All these facilities and opportunities were not, however, available to the Africans. Thus, when in 1901 locusts attacked, African crops failed but the European crops survived. The chief native commissioner for Matebeleland explained: "Locust toxine was only obtainable in such small quantities during past years that we were not able to invite the active co-operation of the natives in its application. [And] the directions for its use were too complicated to impart to the native mind."[11] And in 1907 the chief native commissioner for Mashonaland was still reporting that African cattle were dying as a result of the outbreak of east coast fever.[12] Because of fencing, European cattle were reasonably well protected from mixing with African cattle.

Technologically the European farmer enjoyed a great advantage over the African peasant. Most Africans still used hoes to till the land, whereas European farmers used ploughs drawn by oxen. The disc plough introduced in 1902 had from two to four discs and was drawn by as many as sixteen oxen.[13] Hone tells us that "each disc, in a good day's work, [was] capable of turning over an acre of ground."[14] And yet in 1907 in Mashonaland with a population of 445,316 people, the Africans had only 162 single ploughs,[15] whereas Matebeleland, in 1907, with a population of 221,465, the Africans had 1,097 ploughs.[16] The 1907 commissioner's reports also noted that Africans on the whole had not changed their agricultural methods, and still practiced shifting cultivation.

In 1897 the railway line linking Bulawayo with the rest of South Africa was completed. The line between Salisbury and Umtali, the easternmost city of the country that was already linked by rail with the port of Beira, was completed in 1899. And the line between Bulawayo and Salisbury was finished in 1902. As a result, the company-owned Rhodesia Railways allowed the importation of cattle at very low rates to replace the cattle that had been killed by rinderpest.[17] The railway also speeded up the transportation of urgently needed agricultural machinery. Prior to this, all transportation had been done by ox wagon, but farmers were now able to import fences from South Africa. Without fencing on farms cattle ranching had been difficult. The cattle were herded all day and then were kraaled in muddy pens by night.[18] With fencing not only was cattle ranching made easier but control of cattle disease was easier since diseased cattle were confined to the districts where they were.

The introduction of railways in Rhodesia also encouraged European agriculture in a different way. It opened the local markets in the cities and mines to European produce. Prior to that time African agricultural produce had been sold in these markets. In 1910 there were 1,470 European farmers in the country and the majority had farms within thirty miles of the railway line.[19] Railways also opened the external markets of South Africa, Mozambique, and Europe to European produce. Serious agricultural development in Rhodesia began in 1907. The following export figures for 1909 and 1910 show the effect of railway construction on European agriculture.[20]

	1909 Quantity in Lbs.	Value in £	1910 Quantity in Lbs.	Value in £ [a]
Exports:				
Hides, ox and cow	151,765	£4,908	208,699	£7,292
Skins, Sheep and Goats	85,563	2,804	136,038	4,413
Kaffir Corn	1,413,473	4,090	1,174,261	3,103
Onions	41,123	345	37,948	319
Tobacco (unmanufactured)	190,822	11,022	322,334	27,028
Maize (corn)	2,288,453	6,023	5,911,123	11,973

[a.] Report of the Director of Agriculture, 1910, p. 2. However, included in the exported products were some African produce that European traders had bought from African peasants. No figures indicating total African products sold to Europeans were available— but the total must not have amounted to much.

Most of these products were exported to South Africa. In 1909, 20,300,000 pounds of maize [corn] were exported to Europe.[21]

How had European agriculture become successful in such a short time? What was the policy of the company? To encourage more Europeans to turn to farming, agricultural shows were held in Bulawayo and Salisbury. Between 1900 and 1906 the company administration in Rhodesia undertook experiments in the cultivation of such crops as cotton and tobacco. Success in these experiments was intended to promote the immigration of settlers. Addressing the Legislative Council, Milton, the administrator, revealed the plans of the Company when he said:

The Company is desirous of assisting as far as may be expedient the settlement of suitable immigrants upon its unalienated lands, and with that view is preparing a scheme under which considerable funds will be provided for the purpose. The main objects will be to obtain settlers of the agricultural class with sufficient capital to ensure beneficial occupation of the land, and to assist them by some preparation of their holdings prior to arrival, and by skilled advice while they are gaining experience of the conditions under which farming is carried on in the country.[22]

In December 1905 the board of directors sent C. D. Wise to visit and make a full report on the prospects of Rhodesia as an agricultural country. He spent about four months traveling through the country. Wise's report is of great interest because it shows the attention the company was paying to land as a means to enhance the value of its assets. He concluded: "I believe that Rhodesia is a country capable of enormous development from the agricultural point of view, to say nothing of the cultivation of special crops and the establishment of industries such as tobacco, fibers, oil, flax, hemp and cotton."[23] Rhodesia, since 1890, had imported nearly all its food requirements from South Africa. By 1905 the total value of beef and mutton imports from Transvaal were £732,464 and that of dairy produce was valued at £456,155.[24] Wise argued that Rhodesia was capable of supplying foodstuffs from South Africa.

Local markets in Rhodesia or Salisbury, Bulawayo and Umtali. With their present population the requirements of these towns would soon be filled if the number of farmers in the country was largely increased, but when that happy day comes it will be found that the presence in the country of the farming industry, and other industries in connection with it, will mean an increase in the consumption of foodstuffs.[25]

Wise was aware of the difficulties involved in beginning a new life as a farmer. It was, therefore, important that a special kind of man be recruited if land settlement were to succeed. The first group of agricultural settlers were very important because the success of the agricultural industry depended upon their prosperity. These men, Wise thought, should be men of iron discipline and determination who would not be easily discouraged by a bad season or difficulties in obtaining labor. They should be prepared to suffer and live frugally, not only for their future benefit and the country's but also for the benefit of the company.

Wise suggested that the company assist the new settlers as much as it could. Everything possible should be done to encourage men to come from South Africa to try their fortunes in agriculture.

> The Company should dispose of the land to the first settlers at a low but fair rate, according to the market value of the land today. . . . They should assist these men as far as possible in reason, without spoon-feeding, and make them successful: their success will mean the success of land settlement and the development of their own industry, and they will bring others.[26]

Wise also suggested the idea of alternate block farms, a suggestion that the settlers later opposed bitterly. Under this scheme land surrounding each farm was to be left unoccupied. If a farmer were successful, the value of the surrounding land would increase so that the company could derive additional financial benefit from selling such land.

Another important suggestion from Wise was the idea of a central farm. Under this plan new settlers would come to this farm where they would be taught the rudiments of farming. They would study the nature of the soil and the climate of the region, and learn about the timing of the first rains every season and the time and method of ploughing. They were taught how to build thatched-roof houses. The new settlers also learned how to care for their stock and how to recognize early signs and symptoms of different diseases. The company was to supply the settlers with stock at the market price and they were also to be provided with improved varieties of seeds from the central farm. Wise also suggested the establishment of a general store from which settlers could buy whatever they required and to which they could sell their produce. Nothing was to be left to chance. Wise wrote: "For the benefit of the settlement a general store should be started: this store should supply the necessaries of life . . . implements and all farm requisites. The store should also purchase farm produce of all descriptions from settlers, which, under agreement, should all be sold through the Central Farm Manager."[27] But even after these new settlers left the central farm to start working on their own land, which was near the central farm, the manager of the central farm would visit them periodically to check on their progress and constantly to give them advice. "When they enter on their holdings," Wise wrote, "the Manager should give the settlers assistance and advice, constantly visiting them, taking care, however, not to rush into all sorts of useless experiments."[28]

The new farmers were to be encouraged to practice mixed farming, that is, the farmer would engage in poultry, dairying, and the cultivation of crops and vegetables. Failure in one of these fields would not be absolute disaster for the settler, since he would not have committed himself to one area of agriculture. Wise suggested that the farms should be of 1,000 to 1,500 acres even though he preferred smaller holdings of between 500 to 600 acres.[29] The smaller holdings were better because the new settler could more easily cope with a small farm than with a large one. All these suggestions were seriously taken into account and acted upon by the company.

In 1907 the directors of the company visited Rhodesia in response to the grievances the settlers had against the company and also to determine whether or not Wise's recommendations could be effected. They concluded that the company could no longer hope to realize its financial interests solely through the mining industry. European settlement on the land was essential to reduce the amount of imported food and to increase the value of the company's assets. A Land Bank was established in 1907 to assist farmers with loans for buying stock, agricultural machinery, and seeds, and, in 1908, the company set up an Estates Establishment to promote European settlement. Company reports are full of minute details about the country, its geography, history, people, and economic possibilities, particularly in the field of agriculture. Every year the administrator made a detailed report on the development and difficulties of the agricultural industry. In 1908 the administrator described agriculture as "the industry upon which the country must so largely depend."[30] P. J. Hannon, the secretary of Agricultural Cooperation for the Cape Colony, visited Rhodesia in December 1907. He gave a series of lectures to meetings of farmers at Bulawayo, Gwelo, and Salisbury. He encouraged and advised his listeners to try making cheese and butter and to undertake pig breeding with a view to exporting these products overseas. The reports of his lectures were published by the Agriculture Department and distributed to all the farmers in the country. In 1909 an Englishwoman, Charlotte Mansfield, visited Rhodesia. On her return to England she wrote that Rhodesian agriculture had a great future, arguing that increased agricultural production would underwrite the success of the country.[31] In 1910 the company sent E. A. Maidment to Rhodesia. Maidment was a dairy expert who had traveled extensively throughout Europe and North America and had studied the different methods of dairying practised in the various countries she had visited. She traveled throughout Rhodesia and lectured to farmers, their wives, and children, on the methods for successful dairy farming.[32] Most, if not all, of the new settlers came from South Africa. At the start of their farming career these new settlers needed Africans on their farms either as tenants or as laborers. Many Africans still preferred to be tenants and pay rents; this was satisfactory to the new settlers as rent-paying tenants were a security in case the new settlement failed. In 1909 the administrator reported: "Owners of farms continue to enter into agreements with natives occupying lands thereon, a rent-charge being the more popular form of consideration. . . . Similar agreements have this year been entered into by the British South Africa Company and the natives occupying land the property of the Company."[33] However, it was these new settlers who later were to drive for segregation and who preferred that the Africans be prevented from holding land in their own right.

A few figures indicate the extent of the company's anxiety to raise revenue from the sales of land. Between 1908 and 1912 the company sold 5,247,870 acres to over 2,000 settlers for £486,-739.[34] These figures only show the net total land alienated and the amount paid. However, other settlers came and were given land grants, but for one reason or another gave up their grants and returned to South Africa. This extensive land settlement scheme soon elicited the disapproval of established Rhodesian settlers. Those who had taken up farming found that their produce had no market since the European population in the towns was still very small. The Africans who themselves basically were farmers had no need to buy the agricultural produce of the new settlers. During the first years of European settlement, when European interest was concentrated on mining, African peasants had provided the mines and cities with all their food requirements: mealie-mealie (cornmeal) pumpkins, vegetables, meat, and groundnuts. Food supplies at the mines were now being furnished by European farmers. Because most reserves had poor soil and were situated away from the railway line, African agricultural competition was easily controlled. The external market was almost exclusively a European preserve.[35] "The expansion of the demand for the produce of the white agrarian bourgeiosie depended on the growth of the internal market and the reduction of competition (on both internal and export markets) from the peasantry or from a potential African rural bourgeoisie."[36] Yet it is ironic that the Africans had a lot to do with the growth of the internal agri-cultural market. The Africans, under pressure of tax require-ments, came increasingly to participate in the European economy as farm or mine laborers, or even in a domestic capacity, and provided the white farming community with the market they so urgently desired. The white farmers provided for both European and African demands in the towns and mines. Another major difficulty experienced by both the agricultural and mining indus-tries was a shortage of labor. Because labor was in short supply at the time, new farmers would only have aggravated the already serious problem of excess demand. In 1911 the farmers unan-imously called upon the company to discourage immigration. A letter by a farmer to the editors of the *Bulawayo Chronicle* portrayed the general mood of the settlers in Rhodesia. Arguing against the company's land settlement scheme, he wrote, "We do not want any more farmers producing mealies, potatoes, onions, and so on, as the present number of farmers can grow more than enough to supply the demand. What is wanted is better organiza-tion of the supplies and of distribution, fresh crops and fresh markets . . . The best immigration agent is a prosperous and contented settler."[37] But the company ignored the protest of the farmers, and in fact accelerated its sales. The determination to carry out the land development scheme soon brought a head-on collision with the settlers. The land scheme developed into a political crisis from which the company emerged the loser.

The political crisis over land development is important because it shows how deeply divided the ruling company and the settlers were over the issue of land ownership on which both had become dependent for their economic survival. The company, if it was to recoup the capital it had invested in occupying the country, the money it had spent in subduing African resistance, and the money it had spent in the administration and development of the country, had to sell the land.[38] For Rhodesia to develop into the country that the company had dreamt of, more European settlers were needed. The settlers, aware of their small numbers as compared to the Africans, were in favor of increased immigration. But the farming community was not prepared to accept more settlers as farmers if it were to result in their economic ruin. The Rhodesian farmers thought that it was the company's duty to find additional markets for their products either in South Africa or in England. The company realized that it had an obligation to secure markets for the farmers as well. To promote Rhodesian farm products, the company erected tents at agricultural shows in England to display some Rhodesian products and pamphlets.[39] Yet the company did this primarily to lure more settlers into Rhodesia. Like the settlers, the company put its own economic interest first and that of the other party second.

In 1914 there were 2,059 white farmers in Rhodesia.[40] European agriculture was now well established. "Rhodesian agriculture has established itself on a satisfactory basis; and apart from stock raising, maize, tobacco, citris fruits, and the cultivation of cereals, all promise well for the future."[41] Rhodesian export trade though subject to fluctuations was on steady footing.[42] European farming methods were still improving, whereas African methods remained almost unchanged from what they had been in pre-European times. Africans with a population of 714,000, in 1914, had only 5,075 single ploughs.[43] As further proof of the success of European agriculture by 1919, white farmers had formed specialized associations to improve and secure markets for their farming products. In 1917, a Rhodesian Tobacco Growers Association was formed, and in 1919 a Cattle Breeders Association and a Maize Growers Association were formed.[44] And in 1920 the chief native commissioner was still saying of African Agriculture: "the methods of cultivation leave much to be desired. . . . The natives have not felt any necessity to improve the productiveness of their lands. [And their] methods are crude."[45]

NOTES

1. The British South Africa Company Reports on the Administration of Rhodesia, 1897-1898, p. 3.

2. Report by Arthur Lawley, May 31, 1900, The B.S.A. Co., Reports, 1898-1900, p. 30.

3. Ethel T. Jollie, *The Real Rhodesia* (London: Hutchinson and Co., 1924), p. 130.

4. C. D. Wise, *The British South Africa Company: Report on Land Settlement in Southern Rhodesia;* (London: Waterlow & Sons, Ltd. 1906), p. 3.

5. P. F. Hone *Southern Rhodesia* (London: George Bell and Son, 1909), p. 195.

6. Ibid., p. 198. No figures were given to show how many African cattle died. But the figure must have been considerable since the east coast fever could be spread very easily by both humans and cattle.

7. Report by Arthur Lawley, May 31, 1900. The B.S.A. Reports, 1898-1900, pp. 30-31.

8. African Agriculture was under the Native Department.

9. Guide to Rhodesia for the use of Tourists and Settlers (issued by Authority of): The Beira And Mashonaland Railways, 1914, p. 91. Many white ranchers bought cattle from Africans but they improved their breed by importing European bulls. Ibid., p. 93.

10. For most of the above information, see ibid., pp. 91-92.

11. Report of the Chief Native Commissioner: Matabeleland, For the Year ended 31st March, 1901, p. 5.

12. Report of the Chief Native Commissioner: Mashonaland for the Year ended 31st March, 1907, p. 3.

13. Hone, *Southern Rhodesia*, p. 220.

14. Ibid., p. 220. The old single plough could turn over one acre of ground.

15. Report of the Chief Native Commissioner: Mashonaland for the Year Ended 31st December, 1907, pp. 3-4.

16. Report of the Chief Native Commissioner: Matebeleland for the Year Ended 31st March, 1908, pp. 3-7. Perhaps Africans in Matebeleland had more ploughs because ploughs were cheaper in Matebeleland than Mashonaland and because the former was nearer to South Africa than the latter, from where the ploughs came.

17. In 1901, 1,000 cattle were brought by rail from Mozambique. Unfortunately they brought the east coast fever. Hone, *Southern Rhodesia*, p. 198.

18. Jollie, *The Real Rhodesia*, p. 133.

19. Southern Rhodesia: Report of the Director of Agriculture For The Year Ended 31st December, 1910, p. 1. In 1904 there were about 800 farmers and by 1907 the number had risen to about 1,000. Hone, *Southern Rhodesia*, p. 25.

20. In 1908, Rhodesia had a total of 2,151 miles of railway, ibid., p. 327. And by 1914 there were 2,465 miles of railway, *Guide to Rhodesia 1914*, p. 172.

21. Ibid., p. 2.

22. Southern Rhodesia Debates in the Legislative Council during the First Session of the Third Council, 26 April to 11 May, 1905, p. 2.

23. Wise, *The British South Africa Company* p. 18.

24. Ibid., p. 18.

25. Ibid., p. 19.

26. Ibid., p. 18.

27. Ibid., pp. 21–22.

28. Ibid., p. 21.

29. Ibid., p. 22.

30. Milton's Report: The British South Africa Company Directors' Report and Accounts for the Year Ended 31 March, 1908, p. 39.

31. See Charlotte Mansfield, Via Rhodesia (London: Stanley Paul & Co., 1911).

32. *The Rhodesia Journal* 12, no. 1, (July 21, 1910), p. 3.

33. Milton's Report, The B.S.A. Co., Reports, 1919, p. 37.

34. H. W. Fox, The British South Africa Company Memorandum Containing Notes and Information Concerning Land Policy, 1912, p. 15.

35. Though some African produce was sold in external markets, the amount was very little and Africans sold their produce to Europeans who then exported it.

36. G. Arrighi, *The Political Economy of Rhodesia* (The Hague: Mouton & Co., 1967), p. 24.

37. *The Bulawayo Chronicle*, December 11, 1913, p. 3.

38. See H. W. Fox, Memorandum on Land Settlement, 1912–13, p. 34.

39. See *The Rhodesian Review*, (August 1905–6), p. 59. Also see the B.S.A. Co., Report, 1909, p. 37.

40. Guide to Rhodesia 1914, p. 104.

41. Violet Markham, *The South African Scene* (London: Smith, Elder & Co., 1913), p. 426.

42. Guide to Rhodesia 1914, p. 124.

43. Report of the C.N.C. 1914, p. 6.

44. Report of the director of Agriculture, 1919, p. 8.

45. Report of the C.N.C. for the Year 1920, p. 2.

9
The Quest for Settler Power, 1907–1918

An outstanding feature of the political scene in Rhodesia between 1907 and 1914 was the emergence of organized settler political groups that were preoccupied with discussing what they thought should be the political future of the country. By 1914, when the company's charter was to expire, the settlers had discussed and exhausted all the alternatives; they had made up their minds what they wanted.

The company was the major employer of European labor in the country, particularly in the urban areas. As such, the company's views as to what the future of the country should be indirectly influenced the thinking of its employees, whose very sustenance would be affected should the fortunes of the company fail.[1] This is not to suggest that the settler leaders in business and industry did not oppose the company; they did. But when the time came to take a stand they were not prepared to make the final break. Beginning in 1907, there emerged a new political force in Rhodesia, a political force that drew its strength not from numbers but from the challenge it could present against the company. The farming community, unlike its urban counterpart, was not dependent for its livelihood on the activities of the company. An editorial in *The Rhodesia Journal* of July 1, 1909, entitled "The Coming Political Force in Rhodesia," eloquently described the importance of the developing farming community. The industrial community was no longer to be allowed to speak for the settler community. Industrial spokesmen, The *Journal* argued

represented London Boards and not the resident community. ... When victory for a popular object was almost within sight, then these "politicans" were called off by their London Boards, and their advocacy of the popular causes, generally with them quite a secondary matter, had to cease. No Company representative in Rhodesia can be qualified to act as spokesman for settlers. The farming industry is forging most satisfactorily ahead. The marked development is at present the outstanding feature of Rhodesia. The farmer is localized in every sense of the term. He is his own master, and he represents only himself. His industry is not promoted by the London financier. This country is his permanent home. He cannot be discharged. His industry is the only one industry in our country which does not contain interconflicting interests. It is one which in its ramifications is intimately bound up with those of the residents in the townships upon whose goodwill it can rely with the utmost confidence. It is capable of organization as is no other community in Rhodesia. . . . The political future of the country is in the hands of the farmer, and as time elapses this will prove to be the case.[2]

In 1909 the European population of Rhodesia was slightly over 15,000, and of this number only 1,470 were farmers.[3] But these few farmers were articulate, very well organized, and they had very definite views on what political path they believed the country should take. An example of effective action taken by the farmers may be found in the case of the Labor Tax Ordinance of 1911, which the administration had imposed to raise revenue for the Labor Bureau. To demonstrate their opposition, the farmers refused to pay the tax; their leaders even went to jail rather than pay fines of 2/6. In the end the secretary of state rescinded the tax.[4]

The political importance of the farming community was the result of its financial independence from the company, but more so because of the fact that by 1910 its economic position had greatly improved. The farmers acted as the catalysts; their views aroused the rest of the settlers to take a more active part in politics. Their debates clarified the alternatives for their fellow settlers.

Between 1909 and 1914 two issues dominated the political debates in Southern Rhodesia. From 1909 the implications of the Union of South Africa were explored, and beginning in 1912 the end of charter rule in 1914 became the foremost issue. From the very beginning of settler history in Rhodesia, the country had only been seen as a part of a future United South Africa—the debate in 1909 was about whether or not the time was right for Rhodesia to join the proposed Union. A federated South Africa, under British domination, had been the cardinal point of British South African policy since the middle of the nineteenth century.

In 1906, Lord Selbourne, the British high commissioner for South Africa sent letters to the four provinces of South Africa and Rhodesia proposing that the representatives from the five countries should meet to discuss the possibilities of federation or union. The high commissioner reminded the different administrations of the need to develop a unified African policy. Rhodesia sent Charles Coghlan, a member of the Legislative Council, William Henry Milton, the administrator, and Sir Lewis Lloyd Michell, a member of the board of directors of the Company, as delegates. Here we are interested only in the guidelines that Lord Selbourne put forward as to what he believed should be the policy toward Africans that the British government would find acceptable. In his circular, the high commissioner wrote:

The situation is startling. . . . No reasoning man can live in this country and doubt that the existence here of a white community must from first to last, depend on their success or failure in finding a right solution of the coloured and native questions, or, in other words, upon the wisdom they can show in determining the relative places which the white, coloured and native populations are to fill. History will record no nobler triumph than that of the people of South Africa if they extend the hand of sympathy to the coloured people . . . and to the educated native, and if they succeed in peacefully leading on the upward path of Christianity and of civilization the vast tribes who are beginning to emerge from barbarism . . . the people of South Africa recognize . . . the obligations imposed upon them by the ideals of Christianity and civilization.[5]

The settlers did not see the issue of African policy as a primary concern. They refused to enter the Union for reasons of regional self-interest, arguing that Rhodesia was still young and that its development would be retarded if it joined the more highly developed Union. "Rhodesia is, practically, an undeveloped and unsettled territory, and its people have no political voice or influence even in the internal affairs of their country. We have but a nominal representation. . . . Our concern for some time must be to develop these territories, and to encourage a healthy public interest in our own concerns. . . . In the meantime we shall have ample opportunity of watching the policy and methods of the Union Government."[6] A few farmers, mostly Boers, preferred Rhodesia's entry into the Union for political reasons, hoping that entry would improve their position since it would result in the domination of South Africa by the Boers.[7] Many farmers, however, believed that the Union would be followed by the inundation of Rhodesia with poor whites who would not necessarily create a bigger market but would reduce profits by producing more agricultural goods. Many feared that the labor shortage would become more acute as the Rand would offer better wages than the Rhodesian industries. Politically, they feared domination by the Boers. As early as 1907, the Mashonaland Progressive Association, which had been founded specifically to debate and clarify the implications and alternatives of entry into the Union, issued a pamphlet in which it argued that in the event of inclusion in South Africa,

> by reason of our comparatively small influence, we should lose not alone our independence, but also the political results of our sacrifices we have made as pioneers. . . . Under premature Federation the wings of our ambition must be clipped and that the country and the individual must suffer out of all proportion to the advantage offered. We object to Federation for Rhodesia in the immediate future, because we do not consider ourselves strong enough as yet to hold our own there in and we know that it would result in the control of a small minority by a great majority.[8]

Although it was not a primary determinant, the debate on the Union issue also provided the settlers with a platform to discuss their views on what they believed should be the political role of the African in Southern Rhodesia. The majority of the Europeans were strongly opposed to liberal education for Africans. Education, they feared, would give Africans the vote. Some even argued that education could not change the "raw nature" of the African;

on these grounds it was argued that giving the African the vote was dangerous. The editor of *The Rhodesia Journal* on March 27, 1908, expressed the typical settler attitude when he wrote:

As to the test of education which is implied in the ability of the voter to write his own name and address, it is argued that education means more than mental development through storing of information in the brain, that it means the training of youth under the influence of christian morality in the habits of order self-restraint obedience and in discipline . . . in short the educating of the heart as well as of the mind. Now it is hardly reasonable to suppose that a native who is the product of ages of untrained, unrestrained and careless savagedom can, through the means of a little book learning, acquire the same education, using the fuller sense, as can the white man. . . .[9]

In June 1912, *The Bulawayo Chronicle* in an editorial suggested that Africans should vote only for special representatives (Europeans) who would speak for them in the Council. The Rev. Arthur Cripps in 1914 supported the idea of special African representatives on the grounds that it was unfair that 3/4 million Africans who contributed almost half of the country's revenue in taxes should be without representation.[10] An employer expressed the following views on African education: "Reading and writing, for the mass of natives, will have no wage-earning value for many years to come, but it may be necessary to teach these; if so, all the elementary spelling book lessons should be based on the above subjects, so that, instead of a spelling lesson being taught from a Bible story or a nursery fable and conducted in the local language, it should have to do with the common European standards and be taught in a common language."[11] According to this view, if he was given education at all, the African must be taught a little English so that he would easily understand the orders of his employers.

Addressing a rally in March 1909, Charles Coghlan, to thunderous applause was reported as saying: "they [the Europeans] did not want Rhodesia turned into a blackman's country. They wanted it to be a whiteman's country."[12] White supremacy was the goal, and to maintain it and all the benefits it brought to the settler, it was necessary that political power remain in the hands of Europeans. "We here," said Charles Coghlan, "have made up our minds that we will not have the native franchise."[13]

The following quotation is typical of settler attitude toward African education.

> I have nothing whatever to say against native education, so long as the knowledge imparted runs in channels that will not bring the black into conflict with the white man of South Africa. . . . Personally I regret not seeing the laughing good-tempered, healthy savage of the past, for with all his faults he was perhaps more of a man than the overdressed cheeky product of to-day.[14]

And Hugh Marshall Hole, a company employee from 1898 till 1923, made this graphic description of the kind of African employee that most Rhodesian settlers yearned for:

> The acquistion of an experienced house-boy not only meant an immense increase in one's comfort, but carried indirect advantages of social character. When people took to giving dinner parties I am sure that I frequently owed hospitality—not to any endearing qualities of my own, but to the fact that I was the happy possessor of a "butler" whose table manners were the envy of all my friends. Many a time a letter inviting me to a dinner party has contained a postscript such as this: "Would you be so kind as to bring Alfred with you to help our boys"—a request that I cheerfully complied with as it meant that I, at all events, would be well looked after.[15]

Up to 1905-6, the fear of an African revolt had acted remotely as a lever that forced the Europeans to consider what response their actions might elicit from the Africans. After 1907, with the threat of violent African resistance faded, the settlers paid very little attention to the welfare of the indigenous population. The company administration hardly increased its £1,000 a year grant to African education. The emphasis in education was still on industrial training. In the reserves the company administration did absolutely nothing to train Africans in methods of cultivation that would improve their output, and the use of ploughs was not at all encouraged. The reserves literally became regions where African progress was arrested altogether.[16]

Yet during this pierod the clamor by Africans for education, particularly among the young, was extensive. This report was typical of the many native commissioners made during the period under discussion. "The desire to learn by the younger generation is most marked. The older people, however, do not take to schools, and Chiefs in some districts strongly resent the establishment of schools. . . ."[17] The new forces of education conducted by the missionaries coupled with their antipathy to tribal society was creating a division in African society. And this was encouraged by the company administration. "The only complaints received by me," wrote the chief native commissioner of Mashonaland, "were from Chiefs, who stated that the younger generation is breaking away from the old tribal control, and that they are no longer looked up to as Chiefs, and that they command little or no respect from their following. This is only to be expected as the natives advance in civilization, and should not be interferred with by the Government."[18] The chief native commissioner also observed that educated Africans refused to work as laborers in the mines and on farms—but went to the towns to obtain the kind of employment in which they could exhibit their knowledge and training. The chiefs were well aware that their power was being undermined not only by the education of the young but also by the role the government had asked them to play. Before the company usurped their power, the chiefs had acted as judges in cases brought to them by their followers. But now the company asked the chiefs to report any crimes committed by their followers to the native commissioners. Very often these crimes involved a refusal to pay tax and running away from employment in mines and on farms. These were manifestations, unconscious perhaps, of the Africans' passive resistance against European control. In order to regain the respect of their subjects, the chiefs often refused to reveal the names and the whereabouts of these "criminals" to the officials. "At the present time" the chief native commissioner of Mashonaland again wrote, "chiefs fully realize that their powers are fast disappearing, and it is only natural for them to secrete crime and retain the favour of their people rather than report and lose favour with them."[19]

On a national basis, the Africans remained politically unorganized—and were therefore without a platform and leadership to oppose, with one voice, European power. The attempt in Matebeleland by some Africans to agitate for the restoration of the kingship was callously dismissed and ignored by the administration. In 1909 the chief native commissioner for Matebeleland maintained that the *indunas* were the only legitimate spokesmen for the Matebele. The death of Njube, Lobengula's son and heir, seemed to have left those among the Matebele who sought the resotration of the kingship without a legitimate heir. Njube's death was considered a significant political happening by the administration primarily because it would divide the Matebele on a possible successor. "From a political point of view," commented the chief native commissioner of Matebeleland, "the year has been a most eventful one. In the minds of the natives, the most important event was the death of Njube, the heir apparent to the late King Lobengula. . . . There is no other member of the royal house of Kumalo who is likely to receive anything like the support accorded to Njube by this influential section of the people."[20] The desire by the Matebele to restore the king showed that the Africans had not yet developed a national consciousness necessary to rally all the Africans in Rhodesia and provide a united voice against the settlers.

As 1914 approached, the debate on the political future of Rhodesia became earnest. In 1907 the company had reduced the number of nominated members on the Legislative Council from seven to five, thus giving the elected members a majority of two. But this had not satisfied the settlers because control over finance remained in the hands of the administrator. "These changes effected by the Directors," observed H. T. Longden, an opponent of the company, "were merely palliatives, bringing immediate alleviation but not touching the seat of mischief. Obstructions had been placed across the course of the stream [of settler self-government]; their partial removal increased the flow but did not permit the full volume of water to pass through. Most people were deceived, thinking the waters had been augmented; whereas in fact only a small quantity was being diverted. Discontent soon reared its head again."[21] Of the changes Professor Gann wrote: " . . . from the colonists' point of view the grant of an Elected majority was but a paper victory."[22]

In November 1912 the Rhodesian League was formed in Bulawayo. The League, which wanted rule by the company to end in 1914, called for a representative government under the Crown. But Crown Colony government was only a stepping-stone toward self-government.[23] In January 1913 the Constitutional League was formed in Salisbury. Its aims "were designed to meet the political situation which will arise next year on the expiration of the first 25 years period of the Royal Charter."[24] The Constitutional League also demanded the end of company rule in 1914 and its replacement by responsible government. Many Europeans rejected Crown Colony status for Rhodesia, fearing that Crown Colony status would mean direct control from Britain. To many Europeans, direct British intervention in Rhodesian affairs meant Britain's meddling in African affairs.

And responsible government [was] . . . dismissed. It was the ideal solution, but one which [could] hardly be considered in connection with Rhodesia at the present stage of its development. The Imperial Government would never dream of granting self-government to a mere handful of less than 30,000 whites . . . living side by side with an indigenous population of close upon a million. Further, the Government would be at once beset with financial difficulties.[25]

The company acknowledged the political awareness and the growing power of the settlers. James Rochfort Maguire, a director of the company, speaking of Rhodesia's future said:

It seems to me that the two outstanding factors in Southern Rhodesia are the Chartered Company and the White population. Without the initiative, the resources, the self-sacrifice of the Company securing the occupation, the civilization of the country on the lines we see it to-day would not have taken place in our time. But the object of all these labours and toil was to place in this country a white population . . . fit . . . to take its place among the people of the Empire. In the early days the population . . . was dependent for its existence . . . upon the Company. . . . But as time went on the population grew in numbers and in strength, and the Company has recognized that fact by giving it from time to time an increasing share in political power.[26]

The British government thought that the alternative of entry into the Union of South Africa would moderate the settler's demands. "The fact that any serious difference of opinion between the Elected Members and the Company must inevitably bring to the front the question of entrance of Southern Rhodesia into the Union should in practice be a moderating influence of great value."[27] But the British government was prepared to accept whatever decision the settlers might make.

> His Majesty's Government have, however, felt throughout that their decision must be largely influenced by the opinion of the electors of Southern Rhodesia, who are the persons primarily interested in the form of administration in so far as that part of the Company's territories is concerned. . . . There can be no question of enforcing an immediate change, which the electors of Southern Rhodesia do not at present desire. . . .[28]

The two major Rhodesian newspapers, *The Rhodesia Herald* and *The Bulawayo Chronicle,* favored the continuance of company rule. According to the *Chronicle,* Southern Rhodesia under the charter "has made phenomenal and unprecedented progress for a new country. We do not for a moment believe therefore that the considered judgment of the electorate . . . will be led astray by the display of new and untried form of government, leading no one knows where."[29] In the election of 1914 the settlers voted overwhelmingly to continue company rule on the understanding that the situation would be reviewed within, or at the end of, ten years. Of the twelve seats contested, only one seat was won by an advocate of Crown Colony government. When the Legislative Council met in April 1914 it passed the following resolution: "This Council is of the opinion that under existing conditions a continuation of the Administration of the British South Africa Company is necessary in the interests of the Territory, and humbly prays his Majesty that no change be made in the present form of administration."[30]

Entry into the Union was rejected for the same reason it had been rejected in 1909—the fear of Boer domination. In essence the company was also opposed to entry into the Union because it needed time to realize its economic objectives in Rhodesia. In December 1914, Sir Starr Jameson proposed that Southern Rhodesia, Bechuanaland, and Northern Rhodesia merge.[31] The settlers rejected the idea because "Northern Rhodesia . . . has little hope of becoming a whiteman's country, in the true sense of the term. . . ."[32] When the proposal for merger was made again in 1915, it was rejected again, because the outlook for white supremacy in Northern Rhodesia was bleak. "The fundamental reason for rejecting the proposals was that the settlers sensed a threat to white supremacy. Northern Rhodesia was believed unsuitable for white settlement; therefore in the long run it could not be run by white settlers."[33]

Again, in 1914 as in 1910, the settlers' views decided the immediate political future of both the company and the country. The fact that the company had wanted an extension of its rule was in no way the decisive factor. The decisive factor was that the settlers needed more time and to them continuance of chartered company rule was the best alternative. "Company rule [was] justified . . . because there [was] no practical alternative."[34]

By 1914 the economic position of the settlers had greatly improved. The farmers no longer complained of lack of equipment; they now demanded new markets for their produce. The mining industry (still the major industry in the country) had also greatly improved. Gold was the only export and paid for all the imports. Labor shortage was no longer as acute as it had been previously. Early in 1916 the directors of the company reported, "During the early part of 1916 the supply of labor generally throughout Rhodesia was adequate. . . . Recruiting in Northern Rhodesia was prohibited, owing to the number of natives required for transport work in connection with the military operations in German East Africa."[35] Thus, ironically, the African by his increased participation in the white man's economic endeavor was rapidly strengthening the foundation of settlerism and of his own oppression.

To improve its economic position the company proposed a new land settlement scheme in 1914. Under this scheme, land would be sold to new settlers and the money obtained from these sales would be paid to the shareholders of the company. H. W. Fox, a director of the company, was designated to determine or suggest what land policy the company should follow. He immediately concluded that it was essential for company rule to continue beyond 1914 if the company were to make a profit out of its hitherto rather unsuccessful Rhodesian enterprise. Fox believed that this could best be achieved if the company could convince the settlers that it was trying to help them by its schemes. A tone of accommodation was adopted:

> It is always as well, however, where important interests are concerned, to make assurance doubly sure. There are elements in Rhodesia of a disintegrating character upon which a close watch must be kept, and their existence makes it more than ordinarily necessary to bring about a condition of affairs in which the majority of the population will not only acquiesce in, but wecome, continuance of the Company's rule. How then is this to be done? The answer to this question can, I think, only be found if the answer to the question, "What does the community want?" be first ascertained. As elsewhere, political support must be purchased. People will not support the Company unless it is made worth their while to do so.[36]

The company had to be in a position of power and influence if its maneuvers were to succeed. "It will be obvious," Fox wrote, "that I regard it as an essential feature of the Company's policy to secure the extension of its administrative functions for so long as may be necessary to turn its land assets to account. Otherwise the reward of the shareholders cannot, so far as can be foreseen, be adequate to either their expectations of their sacrifices."[37] The essential feature of the land policy advocated by Fox was that it should be tied to the political settlement to be reached in 1914. As Fox wrote:

> ... it cannot be to the interest of the Company to force the pace of the land sales, and still less of the political development of the country. At the present time, and for some years to come, it is probably that a better policy is to go slow while foundations are being laid. Having regard to . . . the magnitude of the interests at stake, it also follows that reasonable expenditures or sacrifices for the purpose of including the inhabitants of Southern Rhodesia to acquiesce in the prolongation of the Company's administration will be fully justified.[38]

To accelerate the pace of land sales would only prove to the settlers that the company wanted to sell all the land as quickly as possible, and obtain as much money as possible without regard to the settlers' wishes. However, fast sales of the land would not benefit the company financially. If the company were to sell all or most of the unalienated lands at one time, the price would invariably be the same for all the sales, whereas if it sold the land at intervals, the value of the land would increase as the "older" farms prospered. Therefore, it was essential to extend company rule, for time was required to effect these plans. Meanwhile, the company should appear to be making financial sacrifices for the benefit of the country.[39]

Since the building of the railway line linking Rhodesia with South African and Mozambiquan ports, settlers had complained about the high rates charged by the Rhodesian railways.[40] Fox also suggested that the railway rates be reduced, not to the extent that a subsidy would be necessary but only to the extent that railway revenue would cover operating expenses. Such a "sacrifice," Fox thought, would be proof to the settlers that the company was concerned about their grievances. " . . . in respect to the relative values of the Company's assets, it appears to me that the moment has come when the immediate advantage of the railway companies should be sacrificed temporarily in order to secure the far greater ultimate interest of the Company in its land."[41]

The company presented its land settlement scheme to the settlers as one way of increasing the European population. A larger European population would not only increase agricultural production but would also stimulate secondary industries, like cheese and butter making, bakeries, and many other small industries that would provide for the everyday wants of the settlers.

The longer the company administered the country, the more people it would employ. Fox believed that those employed by the company and by its subsidiaries would easily come under the influence of the company; if such people voted, they would tend to vote for those candidates who sympathized with the company. He wrote:

Further it may be sound policy for the Company to utilize the extended period of administrative functions to consolidate its political influence. If the commercial policy of the Company be such as to constitute it the greatest employer in the territory, the fact cannot fail to have an important bearing upon its political influence, especially if its employees are scattered throughout a number of constituencies.[42]

By his proposals Fox not only sought to "buy" the support of the settlers but he also intended to control them through Rhodesian company employees. Ironically a few settlers had advocated the continuation of company rule in 1914, arguing that the company, if it were deprived of its administrative role, might interfere in politics. "Moreover, with a small population," wrote Longden, "there would be a real danger in responsible government. The chartered company, still powerful though deprived of administration, would be a factor to be reckoned with. . . . The Company at election times . . . would be free to take part in the elections without let or hindrance. The Company would be in a better position than ever; it would control the Legislature and overshadow the Administration."[43]

In 1912 subsidiary companies held 8,030,594 acres, most of which were fallow, as only about 1,158,954 of these acres were farmed or used for ranching.[44] The owners of this land, for the most part, were content to lease part of their land to Africans in return for rent. The subsidiary companies were waiting for an opportunity to sell their land in the future when land value would have increased. The chartered company was opposed to this policy and tried, with little success, to persuade the subsidiaries to sell their land to it.

Fox's plan was in reality an extension of Wise's earlier land settlement scheme. Both plans called for a careful selection of settlers and the establishment of demonstration farms. Again the settlers were to be men who were prepared to work hard and who would not flounder in the face of difficulties. "The kind of men who are suitable for Rhodesia are working farmers whose wives and sons and daughters work. They have grit and energy, and some capital. They are thrifty, and they know that the best broom is the master's eye; the best fertilizer, the master's foot; the best bailiff, the master's self. . . ."[45]

Fox also suggested setting up a Land Settlement Board that would be dominated by the company. The board would be composed of nine members, six of whom were to be appointed by the company; two were to be elected members of the Rhodesian

Legislative Council and one member was to be a member of the Agricultural Union. In London a special commission for land settlement was to be set up to prepare and disseminate information. The commission would write about the climate and soil of Rhodesia, various crops that could be grown, and ranching, in general. It would also display photographs of Rhodesia that would be of interest to possible new settlers and generally disseminate propaganda through the agricultural media in Britain.

All these plans to induce new settlers to go to Rhodesia were vigoriously opposed by the Rhodesian whites, who renewed their longstanding argument over the unalienated land. In 1904 the company had claimed ownership of this land based on its conquest of Lobengula; the settlers denied the claim on the grounds that the company held the land only in its capacity as the administering power of the country. The settlers further argued that ownership of the unalienated land would change hands with a change of administration. At the time, Alfred Lyttleton, the secretary for the Colonies, had preferred that the settlers and the company reach an agreement on their own, failing which the matter would be resolved in a court of law.[46] Fox's scheme was based on the assumption that the unalienated lands belonged to the company. Furthermore, his land scheme was intended to give the company enough time in which to sell, if it were possible, all the unalienated lands before relinquishing its administrative powers. "The longer a political settlement," Fox wrote, "that includes a sale by the Company of a large portion of its land can be postponed, the greater will be the area which the Company will have either sold to third parties at full value or be working on its own account. In other words, the smaller will be the area for the new State to acquire."[47]

The attitude of the British government in the quarrel between the settlers and the company is interesting. When H. J. Gladstone, who was now the British high commissioner in South Africa, heard of the scheme, he wrote to the secretary of state urging him to block it. Gladstone rejected the company's claim to the unalienated land based on both the Lippert Concession and Lobengula's defeat arguing for the paramountcy of the 1889 Charter over the Lippert Concession. "Under the Charter they [the Company] are given powers to deal with the land, but not the land itself. . . . But the effect of the scheme is to strengthen if not to establish title without the decision of a Court of Law."[48] Harcourt, the secretary of state for the Colonies, believed that the British government should not intervene. The directors of the company argued that it was for the settlers to accept or reject the plan. The directors were convinced that the proposals that Fox had made would win the support of the settlers. That is why Fox had been very careful in public to identify the scheme with the political and economic development of the country.

The colonial secretary believed that the company was being democratic; it was appealing directly to the settlers for approval of the plans. Harcourt also sympathized with the company. He believed that the company had spent a lot of money in Rhodesia and its shareholders had received nothing in return. This would be a good chance for the company to pay dividends to the patient shareholders. Furthermore, Harcourt believed that the plan, if carried out, would increase the European population in Rhodesia, "I do not think," he wrote, "it would be wise for us to stop any settlement to which the two interested parties may voluntarily come . . . if the settlers think the Company's offer good enough for them it ought to be good enough for us."[49] The British government was agreeable if the company could sell its scheme to the settlers; if it could not, then it was for the settlers to appeal to the British government to resolve the dispute.

The land settlement scheme would serve the interests of the company, and would also increase the white population of the country. But all the money from land sales would go to the shareholders of the company. The settlers rejected the scheme on the grounds that the company was acting as though it was the owner of the unalienated lands, rather than as custodian for the "people" of Rhodesia. The fight against the company was led by the farming community. In December 1913, 1,226 farmers, more than half the farmers in the country, petitioned the colonial secretary:

Your petitioners deliberately affirm with conviction begotten of experience, that the intereets of the Company and those of the people are diverging and . . . the time has arrived when the various questions in dispute between the Company and the people cannot longer remain unsettled without danger and prejudice to the permanent interests of the community. . . . The people claim that the land in question is public domain and that the proceeds of sales should go to the public treasury . . . the Company holding the reins of Government possess an advantage which it is not loth to use for the furtherance of its own interests, and may, by making large grants of land, alienate the whole before the courts or other authorities can determine who the rightful owners are.[50]

The year 1914 was one of crisis for the Rhodesian settlers. The British government was not prepared to grant self-government to Rhodesia because the population of settlers was small and because both the British government and the company maintained that Rhodesia could not stand on its own financially.[51] The British government was neither prepared to be financially involved nor to grant any loans the settlers might ask for. The settlers nevertheless rejected the proposed land settlement scheme and maintained that the company had no right to sell the land and take the money. On April 17, 1914, the elected members of the Legislative Council unanimously passed a resolution calling upon the British government to resolve the dispute in a court of law. The resolution was made on behalf of the inhabitants of Rhodesia. The elected members emphatically resolved:

> that the ownership of the unalienated land in Southern Rhodesia is not vested in, and has never been acquired by, the British South Africa Company as their commercial or private property, and that such powers of taking possession of, dealing with, or disposing of, land in Southern Rhodesia as have been or are possessed by the British South Africa Company have been created by virtue of authority conferred by her Majesty the Queen in Council.[52]

Both the appeal to the Privy Council and the company land scheme were postponed because of the outbreak of World War I. Even before the war had ended, the company had set aside 500,000 acres in Rhodesia for former English soldiers, and only required that each man have £1,000.[53] However, even during the intervening period the Company continued to sell land.

During the year ended 31 March, 1916, 120 farms comprising 494,693 acres were disposed of. . . . On the other hand 58 farms comprising 181,498 acres, previously taken up, were relinquished. During the following nine months 80 farms, comprising 246,153 acres were disposed of, and 55 farms, comprising 173,985 acres were relinquished.[54]

In April 1918, the case was brought before the Privy Council. There were four parties to the dispute; the British government, the company, the settlers, and the Africans. At issue were over 50,000,000 acres of unalienated land. The Africans were represented by the Anti-Slavery and Aborigines Protection Society, which tried to bring African witnesses to England but found the costs for doing this to be prohibitive. The ultimate cost to the Aborigines Protection Society of representing the Africans, between £6,000 and £7,000,[55] included sending someone to Rhodesia to conduct research on the African case. The humanitarians tried to obtain financial aid from the Rhodesian Treasury pointing out that the settlers' expenses came out of the Rhodesian Treasury, and that in 1913 about £300,000 of the Rhodesian revenue out of a total of £750,000 came from African taxation.[56] The British government refused to intervene because it thought that this was a matter between the company and the elected members of the Legislative Council who maintained that they represented all the people of Rhodesia.

The company's case rested on the Lippert Concession and the conquest of Lobengula. The Privy Council rejected the Concession as an agreement between two persons, Lippert and Lobengula, which was not binding to Lobengula's successors, and, therefore, was valueless. The Court dismissed the conquest argument on the grounds "that conquest was on behalf of the Crown."[57] On the winning side, the settlers' case was similar to that of the British government; namely that the company held the land only in its capacity as the administering power, and that when its administrative functions ceased, the unalienated lands would pass into the hands of the new administration.

If the unalienated lands were the property of the Crown; on what basis did this claim rest? In February 1888, Queen Victoria signed a treaty of friendship with Lobengula (the Moffat Treaty). The British government's claim, however, could not be based on the Moffat Treaty, since the company exercised effective authority in Southern Rhodesia only after the defeat of Lobengula in 1894. Since that conquest was undertaken on behalf of the British government, it is reasonable to assume that the claim (a violation of the Moffat Treaty) of the British government rested on Lobengula's defeat. If Britain had followed her West African land policy, in which the defeat of a chief did not alter the customary land rights of the indiginous people, then she would have become the new trustee of the African people of Rhodesia assuming the function of the chief in so far as the land was concerned.

The African claim rested on the argument that the British government had never officially revoked the Moffat Treaty, the Rudd Concession, and the Charter, and that the British government held the land only as trustee of the indigenous population. The Aborigines Protection Society, which argued the African case, maintained that:

1. The natives had never alienated their land rights.
   (a) The only Concessions given by Lobengula were restricted to minerals and waste lands.
   (b) No Concession could apply with equal force to both Mashonaland and Matabeleland.
2. The British Government has never by formal act dispossessed the natives of their land rights.
   (a) Rhodesia is not British territory and the natives are not British subjects. The British Government is bound to the Matebele and Mashona tribes by a treaty of Amity, and nothing in this treaty gives the Protecting Power the right to divest the protected natives of their land rights.[58]

The Aborigines Protection Society also insisted that if the Africans won the case a sum of not less than £100,000[59] that the Africans had paid to their landlords as rent should be refunded.

In July 1918, the Privy Council ruled that the unalienated lands belonged to the Crown and not to the Africans. The Privy Council argued that between 1893 and 1918 the situation, or rather the relations between the Africans and the Europeans, had changed. The Privy Council argued that the Africans who had lived during Lobengula's time had changed and had been scattered all over the country. They further questioned what tribal ownership of land meant. "It seems," they wrote, "to be common ground that the ownership of lands was 'tribal' and 'communal,' but what precisely that means remains to be ascertained."[60] The Council, however, did not inquire into or ascertain what tribal land ownership meant. The Privy Council, which had no respect for African land customary law, argued: "The estimation of the rights of the aboriginal tribes is always inherently difficult. Some tribes are so low in the scale of civilization that their usages conceptions of rights and duties are not to be reconciled with the institutions for the legal ideas of civilized society. Such a gulf cannot be abridged."[61] But why, one may ask, had a civilized British government recognized these rights and institutions earlier? Buell made an appropriate observation when he wrote: "It does not appear, however, that their Lordships made any exhaustive inquiries into the land system of the Matabele. . . ."[62] But the Privy Council maintained that even if the Africans had rights, they were inconsistent with white settlement, which was the purpose of the movement pioneered by the company and approved by the British government.

The ruling of the Privy Council meant surrender to settler pressure. Where European pressure was not as strong, as in Rhodesia, African land rights were more fully observed. In 1921 the Privy Council had a similar case before it; only this time it was the Nigerian Africans *versus* the Crown. The Council in that case ruled in favor of the Africans arguing that African rights, no matter how primitive, were paramount. Comparing the two Privy Council decisions, Buell made the following observation:

> The attitude of the Privy Council in ignoring all native rights in this case [1918] is in striking contrast to its judgment three years later in the Olawa land case in Nigeria where it held that the Crown was obliged to respect the usufructuary rights of native communities in the land. The Nigeria judgment makes no distinction between primitive and more advanced conceptions of land tenure. While it does not grant to the natives rights known to British law, it states that the . . . rights of the natives in land should be respected. In the Rhodesian case, their Lordships sweep away all such rights in favor of the Crown.[63]

Since 1890, the British government had winked when African land rights were trampled upon by the company. In 1918 the British government officially expropriated African land on behalf of the ever vociferous settlers.

NOTES

1. See letter by R. N. Hall, author of *Great Zimbabwe Prehistoric Rhodesia*, to Private Secretary of the High Commissioner, February 25, 1913, C. O. 417/522.

2. *The Rhodesia Journal*, July 1, 1909, pp. 1–3.

3. *The Bulawayo Chronicle*, March 5, 1909, p. 7.

4. See *The Bulawayo Chronicle*, June 21, 1912, p. 7.

5. Cd. 3564, January 1, 1907, "A Review of the Present Mutual Relations of the British South African Colonies," p. 41.

6. *The Rhodesia Journal*, November 3, 1910, p. 5.

7. *The Rhodesia Journal*, September 22, 1910, p. 19.

8. *Rhodesia and Federation* (Salisbury, Rhodesia: Art Printing Works, 1907), pp. 10–11. Also see Guy W. Morris, *The Making of Rhodesia* (Beit Prize thesis, Rhodes House, Oxford University, 1910).

9. *The Rhodesia Journal* 2, no. 10 (March 27, 1908): 245–47.

10. Arthur S. Cripps "Native Interests in Southern Rhodesia," *The Quarterly Review*, no. 586, (October 1914): 540.

11. Tudor G. Trevor, "Native Education from an Employer's Point of View," *NADA*, December 1927, p. 99.

12. *The Bulawayo Chronicle*, March 5, 1909, p. 7.

13. Ibid., p. 1.

14. B. Wilson, "Rhodesia and Its Prospects" in *United Empire*, vol. ii 1911, p. 564.

15. H. M. Hole, *Old Rhodesian Days*, (London: Macmillan and Co., Ltd., 1928) p. 55.

16. See Article by H. S. Keigwin in *NADA: The Southern Rhodesia Native Affairs Department Annual*, vols. 1–4 (Salisbury, Southern Rhodesia, 1923–26), pp.11–12.

17. Report of the C.N.C. Mashonaland For The Year Ending 31st December, 1911, p. 1.

18. Ibid., p. 1.

19. Report of the C.N.C. Mashonaland for the Year Ended 31st December, 1910, p. 1.

20. Report of the C.N.C. Matebeleland for the Year Ended 31st December, 1910, p. 1.

21. H. T. Longden, "The Future of Rhodesia," *The Quarterly Review*, no. 439 (April 1914): 547.

22. L. H. Gann, *A History of Southern Rhodesia: Early Days to 1934 (London: Chatto & Windus, 1965), p. 213.*

23. *The Bulawayo Chronicle*, January 16, 1913.

24. Ibid., p. 1.

25. H. T. Longden, "The Future of Rhodesia," p. 551.

26. C. O. 417/523, 1913.

27. C. O. to B.S.A. Co., February 9, 1911, Cd. 7264 Correspondence Relating to the Constitution of Rhodesia, 1914, p. 6.

28. The Secretary of State (for the Colonies) to the High Commissioner, October 3, 1914. Cd. 7645, Correspondence Relating to the Continuance of the Administrative Provisions of the Charter of the British South Africa Company, pp. 24–25.

29. *The Bulawayo Chronicle,* January 16, 1913, p. 1.

30. Resident Commissioner to High Commissioner May 15, 1914. Cd. 7645, 1914, p. 9.

31. See A. J. Hanna, *The Story of the Rhodesias and Nyasaland,* pp. 150–58.

32. Editorial in *The Bulawayo Chronicle,* January 1, 1914, p. 1.

33. Colin Leys and Cranford Pratt, *A New Deal in Central Africa* (London: Wm. Heinemann, Ltd., 1960), p. 1.

34. Ian D. Colvin, "The Future of Rhodesia," *The Quarterly Review* no. 439 (April 1914), p. 534.

35. The British South Africa Company Reports, 1915, p. 7.

36. H. Wilson Fox, Memorandum Upon Land Settlement in Rhodesia, 1912, p. 35.

37. Ibid., p. 34.

38. Ibid., p. 35.

39. Ibid., p. 35.

40. Quoted In H. T. Longden, "The Future of Rhodesia", p. 554.

	South African Railway Rates for 612 Miles			Rhodesian Railway Rates for 588 Miles		
	Rate per 100 lbs.			Rate per 100 lbs.		
Class	s	d	s	d		
1st class	7	1	per 100 lbs.	14	.8	per 100 lbs.
2nd class	4	1	per 100 lbs.	10	.0	per 100 lbs.
3rd class	3	1	per 100 lbs.	7	.4	per 100 lbs.

41. Fox, p. 35.

42. Ibid., p. 35.

43. Longden, *The Future of Rhodesia,* pp. 551–52.

44. Fox, p. 35.

45. Wilson Fox, Memorandum Upon Land Settlement in Rhodesia, June 21, 1914, p. 59.

46. Reference in C. O. 417–525, 1914.

47. Fox, 1912 Memorandum, p. 34.

48. H. J. Gladstone to Harcourt, October 12, 1913, C. O. 417/525.

49. Harcourt to Gladstone, November 10, 1913, C. O. 417/525.

50. Rhodesian Farmers to Harcourt, December, 1913, C. O. 417/538.

51. See Cd. 7645, 1914, p. 19.

52. Cd. 7509. Papers Relating to a Reference to the Judicial Committee of the Privy Council on the Question of the Ownership of land in Southern Rhodesia, 1914, p. 3.

53. See British South Africa Company Reports 1915–1940, p. 9.

54. Ibid., p. 9.

55. John H. Harris, *The Greatest Land Case in British History: The Struggle For Native Rights in Rhodesia Before Judicial Committee of His Majesty's Privy Council,* (London: The Anti-Slavery and Aborigines Protection Society, 1918), p. 5.

56. Ibid., p. 5.

57. *A. C. 1919, Law Reports: Appeal Cases,* p. 221.

58. John H. Harris, *The Greatest Land Case In British History*, pp. 3-4.

59. Ibid., p. 5.

60. *A. C. 1919 Law Reports: Appeal Cases*, p. 233.

61. Ibid., p. 233.

62. Raymond Leslie Buell, *The Native Problem In Africa* (New York: The Macmillan Company, 1928), vol. 1, p. 212.

63. Ibid., pp. 212-13.

10
African Politics 1918-1923

The main African grievances between 1918 and 1923 were of insufficiency of land, low wages, rising prices, poor working conditions, lack of adequate educational facilities, the Matebele Kingship issue, and the registration of African voters. Unfortunately, we have to rely on the native commissioners' reports as documentary evidence about this new African assertiveness.

The factors that could have speeded up the political awareness of the African people, namely education and economic development of the reserves,[1] were largely ignored by the company. By 1923 the chief native commissioner could report that there were only 86 mission stations with 627 Kraal schools throughout the whole country.[2] And the education received by the Africans was mostly religious and industrial training, which was hardly sufficient to promote the growth of the new political, social, and economic ideas and attitudes that were necessary to transform life in the reserves. Yet in 1923, as he had done in the preceding years, the chief native commissioner also reported: "The desire and demand for education by the younger people continue with unabated insistence. . . ."[3]

Between 1918 and 1923 there were some incidents when African students complained that they spent inadequate time on literary education. In 1922 the director of Native Development reported at Domboshawa, a government industrial training school with an enrollment of 112, that "twelve [students] left in August as the result of a protest against the shortness of time given to schoolroom lessons."[4] Even in the field of industrial training the aim of the Company administration was to produce Africans who would not compete with Europeans. "The native," wrote the chief

190

native commissioner "should be trained not so much as to compete with the white man in the Business life, but as a useful auxiliary to help in the progress of the country."[5] Wilson, a former native commissioner, wrote: "I look forward with a great deal of misgiving to a time when [there will be] a large body of natives, running into several thousands, skilled in the professions and crafts, skilled in farming and business, skilled in rhetoric and logic, intellectually as acute, perhaps as the Greeks . . . [when this happens] we have the stage set for tragedy."[6]

In 1920, H. S. Keigwin, the director of Native Development, wrote a report in which he outlined, in some detail, the kind of industrial training that "he considered" good for the Africans but at the same time would not threaten European enterprise. He suggested that Africans be trained in industries that involved the following: food production, rope and mat making, working hides and skins, basket and chair making, pottery and tiles, carpentry and wagon work, and smithing. As Keigwin noted: "As far as possible, only those industries which do not offer direct competition with Europeans have been considered."[7] Keigwin hoped that this kind of training would eventually encourage the African to seek employment in the towns.

Life in the reserves changed little. Writing in *NADA* in 1923, Keigwin complained that the methods of ploughing used by the Africans were still the same as those they had used in pre-European days. "It is one of the sad things which strikes the observer of native life in this country that there is so little sign of improvement in the home life [after] all these years. . . . Again, in the economic standards . . . little improvement is apparent in their methods of agriculture or care of stock."[8] Keigwin believed that the Europeans had not done enough to help the people living in the reserves. Although about a thousand ploughs had been bought by Africans, there was literally economic stagnation in the reserves.[9]

Most of the Kraal schools were in the reserves. The education the students received there was totally inadequate to produce the new leaders required by modern conditions. The chiefs, the traditional leaders of the Shona, could not supply the needed leadership. Beginning in 1899 their powers and authority had been greatly reduced by the native commissioners. In 1899 the chiefs were reduced to government agents who were appointed and could be dismissed by the company. The authority of the chiefs was further undermined by the work of the missionaries who saw them primarily as standing in the way of their christianizing efforts. The Matebele, on the other hand, had been deprived of their king—hence their rallying cry was "restore the king." But all the agitation by the Matebele for the restoration of the king was, it seems, a desire to restore the past that had been rudely shattered by the arms of the company. It would therefore seem, despite the determination of the organizers of the restoration movement, that the agitation was either a failure or a refusal to acknowledge the new situation. Their program should have called for equal educational social and political treatment for all the people in the country. Such a program could have appealed to all the Africans in the country. But a common African front did not at this stage develop.

The Matebele agitation for the restoration of the kingship was not new, but its significance in 1919, as Ranger noted, lay in the manner in which the demand for the restoration was made.[10] The petition to King George V was made specifically on behalf of the Matebele, whether they resided in Mashonaland or Matebeleland. The petition was made with the assistance of the African National Congress of South Africa and the Ethiopian Church movement of South Africa, which claimed to represent over twenty thousand members.[11] In the deputation of four that presented the petition to the high commissioner in Cape Town, there was only one Rhodesian, S. Hlazo, who was actually a Fingo, not a Ndebele. The high commissioner noted that Hlazo was more concerned with his father's grievances than with the subject matter of the petition.[12] It is not clear why a member of Lobengula's family or any other Ndebele was not in the delegation.

Despite the high commissioners' downgrading of the deputation and the petition, the document is a political indictment against British policy toward the Matebele (and indirectly the Shona) in Southern Rhodesia. The document reflects a certain diplomatic skill on the part of its authors. It begins by congratulating the king on the victory against the Germans and expresses hope that this will lead to freedom and liberty for all the king's subjects throughout the Empire under better conditions than had existed before the outbreak of the war. The petition then criticizes the British government for not checking settler land alienations in Rhodesia. " . . . it pleased Her Gracious Majesty, the late Queen Victoria to allow Great Britain's local representatives in South Africa to parcel out, sell, grant and otherwise dispose of the land in this territory, treating the rights of the late King Lobengula and his tribe therein as of negligible importance, and without giving any appreciable pledge or safeguard to the tribes' vested rights, and their future political status under those new circumstances."[13] The petitioners complained about the location system in which they claimed that their followers lived "under a veiled form of slavery." The petitioners complained about the size and quality of the reserves. "These Reserves, according to the evidence of the Chiefs . . . are situated in unhealthy districts and consist of forests where wild beasts obtain; some places are dry and uninhabitable."[14] The petitioners correctly noted that the British government's representatives did little to disallow discriminatory legislation. "Referring to Native Laws and treatment, Your Petitioners have experienced with great regret that High Commissioners . . . who are the true Representatives of Your Majesty, have acted as disinterested spectators. . . ."[15] The petitioners expressed grave fears as to the future of African affairs in the event of self-government being granted to the Europeans. "Your Petitioners pray that in case Rhodesia is granted any form of Government the Imperial Government take over the Administration of Native Affairs. . . ."[16]

The petitioners decried the ruling of the Privy Council under which the unalienated lands were declared Crown lands by right of conquest. "But in the interest of right and justice," argued the petitioners, "and in pursuance of the fact that the right of conquest (whether justified or not) is now repudiated by the civilized world, Your Petitioners pray that Your Majesty be pleased to hand back the so-called unalienated land."[17] The petition ended with an observation about the inadequacy of the reserves; "And that these areas be so developed in the interests of the people concerned, under their own self-government and self-development and free from passes and taxes and other restrictive regulations."[18]

The petition clearly showed the political weakness of the

Africans. It did not threaten to disturb the peace in Rhodesia if its views were ignored. In the final analysis, the petition appealed to morality and the sense of justice and fair play of the British government. Where vital interests are at stake, usually the strong take action first to preserve those interests and moralize afterwards. The petitioners by cataloguing the excesses of the settlers and the failures of the British government to stop them desperately hoped somehow to rouse the British government to action. However, their appeals, as those of Lobengula before them, were ignored.

Although the petition was ignored by the British government it was, nevertheless, a remarkable political document. It contained, besides the kingship issue, the platform and foundation upon which future African demands would be built. The petition was ignored by the British government because it sought to undo white settlement in Rhodesia, which had been sanctioned by the British government in 1898 and strengthened by the Privy Council ruling in 1918. The Privy Council wrote: "The maintenance of their [African] rights was fatally inconsistent with white settlement of the country, and yet white settlement was the object of the whole forward movement, pioneered by the Company and controlled by the Crown, and that object was successfully accomplished, with the result that the aboriginal system gave place to another prescribed by the Order in Council."[19] Furthermore, the major complaint of the humanitarians, the defenders of African rights, against the European activity in Rhodesia was not the idea of European presence as such but against the excesses of European aggrandizement. Humanitarians would not have supported the dismantling of white settlement which, despite its unfortunate consequences to African freedom, was still seen (by humanitarians) as a civilizing influence.[20]

Perhaps the petition was also ignored because it did not have behind it the masses of the African people. "A small section of the Matabele round about Bulawayo," wrote the chief native commissioner in 1919, "are reported to have made an abortive attempt to collect funds in aid of a movement which had as its object the election as King, Nyamanda, the eldest son of Lobengula."[21] It is conceivable that had the Africans of Southern Rhodesia in 1919 been demonstrating in the streets behind a sort of mass political movement, the document might have attracted the attention it deserved. But in 1919 the era of mass politics had not yet arrived in Rhodesia. The petition was a document of the Matebele aristocracy, exclusively on behalf of the Matebele but without the demonstrable support of the rank and file. It was therefore not the rallying cry it should have been to all the Africans of Rhodesia to resist the further granting of power to the settlers. The petition was of immense benefit, however, to the political development of the African people. For once it became clear in everybody's mind that the evils of settlerism equally affected all the Africans and could only be redressed by the effort of all the African people of Southern Rhodesia—the petition was, in simple terms, a statement of African objectives.

European reaction to the petition was hostile. A European farmer, expressing the general settler attitude, informed the authorities that Nyamanda intended to set up a "black and presumably a blacker Kingdom; that they were proposing to call out the regiments and march on Bulawayo, and that a local Matebele school-teacher and preacher was calling for 'Africa for the black' and announcing that we should have our own king from our own people, and our own laws."[22] Ranger reports that the Rhodesian administration expressed displeasure to those *indunas* who had supported Nyamanda.

Because the traditional powers of the chiefs had been undermined by the Company, and because, despite the valiant struggle, the traditional leadership had not only failed to stem the tide of European expansion in the 1890s but had also failed to assume an aggressive role in the period following defeat, a new African leadership arose in the cities. This new leadership neither looked to the old leadership for inspiration nor solicited its aid in the economic, social, and political battles it waged. There are several reasons for this. The older leadership sought a return to the past. Native commissioners' reports of the period continued to abound with the complaints made by the chiefs of how the new forces in Rhodesian life were undermining their authority. In his 1923 report, the chief native commissioner wrote: "I have previously remarked on the rapidly declining power of the chiefs and headmen. The masses continue to recognize tribal control, but in a less degree. . . . The Younger generation is gradually breaking away from the tribal system."[23] The new African leadership that emerged after World War I, unlike the old leadership, sought to play a greater role in the economic and political future of the country.[24]

Most of the new leadership was composed of Fingoes or Matebele who had either originated, worked, or been educated in South Africa. Ranger points out that the headquarters of this new leadership was Bulawayo,[25] because Bulawayo was more industrialized than Salisbury and because these men had been in contact with the Europeans longer than had the Shona in Salisbury or Umtali. Fingo leaders like the Rev. D. F. Maghatto, leader of the Ethiopian movement in Rhodesia, had earlier supported the Matebele movement to restore the kingship in the years after 1910. Other well-known members of the Fingo community, such as the Hlazos and the Sojinis, had supported the Matebele demands.[26]

Direct appeal to the British government had failed, and in the period after 1923 Africans had to contend with the Europeans on the spot. Abraham Twala, a member of the South African National Congress, observed: "Experience has taught us that our salvation does not lie in Downing Street. I strongly advise our native fledglings in Southern Rhodesia, indulging in politics, to find out and make their friends in Southern Rhodesia. When this has been done we shall see what the harvest will be."[27] Twala was advising Africans in Rhodesia to solicit the sympathy of missionaries and white liberals.

Twala's advice is interesting for it clearly calls upon the new African leadership to change their tactics, and literally calls upon them to abandon their ideas of establishing a Matebele homeland. His advice to the Rhodesian Africans is to work within the European system, advice the old leadership, particularly the Shona leadership, was unwilling to accept. The old leadership lacked the qualifications or at least the incentive to secure the qualifications that were necessary either to enroll as voters or to compete for jobs with Europeans. Both the old and new African leaderships rejected the present state of affairs as it existed at the time under discussion, but their solutions differed. The old sought to return to the past, whereas the new leadership looked to a future when conditions would be better. Henderson and Warhurst were correct in their analysis of Shona politics when they wrote: "We . . . find that modern Shona politics developed in opposition to, not in alliance with traditional secular authorities."[28]

One must, however, not create the impression that by 1923 the majority of Africans in the cities were educated and could qualify for the vote; this is far from the case. By 1923 there were only 25,522 indigenous Africans in the cities at any given time. In fact, in 1922 out of a total of 18,810 voters only about 60[29] were Africans and most of them were Africans of South African origin. In 1912 the franchise qualifications had been doubled and, in 1917, the Treasury Department placated European fears by stating that if in the future the number of qualified African voters should increase to such proportions as would threaten European supremacy, the government would further raise voting qualifications. Very few statistics are available so it is difficult to know exactly why the number of African voters was so low in 1922. Whether it was the result of apathy by qualified Africans who did not register for the vote, or whether it was simply because few Africans had the necessary qualifications is difficult to determine, although the latter reason is more likely. To overcome both of these deficiencies, the Southern Rhodesian Bantu Voters Association was formed in 1922 with the object of encouraging Africans to acquire the franchise qualifications and to register as voters. One of the reasons for the small number of qualified African voters was that more than half of the labor force was provided by alien Africans who worked for a limited time at the end of which they returned to their home. Such Africans would tend not to have any direct political interest in Rhodesian affairs as they were only transients. And because most local Africans went to the cities to work for only a few months to secure money to meet their tax requirements, they could not in most cases meet the financial requirements to be registered voters. Thus, for a long time, even after 1923, the majority of the registered voters and those active in the Southern Rhodesian Bantu Voters Association, continued to be nonindigenous Africans. Yet, the importance of the association lay in the fact that it encouraged Africans to qualify as voters. The weakness of the association was reflected in its very mild demands, which were purely reformist and at no time immediately threatened European hegemony. Nevertheless, the association was a national one that appealed to all the Africans in the country. Its strength lay in the future.

The most potent force was represented by the laborers, even if they did not qualify for the franchise. Again, the leaders in the trade union movement were foreign; the first to organize the Industrial and Commercial Worker's Union was Robert Sambo, from Nyasaland. However, the weaknesses of these leaders resulted from the fact that most of them were nonindigenous Africans, who could be threatened with deportation if they became too vocal. The demands of the laborers were primarily economic. "A feeling of dissatisfaction," the chief native commissioner wrote in 1919, "is caused by the continued rise in the prices of all commodities."[30] If we bear in mind that the African laborers were paid very low wages and that their living conditions were appalling it is easy to understand how the workers were able to organize themselves reasonably successfully. In 1919, the chief native commissioner reported:

> Signs are apparent that some of them [Africans] have begun to realize that they constitute a considerable political, social and economic factor in the development of the country, and occasional agitation is evidence of progress and enlightenment and a desire on their part to make their voice heard in the conduct of certain affairs intimately concerning them . . . recently the native employees of a large mine . . . determined to effect a reduction in the extortionate prices charged by certain local storekeepers. Their first plan of campaign was to picket and forcibly prevent any natives from entering the stores in question. When, however, it was explained to them that this action was illegal, they at once withdrew their pickets and there upon ordered a boycott. The success with which this was attended testifies to the thoroughness of their organization, which embraces natives of many different tribes and tongues. The leaders influence and control the rest by means of harangues and debates, and by circularising them with notices, pamphlets and other propangandist literature. These are signs of the times, but the just and legitimate arguments and methods employed by them are reassuring.[31]

This long quotation shows that the laborers were beginning to organize themselves in a manner that transcended tribal lines.

Their agitation, as the chief native commissioner pointed out, was in accordance with principles accepted and tolerated by the Administration.

In 1923, when Rhodesia was granted responsible government, the Africans were aware of the change. The chief native commissioner noted that Africans "were somewhat agitated in mind as to the extent to which they would be affected by the change of Government. As a matter of policy it was considered desireable to take them into our confidence before the change took place."[32] He, therefore, instructed the native commissioners to explain the change to the chiefs and headmen in their areas. African chiefs were even invited to attend the ceremonies marking the inauguration of the new government. They watched the proceeding and in no way protested: the voice of the Africans was not strong enough in 1923 to oppose the change that took place and these men were least likely to fathom the implications in any case. African political consciousness was still in its earliest embryonic stages when the transfer took place. But there was some movement, as evidenced by the chief native commissioner's report of 1923, which stated "That they are taking a keener interest in matters affecting their political welfare is evidenced by the increasing membership of the various native political organizations."[33]

NOTES

1. See discussion on reserves in Chapter 6.
2. Report of the C.N.C. for the Year 1923, p. 5.
3. Ibid., p. 5.
4. Report of the C.N.C. For the Year 1922, p. 18.
5. Report of the C.N.C. For the Year 1918, p. 4.
6. N. H. Wilson, "The Future of the Native Races of Southern Rhodesia," *South African Journal of Science* 17 (1921): 142.
7. Report by H. S. Keigwin, On the suggested Industrial Development of Natives 1920, p. 5.
8. H. S. Keigwin, "Native Development" in *NADA: The Southern Rhodesian Native Affairs Department Annual*, vols. 1-4, 1923-26, p. 11.
9. Ibid., p. 11.
10. See Terence Ranger, "Traditional Authorities and the Rise of Modern Politics in Southern Rhodesia," eds. Eric Stokes and Richard Brown, *The Zambesian Past: Studies in Central African History* (Manchester: The University Press, 1966), pp. 171-93.
11. C. O. 417/617, 1919.

12. Hlazo's father and other Fingoes had not received the land grants they had been promised by the Company for helping fight the Matebele in 1893, nor were the Fingoes allowed to buy land on the same basis as the Europeans.

13. C. O. 417/617, 1919.

14. Ibid.

15. Ibid.

16. Ibid.

17. Ibid.

18. Ibid.

19. *A. C. Law Reports: Appeal Cases 1919*, p. 234.

20. The building of schools, roads, the ending of Matebele raids—all these were seen as positive achievements. This view was expressed in yearly missionary conferences held in Rhodesia since 1906.

21. Report of the C.N.C. for the Year 1919, p. 1.

22. Wallston to High Commissioner, October 16, 1921; A/18/11 quoted from Rangers' article in *The Zambesian Past*, p. 183.

23. Report of the C.N.C. for the Year 1923, p. 2.

24. See Terence Ranger, *The African Voice in Southern Rhodesia* (London: Wm. Heinemann, Ltd., 1967), chap. V.

25. Ranger, "The Rise of Modern Politics in Southern Rhodesia," in *The Zambesian Past*, p. 181.

26. Ibid., p. 181.

27. *The Rhodesia Herald*, March 3, 1922, p. 3.

28. Ian Henderson and P. R. Warhurst, "Revisions in Central African History to 1953", *The Central Africa Historical Association*, Local Series Pamphlet No. 15 (Salisbury: 1965), p. 31.

29. Proceedings of the Southern Rhodesia Missionary Conference, July 5 to July 8, 1922, p. 24.

30. Report of the C.N.C. for the Year 1919, p. 2.

31. Ibid., p. 1.

32. Report of the C.N.C. for the Year 1923, p. 1.

33. Ibid., p. 2.

11
The Consolidation of Settler Power

The Privy Council decision brought a radical change in the attitude of the company. "With this decision the Company lost interest in the further administration of Rhodesia and began to look for the most profitable settlement."[1] For this reason the company inquired how much the South African government would be prepared to compensate the company if Rhodesia were to join the Union. The company claimed that it had spent £7,866,117 to occupy and develop the country.[2] The Cave Commission appointed by the British government in 1919 to determine how much the company had spent in developing the country suggested that only £3,750,000[3] was owed to the company. The South African government offered to pay the company £6,836,500[4] if Rhodesia joined the Union. The company, beginning in 1918, advocated Rhodesia's entry into the Union. "The Company decided that the most likely chance for it to get its deficits quickly reimbursed was for it to come to an agreement with the Union Government, if only the people of Southern Rhodesia could be persuaded to accept incorporation."[5]

The ruling of the Privy Council once again reopened the debate among whites on the political future of Southern Rhodesia. Although the ultimate decision would be made by the settlers, the interest in the matter of two other forces was great and caused concern among the settlers. The company was interested only in recouping as much as it could and was prepared to sell to the highest bidder. The British government wanted a solution, above all else, that would not leave it financially supporting Rhodesia. Entry of Rhodesia into the Union would meet the requirements of the company and the British government and it would further

201

fulfill the wish that had been expressed by Chamberlain, Milner, and others of strengthening the British voice in South Africa. But the Rhodesian settlers thought and felt differently.

In 1917 a Responsible Government Association was formed to campaign for the introduction of self-government in Rhodesia at the end of chartered company rule. Two of the most prominent leaders of the association were Charles Coghlan and Mrs. Ethel Tawsie Jollie. The argument that entry into South Africa would hamper Rhodesia's economic development was to be heard very often.[6] The association clearly realized that entry into the Union would not retain British preponderance in South Africa since the English were a minority. They appealed to white Rhodesian "British" nationalism and exploited the British fear of Boer domination. The association argued that the history of the Boer-British relationship in South Africa had, from the very beginning of English rule, been one of hostility and strife. "All the rest of the sub-continent," wrote Mrs. Jollie, "has a history of strife between the two white races, a legacy of bitterness which generations to come must still endure."[7] Rhodesia's entry would not resolve the problem. Others argued that between 1888 and 1890, Rhodes, in occupying Mashonaland, had thwarted Boer expansion schemes. The proposed entry into the Union was seen as the revival of Boer expansion schemes of the last decade of the nineteenth century. "The land-hunger of the Dutch is again awake . . . in the old dream of 1880. What has quickened this old ideal once again is the renewed possibility of its realization. . . ."[8]

The fear among the English-speaking Rhodesian settlers of domination by the Boers was indeed real. In a letter to his sister, Bella, Coghlan declared that he was engaged "in the fight . . . for his country and its freedom in the face of tremendous odds."[9] If Rhodesia entered the Union the two official languages would be Afrikaans and English. The Rhodesian settlers were unwilling to learn and speak Afrikaans. There was also the genuine fear that Rhodesia's entry into the Union would be immediately followed by the inundation of Rhodesian agriculture by many poor whites from South Africa.[10]

To further the cause of Rhodesia's entry into the Union, Trevor Fletcher in 1919 formed the Rhodesian Union Association, which represented the Boer farmers who constituted about one fifth of the European population in Rhodesia. The association argued that Rhodesia was a landlocked country and that entry into the Union would provide easy and economic outlets for Rhodesia's products. It was also argued that entry into the Union would not be abandoning the Rhodesian ideal of self-government but that the ideal would be achieved, " . . . for we should then manage our own affairs, not from the narrow point of view of isolation, but from the broader and more worthy aspect of the common good of a united South Africa."[11] Entry into the Union, the association maintained, would not only give the whole of South Africa a uniform policy toward the Africans but it would also provide the ruling authorities with a chance to develop "a more enlightened policy"[12] toward the Africans. The association contended that as long as the ratio between blacks and whites in Rhodesia remained big, the small white minority would be forced to adopt harsher methods to maintain European supremacy. But if this proportion was reduced, by Rhodesia's entry into the Union, it would be unnecessary to adopt harsh policies toward the nonwhites. The association also argued that "as long as the taxpayers of the United Kingdom were called upon to contribute towards the defense of the South African colonies, it forced the Imperial Government to have a native policy."[13] And this would mean that the British government could interfere in Rhodesian's internal affairs. The most important reason that the Rhodesian Union Association advanced for the entry into the Union was probably the financial argument. The association argued that Southern Rhodesia could not stand on its own feet financially and that it could not borrow money for its own development. Furthermore, since Britain was unwilling to grant Rhodesia any loans the country had no alternative but to enter the Union.

Since 1904 the company and the settlers had disagreed as to whether the settlers should foot the bill for some of the administrative functions of the company. The settlers were prepared to pay for such items as public buildings, roads, and general administrative functions, but they maintained that they should not pay for such expenses as the company had incurred in the fighting of 1893 and 1896–97. The settlers also refused to meet any expenses incurred for the company's benefit. The company and the settlers were not agreed on the amount that the new administration in

Rhodesia would owe to the company, which claimed, as noted, that it had spent since 1889 a total of £7,866,117.[14]

In April 1920 a general election was held that further frustrated the company. Out of the thirteen elected members, twelve favored the immediate introduction of self-government and one proposed representative Crown Colony government for Rhodesia. All were against the continuation of chartered rule. Out of a total of 6,765 voters, 4,663 voted for self-government, 420 voted for representative government, 814 voted for entry into the Union, and 868 voted for the continuation of charter rule.[15]

The result of the election prompted the British government to set up a Commission to recommend (1) when and with what limitations responsible or self-government would be granted to Southern Rhodesia, and (2) what procedure would be adopted with a view to working out the future constitution. The commission recommended: "In the interests of Southern Rhodesia and of all concerned, the question whether the Territory is, or is not, prepared to adopt Responsible Government ought to be decided one way or the other at the earliest possible moment. We have further come to the conclusion that, before Responsible Government is actually granted, the electors of Southern Rhodesia should be given a definite opportunity of expressing their opinion for or against its adoption."[16] The results of the last election had clearly shown that the Rhodesian settlers wanted self-government. But the commission believed that in an election many issues are usually debated and therefore the voter's decision is influenced by many considerations. The commission suggested that a referendum be held because in a referendum the voters would be in a better position to realize precisely what responsible government, constitutionally, administratively, and financially would mean to the country, and the voters would thus accept or reject the proposal with the full knowledge of the position and of the step that they were taking.[17]

It is likely that the British government thought that by asking the Rhodesian settlers to decide what the political future of the country would be through a referendum and by explicitly stipulating the conditions, the settlers would be persuaded to vote for joining the Union. The British government published the Rhodesian Draft Constitution at the end of 1921, but refused to guarantee that it would grant loans to a new administration in Rhodesia. Under Article 48 of the Letters Patent of the Draft all the unalienated land in Southern Rhodesia and revenues derived from the sale of the land would remain in the hands of the British government, and proceeds of the sale of land would be handed over to the company to pay for the administrative deficits of the company.

The conditions under which self-government was offered were so difficult that *The Rhodesia Herald* commented that the purpose of the Draft Constitution was to persuade the settlers to join the Union. *The Herald* also found the Draft Constitution more remarkable for its restrictions than for any self-governing principles. J. McChlery, member of the Legislative Council, who also had been a member of the Rhodesian delegation that had met with Winston Churchill, then colonial secretary, observed that as a result of the publication of the Draft Constitution enthusiasm for self-government had lessened. In an interview, McChlery said: "Personally I am less enthusiastic about our ability to apply Responsible Government than I was when I left with the mission."[18] McChlery further stated: "The Imperial Government would certainly, in my opinion, favor the incorporation of Rhodesia into the Union, and the feeling was evident in influential political quarters at Home [England] that it would be a very desirable thing that the matter should be dealt with while a statesman of the calibre and proved loyalty of General Smuts was still in office."[19] And Mrs. Jollie, a bitter opponent of Rhodesia's entry into the Union, wrote: "So far as a self-governing Constitution could be made unattractive, everything was done in the document offered to repel the Rhodesians."[20] The two major daily newspapers in the country, *The Rhodesia Herald* and *The Bulawayo Chronicle*, came out against self-government and for Rhodesia's entry into the Union.

The problem placed before the Rhodesian settlers was complicated further by the attitude of the company and the British and South African governments. The British government let it be known to the settlers that they had an alternative to self-government, that is, entry into the Union: General Smuts also offered to pay the company almost twice as much as the Cave Commission had decided was owed to the company. The South African government was prepared to pay the company £6,836,500.[21] Despite the fact that the Rhodesian population was small, Smuts offered the Rhodesians ten seats in the Union Parliament. On the whole, the settlers would have gained economically if they had entered the Union. The South African government was willing to buy the Rhodesian railways, which would have meant a considerable reduction in railway rates.

Meanwhile the company took a step that clearly was intended to intimidate the settlers into entering the Union. The company appealed to the Privy Council to refuse the Rhodesian settlers self-government before they had paid £3,750,000—the amount the Cave Commission had recommended be paid to the company. The British government had refused to guarantee the settlers a loan and because the settlers could not raise the money it seemed that they might be forced into joining the Union. In an editorial the *Chronicle* remarked: "it appears to us there are only two courses open for patriotic Rhodesians. Either they must accept the generous terms and abundant safeguards offered for an early entry into the Union, or they must recognize that Responsible Government cannot be entered upon until the Courts have decided upon this Petition of Right put forward by the Company."[22]

The attitudes of the British government and the company deepened the suspicions of the Rhodesian settlers. In the campaign speeches of 1922, the issue on which the settlers were called upon to make a decision was clear-cut: entry into the Union or self-government. General Smuts, the South African prime minister, toured Rhodesia vigorously advocating her entry into the Union. Smut's oratory failed to placate the fears of the Rhodesian settlers, the fear of bilingualism and the fear of political domination by the Boers. "The Rhodesians," wrote Davies, "were very conscious of their numerical inferiority and basically were afraid of being swamped by the much larger South in spite of all promises made to them by General Smuts."[23] In October 1922, the settlers voted for self-government. After the clear demonstration of the settler's sentiments the British government did all in its power to transfer political power to the settlers quickly and with as little friction as possible. The British government agreed to pay the company the sum of £3,750,000 before October 1st, 1923—the date when responsible government was to be introduced. The settlers promised to pay the British government a sum of £2,000,-000 with interest at the rate of 5 percent per year not later than January 1, 1926.[24] In 1923, Rhodesia was annexed as a colony and on October 1 of that year she was granted responsible government. Charles Coghlan became prime minister.

What did the grant of Rhodesian self-government mean to the Africans who, because they had no vote despite the fact that they were the majority, had nothing to say in a decision that affected them so deeply? In answering this question we must first look at the position of the British government on African affairs in Rhodesia before the October referendum of 1922.

The outstanding feature of the correspondence concerning self-government between the Colonial Office and the high commissioner on the one hand and the settlers on the other is the almost total lack of attention paid to the political future of the Africans. In the eyes of both the British government and the settlers the important issue between 1920 and 1922 was whether Rhodesia should be granted self-government or enter the Union. The problem of what would happen to the Africans was secondary. In 1923, Mrs. Jollie wrote: "The days of peril from rebellious natives . . . are over. . . ."[25] This sentiment indicates the prevalent feeling among the settlers who took the Africans for granted. When Lord Buxton, the high commissioner, visited Rhodesia in August 1919, Charles Coghlan, the leader of the Responsible Government party, told him: "As regards the difficulty of the native population we do not regard it as insuperable, but we ask for the same measure of control over the natives as the British South Africa Company has today with the same Imperial safeguards. . . . It is, I think, admitted on all sides, that the British South Africa Company Administration of the natives is good." To which the High Commissioner replied, "I think that is so."[26]

The 1921 Rhodesia Committee agreed that the company's administration had been satisfactory and believed that since the settlers asked to continue African administration on the same lines they should be given the same power that had been enjoyed by the company.[27] In the event the settlers chose self-government the British government would grant it with some limitations of African administration. Clause 41 of the draft constitution reads as follows:

No conditions, disabilities or restrictions which do not equally apply to persons of European descent shall, without the previous consent of the High Commissioner, be imposed upon natives (save in respect to the supply of arms, ammunition and liquor), by any Proclamation, Regulation or other instrument issued under the provisions of any law, unless such conditions, disabilities, or restrictions shall have been explicitly prescribed, defined and limited in such law.[28]

The 1898 Order in Council had contained similar theoretical protection for the Africans. But the political social and economic history of Rhodesia from 1898 until 1921, when the draft constitution was published, was filled with more successful than unsuccessful attempts by the settlers to undermine the position of the Africans as protected in the Order in Council. There was no reason to suggest that the Europeans after 1923 would be any different than they had been since 1898.

The British government, in drafting the Rhodesian Constitution in 1921, was faced by two serious problems, the weak financial position of Rhodesia and the African question. The British government was unwilling to involve itself financially in Rhodesia. The African question—the relationship between a small European population and a large African population—was the more serious long-term problem. In 1922 the British government in order to be relieved of both these problems preferred Rhodesia's entry into the Union. Had Rhodesia entered the Union, the South African government would have taken over Rhodesia's finances; another condition for entry was that the British Government would have given up her responsibility to the Africans in Rhodesia, that is, the administration of African affairs would have come directly under the South African government without any further outside interference from Britain.

Afraid that the political position of the Africans might become worse should Rhodesia enter the Union, the Rev. Arthur Shirley Cripps asked the British government to guarantee and safeguard African rights. In a letter to the colonial secretary, he wrote:

I wish . . . to commend to you at this critical time . . . there are, as I believe, many and grave reasons why over 850,000 Natives should not be handed over unreservedly to the Union's self-

governing Dominion, in case of the Union terms offered prov-
ing sufficiently attractive to our tiny European electorate. . . .
Will not the Colonial Office speak out without delay and let it
be clearly understood that (1) though the Union is free to offer
its own terms, (2) and though Southern Rhodesia is free to
decide on accepting such terms . . . (3) yet [the British
Government guarantee] (A) preservation of Natives' access to
franchise (B) Imperial power to veto on increase of Native
Taxation. . . . (D) Preservation of Natives' right to appeal
effectively to the Crown.[29]

When he received no reply from the Colonial Office, Cripps
wrote to a friend in England, G. H. Tremenheere, a pastor at
Oxford, asking him to contact his local member of Parliament so
that he could raise the question in the House of Commons.
Tremenheere wrote to Hugh Cecil, a member of Parliament,
persuading him to ask a question in the House of Commons to
commit the British government to retain control over African
affairs should Rhodesia enter the Union. Cecil wrote a letter to
Churchill, the colonial secretary: "I presume that the natives are
likely to be ill-treated if they are withdrawn from the protection of
the Imperial Government."[30] Churchill replied: "if [Rhodesia
enters the Union] there is no occasion to apprehend that the
natives will be ill-treated. You will no doubt agree that the
suggestion that Imperial control over native affairs should be
retained even if Southern Rhodesia enters the Union is hardly
practicable."[31]

Only a combination of circumstances kept Britain reluctantly
in theoretical charge of Rhodesia's African affairs. The supporters
of responsible government were opposed to entry not because
they were opposed to the Union's African policy but because they
were afraid of the political domination of the Boers. The white
Nationalists in South Africa, the most rampant racists in the
country, opposed Rhodesia's entry into the Union because they
were afraid of increasing the British population, which would
strengthen the British voice in South African affairs.[32] The
Aborigines Protection Society also opposed Rhodesia's entry into
the Union because Rhodesia outside the Union would still,
theoretically at least, be answerable to Britain for her African
policy. For the society it was a choice between the lesser of two

evils since South Africa's African policy at the time was very harsh and Rhodesia's African policy had not yet been developed or written into law. The society also hoped that the British government's theoretical veto powers might act as a moderating influence.

The question then was, could a British government that actually had sought to liquidate its responsibilities be prepared in the future to intervene on the African's behalf should the rights of the Africans be threatened? The policies pursued by the British toward the Africans during the first two decades of the twentieth century held little promise for the possibilities of intervention on the Africans' behalf. It is not surprising that after 1923 the tone of the laws passed by the Rhodesian Legislature was directed at controlling rather than advancing the Africans. In the so-called "White Man's Countries . . . the maintenance of the position, power, prosperity of the white group will rank above all other considerations, and the welfare and progress of his Black wards will come second—and sometimes a very poor second."[33] The Africans could not trust Charles Coghlan, the first prime minister, a man who in 1908 threatened to lynch Africans who were accused of raping white women if the law did not,[34] and who in 1914 had openly expressed his opposition to enfranchising Africans.

Before 1923, settler representatives had expressed their biased opinion and stereotypes about Africans. Before 1923 the governing body had been the company, which was answerable to the board of directors, who in turn were answerable to the British government. After 1923 the Rhodesian members of Parliament were answerable to the settlers who elected them. If London had any influence on the Rhodesian Parliament at all it was remote; the political fortunes of settler representatives were decided by Rhodesian white opinion. After 1923, settler opinions and conventions were turned into law. Hardly ten years had elapsed before the settler Parliament passed the Land Apportionment Act, which divided the land into two—land for Europeans and land for Africans. "At the outset the policy of the Responsible Government tended towards the adoption of the system of territorial segregation which had been developed in South Africa."[35] The act, which became the backbone of segregation in Rhodesia, was a clear violation of Article 41 of the Rhodesian Constitution. As in the past, however, the British government remained silent.

Dougal Malcolm, a company official, writing in *The Quarterly Review* in January, 1924, observed that the settlers had voted to accept "a constitution which save for a pretended and probably illusory reservation to the Imperial authority of control over native affairs, established local Responsible Government. . . ."[36] In 1923 the settlers emerged triumphant in their struggle against both the British government and the company. They were now practically free to write discrimination into law. And indeed such laws were passed with the silent acquiescence of the British government. Mnyanda in his scathing book, *In Search of Truth*, an indictment against the discriminatory laws passed in Rhodesia after 1923, remarked that after 1923 Africans lost more freedom than they had previously enjoyed. "Ever since responsible government was achieved in Southern Rhodesia," he wrote, "there has been a tendency on the part of the administration to encroach increasingly on the right of the Africans. As a consequence, not only are they less free than they were before, but they also come to depend helplessly on Government. Laws have been enacted which aim at keeping the Africans in a permanent status of inferiority."[37]

NOTES

1. Theodore Bull, ed., *Rhodesian Perspective* (London: Michael Joseph Ltd., 1967), p. 12.

2. Cmd. 1129, Papers Relating to the Commission Appointed to Take an Account of What Would Have Been Due to the British South Africa Company If the Administration of Southern Rhodesia by the Company Had Been Determined on 31st March 1918. Correspondence and Report, 1921, p. 2.

3. Cmd. 1914. Correspondence Regarding a Proposed Settlement of Various Outstanding Questions Relating to the British South Africa Company's Position in Southern and Northern Rhodesia, 1923, p. 2.

4. Annexure No. 1 to British South Africa Company's Meetings April 27, 1922. C. O. 417/689.

5. M.A.G. Davies, *Incorporation in the Union of South Africa or Self-Government: Southern Rhodesia's Choice, 1922* (Pretoria: Communications of the University of South Africa, 1965), p. 14.

6. See Ethel Tawsie Jollie, *The Real Rhodesia* (London: Hutchinson & Co., Paternoster Row, 1924).

7. Ethel Tawsie Jollie, "Trust General Smuts," *The National Review* (October 1922): 306.

8. Iver McIver, "Rhodesia," *The National Review*, (April 1922): 303.

9. Quoted in M.A.G. Davies, *Incorporation in the Union of South Africa*, p. 34.

10. See Robert C. Tredgold, *The Rhodesia That Was My Life* (London: George Allen & Unwin Ltd., 1968), p. 86.

11. Trevor Fletcher, "Rhodesia and the Union," *The Rhodesian Union Association*, 1919, p. 5.

12. Ibid., p. 6.

13. Ibid., p. 7.

14. Cmd. 1129, the Cave Commission, 1919, p. 2.

15. Cmd. 1273, First Report of a Committee Appointed by the Secretary for Colonies to Consider Certain Questions Relating to Rhodesia, 1921, p. 2. The total number of registered voters was 11,098.

16. Ibid., p. 5.

17. Ibid., p. 5.

18. *The Bulawayo Chronicle*, January 21, 1922, p. 4.

19. Ibid., p. 4.

20. Ethel Tawsie Jollie, "Trust General Smuts," *The National Review* (October, 1922): 310.

21. C. O. 417/689.

22. *The Bulawayo Chronicle*, August 21, 1922, p. 1.

23. M.A.G. Davies, *Incorporation in the Union of South Africa*, p. 36.

24. *The Bulawayo Chronicle*, July 14, 1923.

25. Jollie, *The Real Rhodesia*, p. 8.

26. C. O. 417/622, 1919.

27. Cmd. 1273, First Report of a Committee, 1921, p. 13.

28. Winston Churchill to High Commissioner, Prince Arthur of Connaught, December 22, 1921. Cmd. 1573, p. 15.

29. Cripps to Colonial Secretary March 11, 1922. C. O. 417/691.

30. Cecil to Churchill, April 7, 1922, ibid.

31. Churchill to Cecil, April 26, 1922, ibid.

32. *The Bulawayo Chronicle*, February 26, 1921, p. 1.

33. R. F. Alfred Hoernle, "The Relationship Between Black and White," *The African Observer* (May–October, 1934): 14.

34. *The Bulawyao Chronicle*, March 5, 1909.

35. Malcom Hailey, *An African Survey: A Study of Problems Arising in Africa South of the Sahara* rev. ed. (London: University Press, 1957), p. 439.

36. Dougal Malcolm, "The British South Africa Company," *The Quarterly Review* no. 478 (January 1924): 89.

37. B. S. Mnyanda *In Search of Truth: A Commentary on Certain Aspects of Southern Rhodesia's Native Policy* (Bombay: Hind Kitab's Ltd., 1954), p. 4.

12
Conclusion

When Rhodesia was occupied in 1890, the British government hoped to use both the settlers and the Company to achieve its overall policies in South Africa, that is, to retain British preponderance. This was the main reason why Britain limited its role as protector of African rights. To have come out openly and strongly in defense of African rights would have aroused opposition among the whites in Rhodesia and in South Africa.

After 1910 if Rhodesia were to join the Union, as the British government wished, she could not do so under Company rule. Before she could enter the Union, Rhodesia had to have the same political status as the other four provinces, namely self-government. Hence whenever a change of government was discussed the voice of the settlers was more important and decisive than that of the company.

The ideals of British policy toward the Africans in Southern Rhodesia beginning in 1890 were clearly stipulated in the Royal Charter of 1889. The charter, the document that empowered the company to carry on its economic activities, affirmed in no uncertain terms the prior political rights of Lobengula and therefore of the Africans. The British government had the power to revoke the charter if the company strayed from its important provisions. During the first eight years of its operations, the company literally ignored the provisions of the charter. It provoked the Matebele to fight in 1893, and in 1896–97 the Africans in Rhodesia fought to liquidate its rule. And yet, the British government did not revoke the charter, or even condemn the company's actions that had violated the 1889 Charter's provisions and had caused the fighting. In 1898 the British government

213

passed an Order in Council which recognized the company as the governing power in Rhodesia. By the high commissioner's Proclamation of 1899, the British government further strengthened the company's hand in dealing with the Africans by empowering the administrator to appoint or dismiss African chiefs.

The year of 1898 saw a total surrender of initiative by the British government to the company and to the settlers. Commenting on the company's disregard of the charter's provisions, Lord Olivier wrote: "The Company from the outset entirely ignored this injunction. . . . The Colonial Office acquiesced, hypnotized by the aura of the impeccable personages whose figures decked the Company's office window, and an Order in Council of 1898 ignored all existing rights. . . ."[1] The 1898 Ordinance gave the settlers a say in the running of the country. The company was given the power to establish African reserves, which were used to prevent African economic and political progress. Even Lewis Gann, an apologist for the company, has admitted: "Chartered Company theoreticians, for economic and ideological reasons, opposed the idea of building up or strengthening native institutions in any form."[2]

The setting up of reserves and a "well organized Native Department" have been praised as some of the major achievements of the company's African administration.[3] Indeed, these were major achievements; but we should ask why were they set up—what did these institutions intend to achieve? The Native Department was reorganized after the 1896–97 Chimurenga, which took the company officials by surprise; they had not anticipated the war because they did not know what the Africans were thinking. Further African revolt would have greatly endangered the company's future. Therefore, to prevent further revolts and to protect the image of the company, the Native Department was reformed to keep the administration informed on what the Africans thought or intended to do. And whenever African grievances were found, something should be done about them. Africans' grievances were sometimes relieved, not because the company at heart cared for the welfare of the people but because it primarily feared the consequences of not "caring." Whenever the company found chiefs difficult to deal with it dismissed them.

The evidence that the chiefs presented to the 1914 Reserves

Commission indicated that they were dissatisfied with the reserves as they were constituted, but the Commission, by its own admission, ignored the evidence. As far as the company was concerned, the reserves were primarily centers of control. Reserves were places where Africans would live under their own tribal institutions but under the ever watchful eye of a native commissioner. In the reserves, Africans could not compete economically with the Europeans. And because transportation and educational facilities were poor, the Africans in the reserves could not meet the educational and financial qualifications of the franchise. Thus, politically, the reserves denied the Africans a role in the running of the country.

The reserves unfortunately also introduced the principle of discrimination. Writing about the 1898 Ordinance and the power given to the company to establish reserves, Olivier said: "This was interpreted solely as a direction to establish Native Reserves into which the native were to be penned: thus laying the foundation of the principle of segregation."[4]

Debates in the Legislative Assembly in the period from 1900 to 1923 showed that Europeans were opposed to liberal education for the Africans. In 1907 the Africans paid £190,000 in taxes, and of this amount only £1,500 was spent on African education[5] Europeans feared that Africans might clamor for the same social, economic, and political privileges that were enjoyed by the Europeans. In 1920, H. S. Keigwin, a former native commissioner, suggested that Africans should not receive the kind of education that could make them challenge the European's dominant position.[6]

Some historians have claimed that Africans benefited enormously under company rule. Gann and Duignan pointed out in *Burden of Empire* that Matebele warriors under the company became wage-earning laborers who could clothe themselves in European dress. The Shona were saved from annihilation by the Matebele. Both tribes, as a result of European conquest, were liberated from the despotism of tribal authority and their life in general improved.

Gann and Duigan also tell us that the Matebele, prior to the coming of the Europeans, could become renowned warriors, could accumulate wealth by plunder, or acquire many wives.

But these achievements exhausted the limits of his choice. . . .
It is our contention that imperial rule helped to bring about
major social, economic and ideological changes which in turn
vastly extended social opportunity. The Matebele warriors'
modern descendants can make a living as a teacher, a trader . . .
a farmer or a tailor: This advance was not only relative, but
absolute. It was made possible by a great cultural transfusion in
which the West took the leading part.

However, Gann and Duignan do not tell us what the Africans
thought of Western civilization. Above all, they do not acknowledge under what terms the Europeans imposed their civilization
on the Africans. The Africans had no alternative; they were
headed into the reserves and were required to carry passes in the
cities. Taxes were imposed on the Africans to force them to work
for the Europeans. It is difficult to accept the assertion by Gann
and Duignan that the advancement made by the Africans was
absolute. Racial discrimination in Southern Rhodesia frustrated
this "advancement."

Unfortunately, these views were advanced primarily to justify
the social order that was imposed on the Africans since the
European conquest in Rhodesia. The primary task of the historian
should be to tell what really happened and why it happened. No
reasonable historian or commentator of Rhodesian events between 1898 and 1923, or after, would refuse to admit that European conquest significantly altered the African's life. Two very
important qualifications should, however, be made. How did this
change come about? and why? Perhaps one should also ask, and
this is crucial, what did the Africans themselves think of the
changes? And, in addition, what have been the long-term results
of settlerism in Rhodesia?

The answer to these questions forms an adequate evaluation
not only of British policy toward the Africans between 1898 and
1923 but also of the company's African administration during the
same period. The changes forced upon the Africans through the
1893 War and the 1896–97 Chimurenga were institutionalized
through the reserves; the labor, education, and political policies
of the Company; and the settlers.

The franchise qualifications were so high that they practically
excluded the Africans from playing an effective role in the

country. In 1903 there were 5,199 European voters and only 51 African voters.[9] And yet in 1912, the franchise qualifications were raised. In 1922 out of a total of 18,810 voters, only 60 were Africans.[10]

From 1907 onward the voice of the settlers became increasingly important in determining the future economic and political development of the country. In 1909, the settlers voted against entry into the Union, and in 1914 they voted to extend company rule for another ten years. In 1914 the elected members of the Legislative Assembly unanimously voted on a resolution to challenge the company's claim to ownership of the alienated lands before the Privy Council. The company lost the case in 1918. And finally in 1923, the settlers rejected entry into the Union and voted for self-government with the same powers over African affairs as had been exercised by the company.[11]

In 1923 both the new African leadership that was just emerging in the towns and the traditional leadership, as evidenced by their complaints, rejected the state of affairs in which they, as Africans as opposed to the Europeans, saw themselves on the eve of the granting of self-government. The traditional leadership unrealistically preferred the restoration of the past. The new leadership looked to the future when they hoped the gates to the social, economic, and political process that were then closed to them would be open.

We are now in a position to radically qualify Gann's and Duignan's views; that is, changes did occur in the African way of life, but these changes were not the direct result of policies clearly formulated in advance but rather changes intended by force and in some cases by reform to arrest the economic and political advancement that would have resulted from the African's contact with the Europeans.

Before further evaluating Gann's, Duignan's, or Mason's conclusions about the results of European settlement in Rhodesia, it would be useful to discuss briefly the theory of the Africanization of African history, which is gaining popularity among young African historians today. In the introduction to *Revolt in Southern Rhodesia 1896–97*, Ranger wrote that he thought that it was very important for Africans to write about their own experience, in short, their own history. Africanization of African history means above all, honestly recording what happened in and to African society but emphasizing the initiatives, reactions, and resistance of the African people to European encroachment on their traditional institutions. What was decided in London or Cape Town or in the settler assembly in Salisbury is important only insofar as it shows the factors at play in the evolution of traditional African society. African history does not begin with European colonization of Rhodesia. Colonization may have greatly changed the course of African society, but it did not, as the history of independent Africa clearly shows, destroy or alter the basic fabric of African traditional life (social customs, communal tendencies, and the like) at least for the majority of Africans living in the rural areas. Since history records change, the historian of African society must primarily be concerned with the fundamental and not superficial changes that took place in that society. The historian should also faithfully record the factors that were responsible for the changes, such as European colonization, wars, slavery, and the rise and fall in economic production.

The preceding paragraph is a criticism of most European historians of Rhodesia and Africa, whose emphasis is upon what the Europeans decided and upon what they hoped their decisions would mean to the Africans, and not upon what those decisions actually meant. Gann and Duignan say that colonization brought Western dress to the Africans, but the important consideration should be what basically happened to the African way of life in Rhodesia after 1890. Did the Africans lose anything? If so, what? and was their loss compensated by whatever they gained (clothes, education, and so on) from their contact with the Europeans? And above all, what did the Africans of the time and their descendants think about the changes that occurred in their society?

In 1896–97, the Africans of Rhodesia fought to regain their freedom. I have documented the refusal of the old African leadership to accept the loss of their way of life. The new African leadership rejected settlerism as well, which basically means oppression and segregation and rule by foreigners. The Africans, then, lost their freedom.

Anyone who argues that European colonization freed the Africans from tribal dictatorship makes the mistaken assumption that the chief in traditional society was a dictator. Gann, who explicitly stated his dislike of tribal society, also believes that Western imperialism was on the whole good for the Africans. Of the dissolution of the British Empire, Gann has written, "I derive no satisfaction from its demise." And of the Rhodesian settlers, Gann says " . . . as a European, I am sympathetic to (them) and their problems; this attachment has been reinforced by long residence in the country."[12] Gann is also projecting his own attitudes and views of society, which may not be the best for African society. Why would anyone fight for his own way of life if he does not like it? That the young after the conquest of their society went to work for the Europeans or to school was the result of direct or indirect European pressure. Cornelius De Kiewiet, the historian wrote: "To labour was to learn. How could savages better acquaint themselves with white civilization than by becoming its apprentices? Within the tribe they could only remain the prisoner of their own primitive habits. The more completely they were withdrawn by holy ennobling labour from the influence of chiefs and witchdoctors, the swifter would be their emencipation."[13] But the "dictatorship" of the chiefs was replaced by another dictatorship that was more real and terrible under the banner of Christian civilization. De Kiewiet confessed: "The process of European colonization was not a process that enlightened the natives, or emancipated them or enriched them. The . . . land-hungry Europeans turned the bulk of the natives into a proletariat, governed by laws that bound rather than unloosed, that restricted their liberties rather than widened their opportunities."[14]

In addition to the loss of their freedom, the Africans lost their land, the mainstay of their economic activity. Under European occupation, the area the Africans cultivated was greatly and unproportionately reduced.

These then are the major results of European settlement in Rhodesia. What the Africans gained from European settlement, such as education and the building of roads and hospitals, was minimal in comparison. And even these services were neglected and grudgingly given by the new dictators.

The question as Gann and Duigan raise it is one of priorities, whether "equality now" as an absolute, as the Africans argue, or not, as the settlers maintain.[15] Conservatives argue that time is necessary for Africans to learn technical skills and "principles of democracy," but the history of Southern Rhodesia shows that time itself was used to keep the Africans of Rhodesia from the economic, social, and political mainstream of the country.

We may conclude from the foregoing that perhaps the most important result of the contact between the whites and the blacks in Rhodesia is not that some blacks have white-collar jobs, but rather the challenge of the entrenched European position by the African. Throughout Rhodesian history, beginning in 1890, it is this challenge that is central to an understanding of company administration African policies and after 1923 settler African policies. Since 1965, this challenge has errupted into guerilla war.

To regulate white-black relations in Rhodesia, Britain, after 1898, adopted a policy of restraint. The policy failed. The British decision makers were six thousand miles away and therefore were not accurately informed about what was going on in Southern Rhodesia. But this book was written primarily on the materials that were found in the Public Record Office—which materials had passed through the various levels of British decision makers. British policies then can be explained by Britain's attitude to South Africa and the policies she advocated there, and by her acquiescence to the pressure of the settlers. Furthermore, the British government advocated outright racial policies. Milner did not want whites to do menial work, which he believed should be done by Africans.[16] His political policies called for the racial domination of the Boers by the British and of the blacks by the whites. When, in 1906, the Rhodesian administration proposed a bill to prevent more Africans from getting the franchise, Selbourne, the high commissioner, did not object, but to avoid the colonial secretary's disapproval, he advised Milton: "This cannot very well be stated. The ostensible object therefore must be something quite different but at the same time plausible. There must not be anything either in the official correspondence or in Council debates, any hint of a disability on natives if you want to avoid bringing Exeter Hall on your backs."[17] The colonial secretary allowed the qualifications to be raised. The British liberals hoped to secure an enlightened policy toward the Africans in Rhodesia not through direct involvement but through influence.

The situation was not helped by the conspicuous silence of the missionaries in Southern Rhodesia. Missionaries are usually the voice of conscience in a society. In Rhodesia, only Rev. Arthur S. Cripps and Rev. John White fought unceasingly for the rights of the Africans. The missionaries had a very slight foothold in Rhodesia before 1897. After that time their efforts were dependent on the company. They received land grants from the company—and in the case of trouble they looked to the company for protection. In the kraal schools the company required the missionaries to teach discipline and obedience. The missionaries themselves, knowing little about African culture, despised the African way of life. To convert Africans, the missionaries also tried to change totally the African's way of life—hence they had little sympathy with the African's resistance to European encroachment upon his institutions.

On the whole, the missionaries were agreed that Africans were, at the time, not ready to take part in the governing process of the country. In the missionaries' annual conferences, which began in 1906, the main items on the agenda were concerned with the problems of beer drinking among the Africans, lobola, polygamy, and the conversion of Africans to Christianity.

In 1922 the missionaries passed ineffective resolutions by which they hoped to protect African interests after Rhodesia gained self-government. At the 1922 conference, the Rev. John White, in a paper entitled "A Dumb People," proposed that African advisory councils be set up which eventually would elect Europeans to represent them (Africans) in the Legislative Assembly.[18] He also proposed that nominations of council members should be done by the high commissioner because, as he believed, Africans were still too immature to be trusted with the elections of their own councillors to select European representatives. But in 1924, White changed his mind and proposed that "two Europeans nominated by the Crown could directly represent these [African] politically dumb people in the Parliament of the Colony."[19] Cripps suggested that before the appointment of the two European representatives, the secretary of the (1924) Missionary Conference be appointed "parliamentary business secretary for Conference, to watch native interest . . . "[20] In 1922 as in 1924, White's and Cripp's proposals were unanimously adopted without debate; nothing, however, came out of these suggestions.

In 1925 the various missionary bodies in Rhodesia gave evidence before the Native Education Committee of Enquiry. All the missionary groups, with the exception of the American Methodists, said nothing about their role in the political development of the Africans. The American Methodists explained their educational goals when they said: "A large part of (their) educational work is to train and educate Natives to take the proper place they must take in the political body. The aim would be training Natives to fit them to get the franchise and to take part in the administration of the country. . . . We teach them civics and methods of self-government, and have always done so."[21]

The missionaries themselves practiced discrimination. African ministers of religion were not given the same pay as their European counterparts and Sunday services in the towns were segregated. The voices of conscience could not, without exposing themselves as hypocrites, attack the social segregation that was practiced by the settlers. The missionary Conference in 1925 regretted that the missionaries had done very little to protect Africans' rights. Then, because of the violent manner in which Europeans had expropriated African land, the social conflict, and the miscarriage of justice whenever Africans and Europeans were involved in criminal cases, the missionaries tragically supported segregation of the races as a solution. A few quotations from Father Cotton show the misguided missionary reasoning in favor of segregation as a solution to the race problem. Father Cotton, who had lived in South Africa, was an Anglican priest at St. Augustine's Mission in Southern Rhodesia. His book, *The Race Problem in South Africa*, was a search for a solution to the black-white problem in both Rhodesia and South Africa. Father Cotton observed that the Europeans feared that "were the blacks given the franchise on the same terms as the whites, they would dominate the country; and that if they were allowed unrestricted admittance to skilled grades of labour they would oust the Whites."[22] According to Father Cotton, there were two alternatives to the race problem. "One is a territorial segregation that gives also an economic severence. And the other is race assimilation, race blending, and fusion."[23] Father Cotton condemned the harsh European policies toward the Africans and he denounced land expropriation. But if the Africans came to power might they not do the same to the Europeans? Father Cotton's solution was "that the white and black races segregate themselves from one another and separate in peace."[24] Because of the inability of the whites to live without exploiting the blacks, which blacks were also capable of if they came to power, Father Cotton advised that "the dream of a single great dominion, extending from the Cape to the Zambezi, would have to be abandoned."[25] He concluded that segregation would be "a bold stroke of statesmanship, a high call to sacrifice for an intelligible and not ignoble end, this only has hope of success."[29]

Another pressure group on the British government, the Anti-Slavery and Aborigines Protection Society, needs special mention. The society bravely and loudly fought for the rights of the African people of Southern Rhodesia. But the society was considered too radical in Britain, and it no longer enjoyed the influence that the evangelical movement had had in the 1820s and 1830s. In its arguments on behalf of African rights in Rhodesia, the society often appealed to universal principles of justice that made little impression on the British decision makers who thought that the problems in Rhodesia were not universal but were unique. But Harris, among others, correctly predicted that the Rhodesian problem, further aggravated by giving a handful of Europeans responsible government, would seriously shake the future of the British Commonwealth.

In 1923 the well-organized and vociferous settlers emerged triumphant over both the company and the British government as well as the moral opposition of Cripps and the Anti-Slavery and Aborigines Protection Society. After the decision of the settlers, as far as the British government was concerned, there was no alternative to self-government, particularly since the political voice of the Africans was not loud and strong enough to oppose the establishment of the new order. The officials in London hoped and believed that by drafting a constitution that theoretically guaranteed equality to all people, they could somehow contain settler ambitions. The settlers, on the other hand, accepted the constitution because in it they saw practical inequality. And hardly had ten years elapsed when this inequality was put into law by the enactment of the Land Apportionment Act in 1930, which unproportionately divided all the land in Southern Rhodesia into land for the exclusive use of the Europeans and land exclusively for African use.[27] The act is the backbone of racial discrimination in Rhodesia. Under the act, Africans are excluded from owning businesses and from trading in the rich Europeans areas. The act legalized residential discrimination against the Africans, and prevented the Africans from exercising a basic fundamental right enjoyed by most free people in the world, the right to live and work freely where they liked in the land of their birth, a right that had been guaranteed by the 1922 Constitution. The act can be seen as the climax and logical outcome of the rise of settler power.

NOTES

1. Lord Olivier, "Native Land Rights in Rhodesia," *The Contemporary Review*, no. 728 (August, 1926): 147.

2. L. H. Gann, *A History of Southern Rhodesia: Early Days to 1934* (London: Chatto & Windus, 1965), p. 148.

3. Cmd. 1273, *The Rhodesia Committee*, p. 13.

4. Lord Olivier, "Native Land Rights in Rhodesia," pp. 147–48.

5. Southern Rhodesia Debates, May 10, 1907, pp. 56–57.

6. Report by H. S. Keigwin, On the Suggested Industrial Development of Natives, 1920, p. 5.

7. L. H. Gann and P. Duignan, *Burden of Empire: Appraisal of Western Colonialism in Africa South of the Sahara* (New York: Frederick A. Praeger, 1967), p. vii.

8. Ibid., p. vii P. Mason in his book, *The Birth of a Dilemma: The Conquest and Settlement of Rhodesia* (London: Oxford University Press, 1958) expresses a somewhat similar view.

9. Cd. 2399, 1905, p. 65.

10. Proceedings of the Southern Rhodesia Missionary Conference July 5 to July 8, 1923, p. 24.

11. In 1919, in a petition ignored by the British government, Nyamanda asked the British government to take over control of African affairs should Rhodesia be granted self-government. C.O. 417/617, 1919.

12. Lewis H. Gann, *Central Africa: The Former British States* (Englewood Cliffs, N.J.: Prentice Hall Inc., 1971), p. ix.

13. Cornelius De Kiewiet, *A History of South Africa: Social and Economic* (Oxford: The Clarendan Press, 1941), p. 85.

14. Cornelius De Kiewiet, *The Imperial Factor in South Africa: A Study in Politics and Economics* (Cambridge: University Press, 1937), p. 3.

15. See L. H. Gann and P. Duignan, *White Settlers in Tropical Africa* (London: C. Nicholls & Company Ltd., 1962), chap. 4.

16. C.O. 417/391, 1904. Also see C. Headlam, ed., *The Milner Papers, 1897–1899* (London: Cassell & Company, Ltd., 1921), vol. 2, p. 459.

17. Lord Selbourne to Sir H. W. Milton: February 22, 1907. Quoted in Gann, *A History of Southern Rhodesia, Early Days to 1934*, p. 224.

18. Proceedings of the Southern Rhodesia Missionary Conference, July 5–July 8, 1922, p. 24.

19. Proceedings of the Southern Rhodesia Missionary Conference, May 30–June 4, 1924, p. 9.

20. Ibid., p. 9.

21. Southern Rhodesia: Report of the Commission Appointed to Enquire into the Matters of Native Education in all Its Bearings in the Colony of Southern Rhodesia, 1925, p. 35.

22. Walter Aidan Cotton, *The Race Problem in South Africa* Edinburgh: Turnbull & Spears, 1926), p. 5. In 1921, the Rhodesia Committee, Cmd. 1273 wrote, "The existing Franchise . . . is a high one. We propose that the franchise should remain as at present, but that the Legislative Assembly should have unrestricted power to alter if they so desired," p. 8. And whenever the settlers have felt threatened by more Africans meeting the franchise qualifications, they have altered them. See A. J. Hanna, p. 171, where he shows that in 1912 and 1951 the franchise qualifications *The Story of the Rhodesians and Nyasaland* (London: Faber and Faber, Ltd., 1960), were raised.

23. Ibid., p. 23.

24. Ibid., p. 115.

25. Ibid., p. 118.

26. Ibid., p. 122.

27. The 1930 Land Apportionment Act has subsequently been repealed. But it has been replaced by a similar act with similar restrictions, the Land-Tenure Act passed in 1969. And although the Land Tenure Act has now been abolished only very few Africans can afford to live and do business in areas previously set aside for Europeans only.

Bibliography

OFFICIAL SOURCES

A: BRITISH

Appeal Cases, 1919 Law Reports.

A. C. 1919 *Law Reports: Appeal Cases.*

Public Record Office
Resident and High Commissioner's Despatches C.O. 879/484, 1894.
C.O. 417/168, 1896–C. O. 417/691, 1922.

Command Papers
1888, C. 5363. "Further Correspondence Respecting the Affairs of Bechuanaland and Adjacent Territories."

1888, C. 5524. "Further Correspondence Respecting the Affairs of Bechaunaland and Adjacent Territories."

1892, C. 6645. "Ordinances made by the British South Africa Company."

1893, 7171. "Copies and Extracts of Correspondence Relating to the British South Africa Company in Mashonaland and Matebeleland."

1893, C. 7284. "Correspondence Respecting the Death at Tati of Two Indunas in October, 1893."

1893, C. 7290. "Papers Relating to the Administration of Matebeleland and Mashonaland."

1894, C. 7555. "Report by Mr. F. J. Newton, C.M.G., upon the Circumstances Connected with the Collision between the Matebele and the Forces of the British South Africa Company at Fort Victoria in July, 1893, and the Correspondence Connected Therewith."

1896, C. 8060. "Instructions Issued to Colonel Sir R.E.R. Martin, Relative to the Control of Armed Forces in the Territories of the

British South Africa Company, and His Future Position There; Instructions Issued to Major General Sir Frederick Carrington, Relative to the Military Operations Against the Matebele; with Copy of Despatch to Sir Hercules Robinson on These Subjects."

1896, C. 8130. "Report of the Land Commission of 1894, and Correspondence Relating Thereto."

1897, C. 8547. "Report by Sir R.E.R. Martin, F.C.M.G., on the Native Administration of the British South Africa Company, with a letter from the Company Commenting on the Report."

1898, C. 8732. "Correspondence Relating to the Proposed Changes in the Administration of the British South Africa Company."

1898, C. 8773, "I. Charter of the British South Africa Company; II. Order in Council, May 9, 1891; III. Order in Council, June 18, 1894."

1899, C. 9138. "Papers Relating to the British South Africa Company: I. Southern Rhodesia Order in Council, dated 20th October 1898; II. Proclamation, dated 25th November, 1898, Promulgating Native Regulations for Southern Rhodesia; III. Proclamation dated 25th November, 1898, Making Provision for an Electoral System in Southern Rhodesia; IV: Draft of Supplemental Charter of the British South Africa Company."

1902, Cd. 1200. "Correspondence Relating to the Regulations and Supply of Labour in Southern Rhodesia."

1904, Cd. 2028. "Correspondence Relating to the Proposed Introduction of Indentured Asiatic (Chinese) Labour into Southern Rhodesia."

1904-5, Cd. 2684. "Colonial Reports. No. 472. British Central Africa Protectorate."

1905 Cd. 2399. "Report of the South African Native Affairs Commission, 1903-1905."

1905-6, Cd. 2684. "Colonial Reports. No. 499. British Central Africa Protectorate."

1906-7, Cd. 3729. "Colonial Reports. No. 537. British Central Africa Protectorate."

1914, Cd. 7262. "Correspondence (between Sir Starr Jameson of the British South Africa Company, and the Colonial office) Re-lating to the Constitution of Southern Rhodesia."

1914, Cd. 7509. "Papers Relating to a Reference to the Judicial Committee of the Privy Council on the Question of the Ownership of Land in Southern Rhodesia."

1914–1916, Cd. 7645. "Correspondence Relating to the Continuance of the Administrative Provisions of the Charter of the British South Africa Company (with copies of the Charters of 1889 and 1900)."

1914–1916, Cd. 7970. "Supplementary Charter to the British South Africa Company, dated 13th March, 1915."

1917–1918, Cd. 8694. "Papers Relating to the Southern Rhodesia Native Reserves Commission, 1915."

1920, Cmd. 547. "Correspondence with the Anti-Slavery and Aborigines Protection Society Relating to the Native Reserves in Southern Rhodesia."

1920 Cmd. 1042. "The Despatch to the High Commissioner for South Africa Transmitting the Order of His Majesty in Council, dated 9th November, 1920 Relative to Native Reserves in Southern Rhodesia."

1921, Cmd. 1129. "Papers Relating to the Commission Appointed to Take an Account of What Would Have Been Due to the British South Africa Company If the Administration of Southern Rhodesia by the Company Had Been Determined on 31st March, 1918. Correspondence and Reports."

1921, Cmd. 1273. "First Report of a Committee Appointed by the Secretary of State for Colonies to Consider Certain Questions Relating to Rhodesia."

1921, Cmd. 1471. "Second Report of the Committee Appointed by the Secretary of State for Colonies to Consider Certain Questions Relating to Rhodesia."

1922, Cmd. 1573. "Despatch to the High Commissioner for South Africa Transmitting Draft Letters Patent Providing for the Constitution of Responsible Government in the Colony of Southern Rhodesia, and Other Draft Instruments Connected Therewith."

1923, Cmd. 1914. "Correspondence Regarding a Proposed Settlement of Various Outstanding Questions Relating to the British South Africa Company's Position in Southern and Northern Rhodesia."

1923, Cmd. 1984. "Agreement between the Secretary of State for the Colonies and the British South Africa Company for the Settlement of Outstanding Questions Relating to Northern and Southern Rhodesia, dated 29th November, 1923."

B: SOUTHERN RHODESIA DOCUMENTS

Legislative Council Debates, 1898–1923.

Reports of the Chief Native Commissioner, Mashonaland, 1903–1912.

Reports of the Chief Native Commissioner, Matabeleland, 1903-1912.

Reports of the Chief Native Commissioner, Southern Rhodesia, 1913-1923.

Reports of the Inspector of Native Compounds, 1903-1922.

Reports of the Labour Board of Southern Rhodesia, 1901.

Reports of the Rhodesian Native Labour Bureau, 1904-1919.

Report of the Native Labour Enquiry Committee, 1906.

Report of the Committee Appointed to Enquire into the Prevalence and Prevention of Scurvy and Pneumonia amongst Native Labourers, 1910.

Reports of the Director of Agriculture, 1910-1919.

Report of the Native Affairs Committee of Enquiry, 1910-11.

Report by H. S. Keigwin, Esq., Native Commissioner, on the Suggested Industrial Development of Natives, 1920.

Report of the Commission Appointed to Enquire into the Matters of Native Education in all Its Bearings in the Colony of Southern Rhodesia, 1925.

C: COMPANY REPORTS AND MEMORANDA

The British South Africa Company

Reports of the Administration of Rhodesia. London, 1897-1902.

Reports on the Company Proceedings and the Conditions of Its Territories within the Sphere of its Operations. London, 1889-1907.

The Guide to South Africa for the Use of Tourists, Sportsmen, Invalids and Settlers. London, 1900-1923.

Memorandum Containing Notes and Information Concerning Land Policy. (H. Wilson Fox) London, 1912.

Memorandum on Position, Policy and Prospects of the Company. London, 1907.

Memorandum upon Land Settlement in Rhodesia with Accompanying Papers and Maps. London, 1913.

UNPUBLISHED MATERIALS

Fage, J. D. "The Achievement of Self-government in Southern; Rhodesia; 1893-1923, dissertation, "Cambridge University Ph. D, 1949."

Kapenzi, Geoffrey Zvirikunzeno. "A Study of the Strategies and Methods Used by the American Methodist Missionary Society in its Religious Education Program from 1898-1967." D.Ed. diss., Boston University, 1970.

Lee, M. E. "The Abrogation of the Charter Movement in South Rhodesia, 1898-1907." Henderson Seminar no. 16, November 6, 1971.

Matipano, Francis P. "A History of the Matabeles' Diplomatic Relations with the White Concessionaires and Treaty Seekers, 1836-1900" Ph.D. dissertation, Howard University, 1978.

McGregor, R. "Native Segregation in Southern Rhodesia, a study of Social Policy." dissertation, London University, Ph.D., 1940.

Morris, Guy W. *The Making of Rhodesia*. Oxford University Prize, Beit Thesis, 1910.

Moyana, Henry V. "Land Apportionment in Rhodesia 1920-1960" Ph.D. dissertation, Columbia University, 1975.

Mutambirwa, James Alfred. "Rhodes and the British Conquest of Rhodesia: 1888-1896." M.A. thesis, Columbia University, 1967.

Palmer, Robin Henry. "The Making and Implementation of Land Policy in Rhodesia: 1890-1936." Ph.D. dissertation, London University, 1968.

Touzalin, Charlotte Maurice. "The Rise of the Empire Builders: 1870-1899." M.A. thesis, Columbia University, 1921.

PUBLISHED MATERIALS (PRIMARY SOURCES)

Barklie, John. *The Title Tangle in Southern Rhodesia*. Bulawayo: The Central Executive Committee of the Rhodesian League, 1913.

Battaliou, H. A. *Political Letters on the South African Situation*. Cape Town: A. E. Heyer, 1900.

Boyd, Charles W., ed. *Mr. Chamberlain's Speeches*. 2 vols. London: Constable and Company Ltd., 1914.

Brown, William Harvey. *On the South African Frontier*. London: Sampson Low, Marston & Company Ltd., 1899.

Bryce, James. *Impressions of South Africa*. 3rd ed. London: Macmillan and Co., Ltd., 1899.

Chamberlain, Joseph. *Foreign and Colonial Speeches*. London: George Routledge & Sons Ltd., 1897.

Colquhoun, Archibald R. *The Africander Land*. New York: E. P. Dutton and Company, 1906.

Eybers, G. W., ed. *Select Constitutional Documents Illustrating South African History: 1795-1910.* London: George Routledge & Sons., Ltd., 1918.

Fletcher, Trevor. "Rhodesia and the Union." *The Rhodesia Union Association.* Salisbury: 1919.

Harris, John H. *The Greatest Land Case in British History: The Struggle for Native Rights in Rhodesia Before the Judicial Committee of His Majesty's Privy Council.* London: The Anti-Slavery and Aboriginies Protection Society, 1918.

Headlam, C., ed. *The Milner Papers. 1897-1905.* 2 vols. London: Cassell & Co. Ltd., 1931-1933.

Mashonaland Progressive Association. *Rhodesia and Federation.* Salisbury, Rhodesia: Art Printing Works, 1907.

Onslow-Carleton, W. M. *Land Settlement Scheme for the Matebele.* Cape Town, South Africa: Townshend, Taylor & Snashall, 1910.

Scott, Leslie. *The Struggle for Native Rights in Rhodesia: Extracts from the Argument of Mr. Leslie Scott before the Judicial Committee of the Privy Council April 16 to May 2, 1918.* London: The Anti-Slavery and Aborigines Protection Society, 1918.

Thomson J. Mudie. *Political Reorganization: A Study Towards Self-Government,* Balawayo, Rhodesia: Rhodesia Review Co., Ltd., 1898.

Vindex, ed. *Speeches of Cecil Rhodes.* London: Chapman and Hall, Ltd., 1900.

Wise, C. D. *The British South Africa Company: Report on Land Settlement in Southern Rhodesia.* London: Waterlow & Sons Ltd., 1906.

CONTEMPORARY PERIODICALS

African Advance (American Methodist Quarterly Journal), 1916-1919.

African Commerce, 1901.

NADA (Native Affairs Department Annual), 1920-1926.

Proceedings of the Southern Rhodesia Missionary Conference. 1915-1924.

Rhodesia Agricultural Union, 1905-1919.

Rhodesia Missionary Advocate (American Methodist Quarterly Journal), 1909-1914.

Southern Rhodesia Quarterly Paper (Anglican) 1916-1923.

The Rhodesian Journal, 1903-1923.

CONTEMPORARY NEWSPAPERS (ALL WEEKLY EDITIONS)

Bulawayo Observer	1902-1910
Gwelo Times	1914-1923
Rhodesia Times	1902-1906
The Bulawayo Chronicle	1895-1923
The Rhodesia Herald	1895-1923

GENERAL WORKS

Amery, L. S., ed. *The Times History of the War in South Africa.* London: Sampson Low, Marston and Co., 1900-1909.

Anonymous. *The Matabele-Scandal.* Cambridge, 1894.

Arrighi, G. *The Political Economy of Rhodesia.* The Hague: Mouton & Co., 1967.

Barnes, Leonard. *The Duty of Empire.* London: Victor Gollancz Ltd., 1935.

———. "Skeleton of Empire." *Fact* (June 1937).

———. *Empire or Democracy? A Study of the Colonial Question.* London: Victor Gollancz Ltd., 1939.

Benson, W. "The African Labourer." *The Nineteenth Century and After: 1877-1930* 108, no. 641 (July 1930).

Blake, Robert. *A History of Rhodesia.* New York: Alfred A. Knopf, 1978.

Boggie, A. *From Ox-Wagon to Railway: Being a Brief History of Rhodesia and the Matebele Nation.* Bulawayo, Rhodesia 1897.

Brand, R. H. *The Union of South Africa.* London: The Clarendon Press, 1909.

Bryant, Margaret, ed. *The Colonial Problem. A Report by a Study Group of Members of the Royal Institute of International Affairs.* London: Oxford University Press, 1937.

Buell, Raymond Leslie. *The Native Problem in Africa.* 2 vols. New York: The Macmillan Company, 1928.

Bull, Theodore, ed. *Rhodesian Perspective.* London: Michael Joseph, Ltd., 1967.

Bulpin, T. V. *The White Whirlwind.* Cape Town, South Africa: Cape Times Limited, 1961.

Cana, Frank. *South Africa from the Great Trek to the Union.* London: Chapman & Hall Ltd., 1909.

Carnegie, David. *Among the Matabele.* London The Religious Tract Society, 1894.

Colvin, Ian D. "The Future of Rhodesia." *The Quarterly Review.* no. 439 (April 1914).

Cotton, Walter, Aidan. *The Race Problem in South Africa.* Edinburgh: Turnbull & Spears, 1926.

Crankshaw, Edward. *The Forsaken Idea.* London: Longmans Green and Co., 1952.

Creighton, T. R. M. *Southern Rhodesia and the Central African Federation: The Anatomy of Partnership.* New York: Federick A. Praeger, 1961.

Cripps, A. S. "Native Interests in Southern Rhodesia." *The Quarterly Review,* no. 586 (October 1914).

———. "An Africa of the Africans." *The International Review of Missions,* 10 1921.

———. "The Dispossession of the African." *East and West* 20 (1922).

———. "Native Rights Under a New Government in Southern Rhodesia." *The South African Quarterly.* 4, no. 3 (September 1922).

———. *An Africa for Africans: A plea on behalf of Territorial Segregation Area and of Their Freedom in a South African colony.* London: Longmans, Green and Co., 1927.

Darragh, J. T. "The Native Problem in South Africa." *The Contemporary Review* (January, 1902).

Darter, A. *The Pioneers of Mashonaland: Man who made Rhodesia.* London: Simpkin, Marshall, Kent & Co. Ltd., 1914.

Davies, N.A.G. *Incorporation in the Union of South Africa or Self-Government: Southern Rhodesia's Choice 1922 Pretoria,* Communications of the University of South Africa, 1965.

De Kiewiet, Cornelius. *The Imperial Factor in South Africa: A Study in Politics and Economics.* Cambridge: University Press, 1937.

———. *A History of South Africa: Social and Economic.* Oxford: The Clarendon Press, 1941.

De Thiery, C. "Rhodes." *The Empire Review.* vol. 3, 1902.

Dilley, Marjorie Ruth. *British Policy in Kenya Colony.* 2nd ed. London: Frank Cass & Co., Ltd., 1966.

Evans, Maurice S. *Black and White in South East Africa.* London: Longmans, Green and Co., Ltd., 1911.

Gale, W. D. *Heritage of Rhodes.* London: Oxford University Press, 1964.

Gann, L. H., and Duignan, P. *White Settlers in Tropical Africa.* London: C. Nicholls & Company Ltd., 1962.

———. *Burden of Empire: Appraisal of Western Colonialism in Africa South of the Sahara.* New York: Frederick A Praeger, 1967.

Gann, L. H. *A History of Southern Rhodesia: Early Days to 1934.* London: Chatto & Windus, 1965.

———. *Central Africa: The Former British States.* Englewood Cliffs, N.J.: Prentice-Hall, Inc., 1971.

Garvin, J. L. *The Life of Joseph Chamberlain.* London: Macmillan and Co., Ltd., 1932.

Gibbs, Peter. *A Flag for the Matabele: A Story of Empire-Building in Africa.* London: Frederick Muller, Ltd., 1955.

Gray, Richard. *The Two Nations: Aspects of the Development of Race Relations in the Rhodesias and Nyagaland.* Oxford University Press, 1900.

Gross, Felix. *Rhodes of Africa.* New York: Frederick A. Praeger, 1957.

Hailey, Malcom. "Nationalism in Africa." *United Empire.* vol. 28, 1937.

———. *An African Survey: A Study of Problems Arising in Africa South of the Sahara.* rev. ed. London: Oxford University Press, 1957.

Halperin, Vladimir. *Lord Milner and the British Empire: The Evolution of British Imperialism.* London: Oxford University Press, 1952.

Hanna, A. J. *The Story of the Rhodesias and Nyasaland.* London: Faber and Faber Ltd., 1960.

Harris, John H. *The Chartered Millions: Rhodesia and the Challenge to the British Commonwealth.* London: Swarthmore Press, Ltd., 1920.

———. *Slavery or Sacred Trust.* London: Williams and Norgate, Ltd., 1926.

———. *Dawn in Darkest Africa.* New Ed. London: Frank Cass & Co. Ltd., 1908.

Hawkin, R. C. "The Rhodesian Problem." *The Contemporary Review* (April 1922).

Henderson, Ian, and Warhurst, Philip R. *Revisions in Central African History.* Salisbury, The Central Africa Historical Association, Local Series Pamphlet no. 15, 1965.

Hoernle, R. F. Alfred. "The Relationship Between Black and White." *The African Observer* 1 (May–October 1934).

Hofmeyr, Jan H. *South Africa.* London: Ernest Benn Ltd., 1931.

————. *South Africa Native Policy and the Liberal Spirit.* Cape Town, South Africa: University of Cape Town, 1939.

Hole, H. M. *The Making of Rhodesia.* London: Macmillan and Co., Ltd., 1926.

————. *Old Rhodesian Days.* London: Macmillan and Co., Ltd., 1928.

Hone, P. F. *Southern Rhodesia.* London: George Bell and Son, 1909.

Jackson H.M.G. "The Natives of Southern Rhodesia: Their Position After Ten Years Under Responsible Government." *The African Observer* 1 (May–October, 1934).

Johnson, (Bishop) James. "Political and Social Conditions of Missionary Work: The Relations of Mission Work to Native Customs." *Pan Anglican Congress,* 1909.

Jollie, Ethel, Tawsie. *The Real Rhodesia.* London: Hutchinson and Co., Paternoster Row, 1924.

————. "Trust General Smuts." *The National Review* (October 1922).

————. "African Dilemma." *African Observer* 6, no. 4 (November 1936–April 1937).

————. "Native Policy." *United Empire* (January 1937).

Jones, Neville. *Rhodesian Genesis.* Glasgow: The University Press, 1953.

Kane, Nora. *The World's View: The Story of Southern Rhodesia.* London: Cassell & Co., Ltd., 1954.

Kapungu, T. Leonard, *Rhodesia: The Struggle For Freedom* New York: Orbis Books, 1974.

Keatley, P. *The Politics of Partnership.* London: Penguin Books Ltd., 1963.

Kidd, Benjamin. *The Control of the Tropics.* London: Macmillan & Co., Ltd. 1898.

Kidd, Dudley. *Savage Childhood.* London: Adam & Charles Black, Ltd., 1906.

————. *The Essential Kafir.* 2nd ed. London: Adam & Charles Black, Ltd., 1925.

————. *Kafir Socialism.* London: Adam & Charles Black, Ltd., 1908.

Knight, E. F. *South Africa After the War.* London: Longmans, Green and Co., Ltd., 1903.

Leys, C. *European Politics in Southern Rhodesia.* Oxford: The Clarendon Press, 1959.

Lockhardt, J. G., and Woodhouse, C. M. *Cecil Rhodes: The Colossus of Southern Africa.* New York: The Macmillan Company, 1963.

Longden, H. T. "The Future of Rhodesia." *The Quarterly Review*, no. 439 (April 1914).

Luke, W. B. *Lord Milner*. London: S. W. Patridge & Co., 1901.

MacCrone, I. D. *Race Attitudes in South Africa*. London: Oxford University Press, 1937.

Macmillan, W. M. *Democratise the Empire: A Policy of Colonial Reform*. London: Kegan Paul, Trench, Trubner & Co., Ltd. 1941.

Mair, L. P. *Native Policies in Africa*. London: George Routledge & Sons Ltd., 1936.

Malcolm, Dougal. "The British South Africa Company." *The Quarterly Review*, no. 478 (January 1924).

———. *The British South Africa Company: 1889-1939*. London: Herbert Fitch & Co., Ltd., 1938.

Marris, Murrell N. *Joseph Chamberlain: Imperialist*. London: George Routledge & Sons Ltd., 1905.

Marx, Karl, and Engels, Frederick. *Manifesto of the Communist Party*. 2nd ed. Peking: Foreign Language Press, 1968.

Mason, P. *The Birth of a Dilemma: The Conquest and Settlement of Rhodesia*. London: Oxford University Press, 1958.

McIver, Iver. "Rhodesia." *The National Review* (April 1922).

———. "The Future of the Two Rhodesias." *Fortnightly Review* (June 1923).

Milner, (Lord). *The Nation & Empire*. London: Constable & Company, Ltd., 1913.

Mlambo, Eshamael. *Rhodesia: The Struggle for a Birthright*. London: C. Hurst & Co., 1972.

Mnyanda, B. S. *In Search of Truth: A commentary on Certain Aspects of Southern Rhodesia's Native Policy*. Bombay: Hind Kitabs Ltd., 1954.

Morel, E. *The Blackman's Burden*. London: The National Labour Press, Ltd., 1954.

Mumford, Bryant. "Education and the Social Adjustment of the Primitive Peoples of Africa to European Culture." *Africa: Journal of the Institute of African Languages and Cultures* 2 no. 2 (April 1929).

Newman, C. L. Norris. *Matabeleland and How We Got It*. London: T. Fischer Unwin, 1895.

Neilsen, Peter. *The Matabele at Home*. Bulawayo: Davis & Co., (no date).

———. *The Blackman's Place in South Africa*. Cape Town: Juta & Co., Ltd., 1922.

Olivier, (Lord). *The League of Nations and Primitive Peoples*. London: Oxford University Press, 1918.

―――. "Are We Going to Act Justly in Africa." *The Contemporary Review*, no. 728 (August 1920).

―――. "Native Rights in Rhodesia." *The Contemporary Review* (August 1926).

―――. *Anatomy of African Misery*. London: Leonard and Virginia Woolf, 1927.

―――. *White Capital and Coloured Labour*. London: Hogarth Press, 1929.

Orde-Browne, G. J. "The African Labourer." *Africa: Journal of the International Institute of African Languages and Culture* 3 no. 1 (January 1930).

Outhwaite, R. L. *Lord Milner's Record*. London: Echo Office, 1904.

Palley, C. *The Constitutional History and Law of Southern Rhodesia, 1888–1965*. Oxford: The Clarendon Press, 1966.

Palmer, Robin. *Land & Racial Domination in Rhodesia*. Berkley and Los Angeles: University of California Press, 1977.

Posselt, F.W.T. *Fact and Fiction: A Short Account of the Natives of Southern Rhodesia*. Bulawayo, Rhodesia 1935.

Ranger, Terence. *Revolt in Southern Rhodesia: 1896–7*. London: Heinemann, 1967.

―――, ed. *Aspects of Central African History*. London: Wm. Heinemann, Ltd., 1968.

―――. *The African Voice in Southern Rhodesia*. London: Wm. Heinemann, Ltd., 1970.

Rayner, William. *The Tribe and Its Successors: An Account of African Traditional Life and European Settlement in Southern Rhodesia*. London: Faber and Faber, Ltd., 1962.

Robinson, Ronald, and Gallagher, John. *Africa and the Victorians*. New York: St. Martin's Press, 1961.

Roder, W. "The Division of Land Resources in Southern Rhodesia." *Annals of the Association of American Geographers* 54 (1964).

Rodney, Walter. *How Europe Underdeveloped Africa*. Dar-es-Salaam, Tanzania: Tanzania Publishing House, 1972.

Rogers, Cyril A., and Rogers, Frantz. *Racial Themes in Southern Rhodesia: The Attitudes and Behavior of the White Population*. New Haven, Conn.: Yale University Press, 1962.

Samkange, Stanlake. *On Trial for My Country*. London: Wm. Heinemann Ltd., 1967.

―――. *Origins of Rhodesia*. London: Wm. Heinemann, Ltd. 1968.

Savage, Murray J. *Achievement: Fifty Years of Missionary Witness in Southern Rhodesia*. Wellington, New Zealand: A. H. & A. W. Reed, 1949.

Schapera, I. "Economic Changes in South African Native Life." *Africa: Journal of the International Institute of African Language and Cultures* 1 (January 1928).

Shamuyarira, Nathan. *Crisis in Rhodesia*. London: Andre Deutsch, 1965.

Smith, Edwin W. *The Way of the White Fields in Rhodesia: A Survey of Christian Enterprise in Northern and Southern Rhodesia*. London: World Dominion Press, 1928.

Stokes, Eric, and Brown, Richard, eds. *The Zambezian Past: Studies in Central African History*. Manchester: The University Press, 1966.

Tabler, Edward C. *The Far Interior*. Cape Town, South Africa: A. A. Balkema, 1955.

The Central Africa Examiner 3 no. 25, (May 7, 1960).

The Rhodesia Review (1905‑6).

Thompson, L. M. *The Unification of South Africa: 1902‑1910*. Oxford: The Clarendon Press, 1960.

Thomson, J. Mudie. *Political Reorganization: A Study Towards Rhodesian Self-Government*. Bulawayo, Southern Rhodesia: Review Co., Ltd., 1898.

Thorpe, Clarence. *Limpopo to Zambezi: Sixty Years of Methodism in Southern Rhodesia*. London: Cargate Press, 1951.

Townsend, Mary Evelyn. *European Colonial Expansion Since 1871*. New York: J. B. Lippincott Company, 1941.

Tredgold, Robert C. The Rhodesia That Was My Life. London: George Allen & Unwin Ltd., 1968.

Trevor, Tudor G. "Native Education from an Employer's Point of View *NADA* (December 1927).

Vambe, Lawrence. *An Ill-Fated People*. Pittsburgh, Penn.: University of Pittsburgh Press, 1972.

Van Der Horst, Sheila T. *Native Labour in South Africa. New Impression* London: Frank Cass & Co., Ltd., 1971.

Van Onselen, Charles. *Chibaro: African Mine Labour in Southern Rhodesia 1900‑1933*. London: Pluto Press, 1976.

Walker, Eric. A. *Lord Milner and South Africa*. London: Humphrey Milford Amen House, E. C., 1942.

———. *A History of Southern Africa*. 3rd. ed. London: Longmans, Green and Co., Ltd., 1964.

———. *The Great Trek*. London: Adam & Charles Black, Ltd., 1934.

Wallis, J.P.R. *One Man's Hand: The Story of Sir Charles Coghlan and the Liberation of Southern Rhodesia*. London: Longmans, Green and Co., Ltd., 1950.

Williams, Basil. *Cecil Rhodes*. New ed. London: Constable and Company Ltd., 1938.

Wilson. B. "Rhodesia and Its Prospects." *United Empire* 2 (1911).

Wilson, N. H. "The Future of the Native Races of Southern Rhodesia." *South African Journal of Science* 17 (1921).

Witts, Frank H. "The Native Labour Question in Southern Rhodesia." *The Empire Review* 22 (1912).

Worsfold, W. Basil. "British Policy in South Africa." *The Monthly Review no. 31 (April 1903)*.

———. *Lord Milner's Work in South Africa: 1897–1902*. London: Hazell, Watson & Viney Ltd., 1906.

———. *The Union of South Africa*. London: Sir Isaac Pitman & Sons, Ltd., 1912.

Wrench, John Evelyn. *Alfred Milner: The Man of No Illusions*. London: Eyre & Spotliswoode, Ltd., 1958.

Yudelman, Montague. *Africans On the Land. Economic Problems of Agricultural Development in Southern, Central, and East Africa with Special Reference to Southern Rhodesia* London: Oxford University Press, 1964.

Index